VOL. 2

AMNESTY

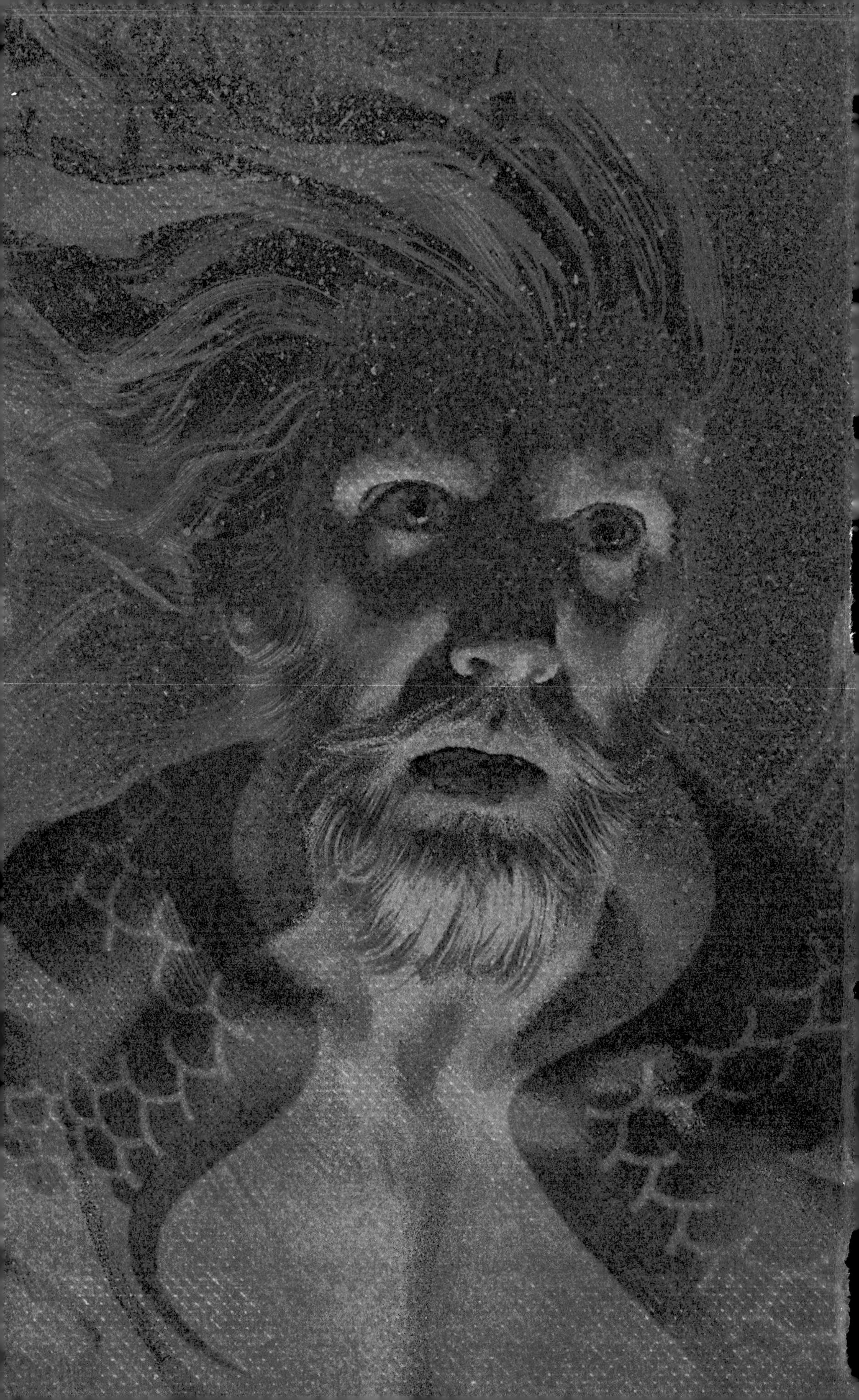

AQUAMAN

AMNESTY

KELLY SUE DeCONNICK writer

VIKTOR BOGDANOVIC

ROBSON ROCHA

DANIEL HENRIQUES

EDUARDO PANSICA

JULIO FERREIRA

JONATHAN GLAPION

RYAN WINN

artists

SUNNY GHO colorist

CLAYTON COWLES letterer

**ROBSON ROCHA, JASON PAZ &
ALEX SINCLAIR** collection cover artists

AQUAMAN CREATED BY PAUL NORRIS

VOL.

ALEX ANTONE Editor – Original Series
ANDREA SHEA Assistant Editor – Original Series
JEB WOODARD Group Editor – Collected Editions
SCOTT NYBAKKEN Editor – Collected Edition
STEVE COOK Design Director – Books
LOUIS PRANDI Publication Design
TOM VALENTE Publication Production

BOB HARRAS Senior VP – Editor-in-Chief, DC Comics
PAT McCALLUM Executive Editor, DC Comics

DAN DiDIO Publisher
JIM LEE Publisher & Chief Creative Officer
BOBBIE CHASE VP – New Publishing Initiatives & Talent Development
DON FALLETTI VP – Manufacturing Operations & Workflow Management
LAWRENCE GANEM VP – Talent Services
ALISON GILL Senior VP – Manufacturing & Operations
HANK KANALZ Senior VP – Publishing Strategy & Support Services
DAN MIRON VP – Publishing Operations
NICK J. NAPOLITANO VP – Manufacturing Administration & Design
NANCY SPEARS VP – Sales
MICHELE R. WELLS VP & Executive Editor, Young Reader

AQUAMAN VOL. 2: AMNESTY
Published by DC Comics. Compilation and all new
material Copyright © 2019 DC Comics. All Rights
Reserved. Originally published in single magazine
form in *Aquaman* 48-52. Copyright © 2019 DC
Comics. All Rights Reserved. All characters,
their distinctive likenesses, and related elements
featured in this publication are trademarks of DC
Comics. The stories, characters, and incidents
featured in this publication are entirely fictional.
DC Comics does not read or accept unsolicited
submissions of ideas, stories, or artwork.

DC Comics, 2900 West Alameda Ave.,
Burbank, CA 91505. Printed by LSC Communications,
Kendallville, IN, USA. 11/15/19. First Printing.
ISBN: 978-1-4012-9533-2

Library of Congress Cataloging-in-Publication Data
is available.

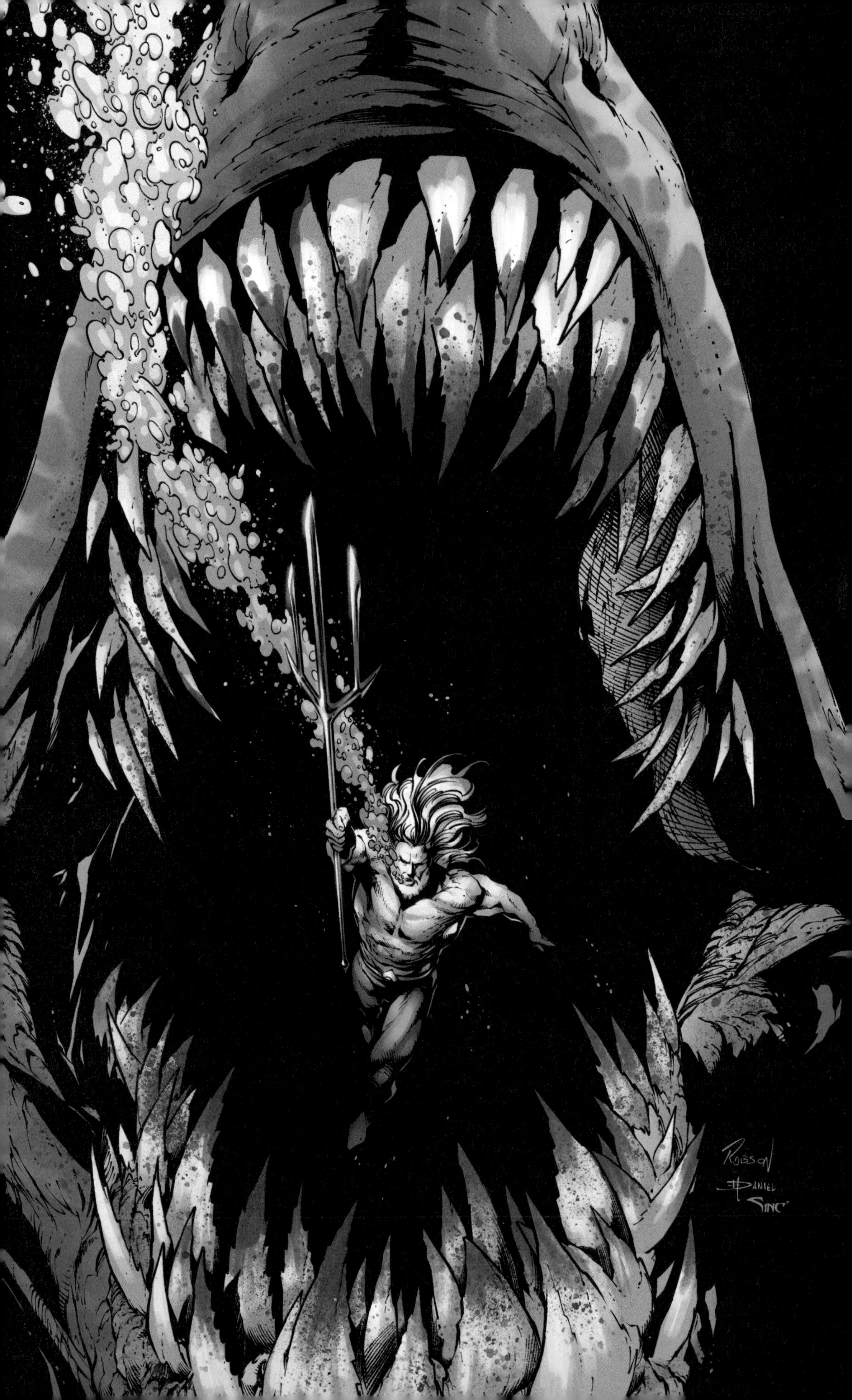
ROBSON
DANIEL
SINC'

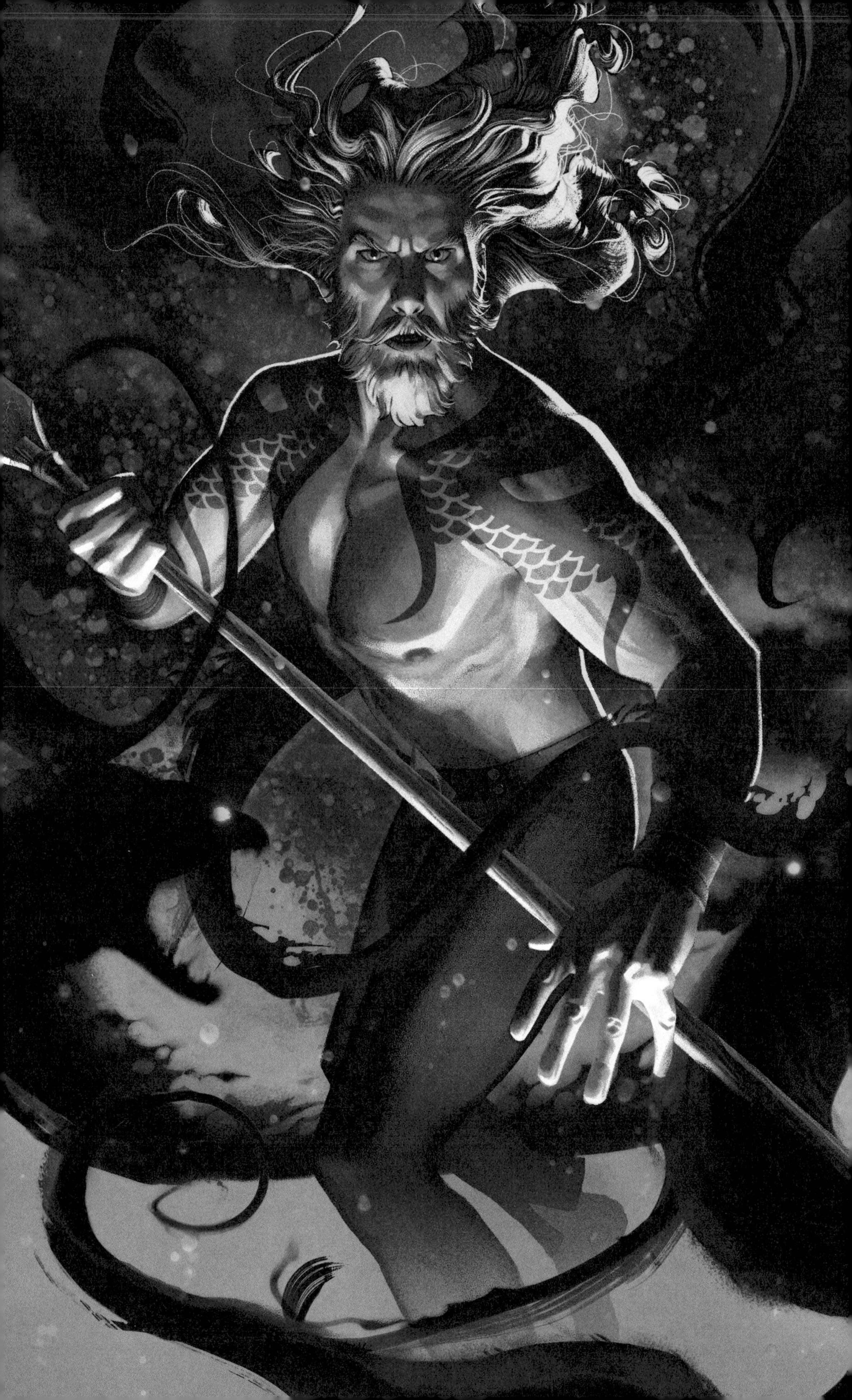

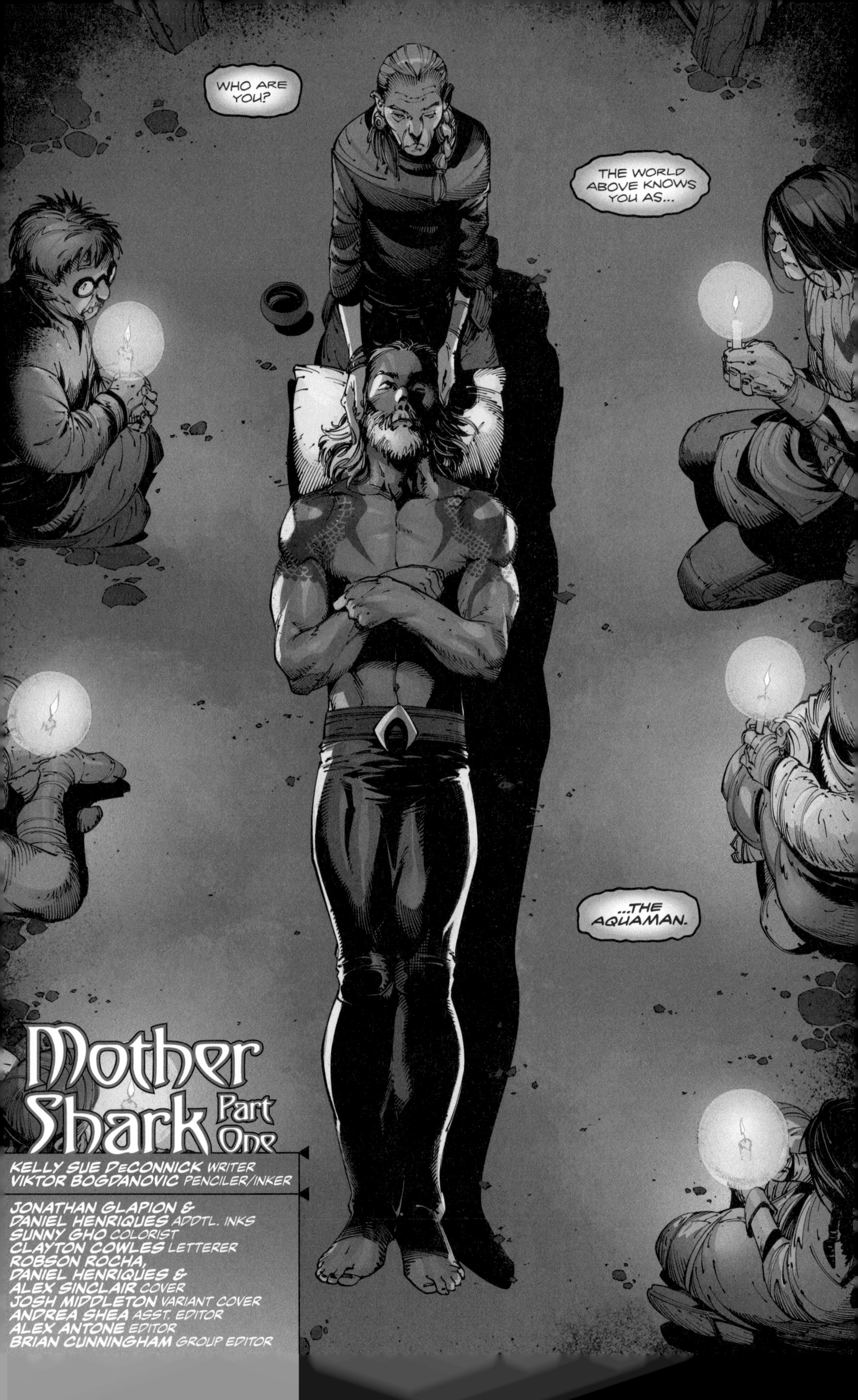
WHO ARE YOU?
THE WORLD ABOVE KNOWS YOU AS...
...THE AQUAMAN.
Mother Shark Part One
KELLY SUE DeCONNICK WRITER
VIKTOR BOGDANOVIC PENCILER/INKER
JONATHAN GLAPION & DANIEL HENRIQUES ADDTL. INKS
SUNNY GHO COLORIST
CLAYTON COWLES LETTERER
ROBSON ROCHA, DANIEL HENRIQUES & ALEX SINCLAIR COVER
JOSH MIDDLETON VARIANT COVER
ANDREA SHEA ASST. EDITOR
ALEX ANTONE EDITOR
BRIAN CUNNINGHAM GROUP EDITOR

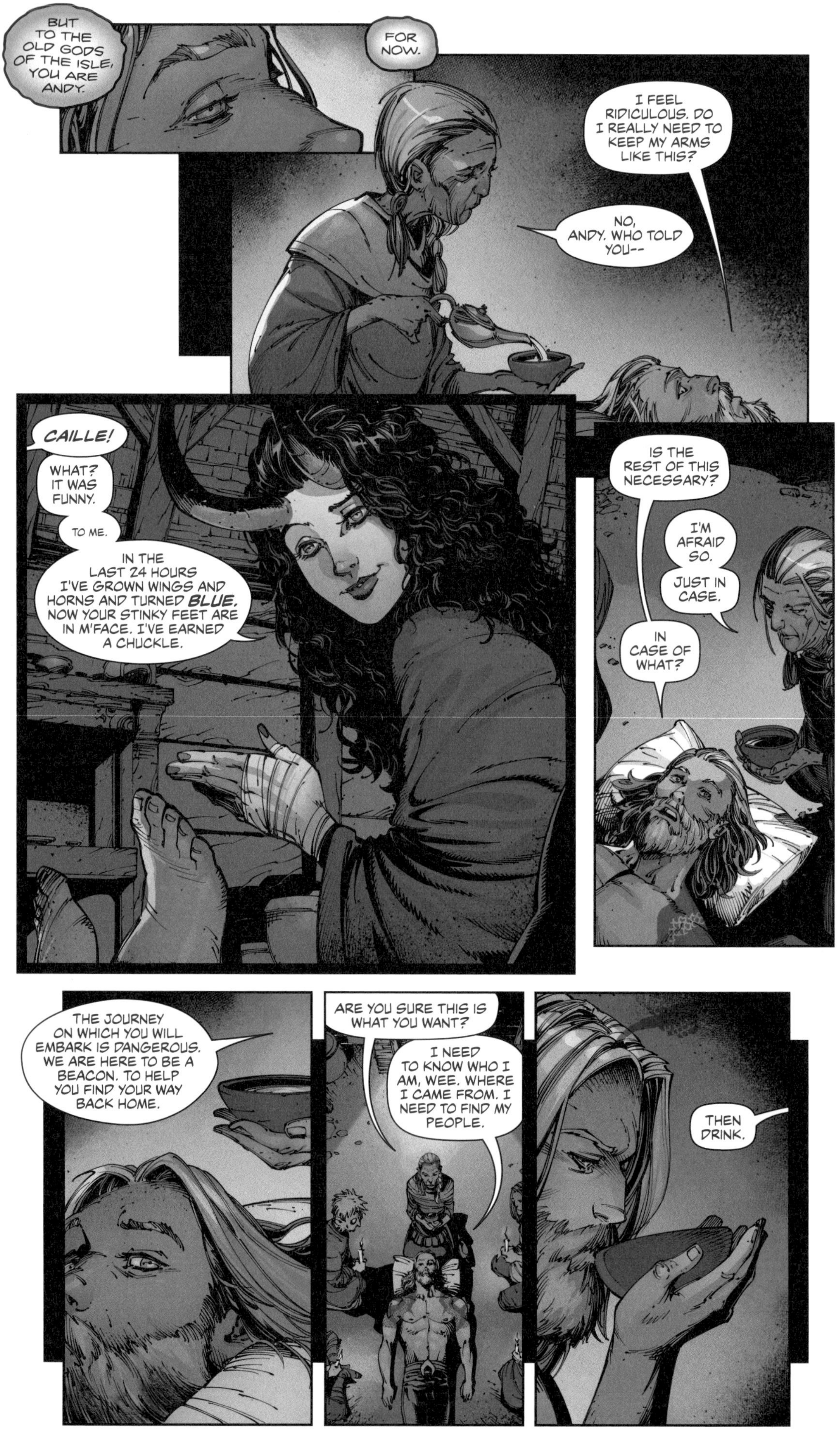
BUT TO THE OLD GODS OF THE ISLE, YOU ARE ANDY.
FOR NOW.
I FEEL RIDICULOUS. DO I REALLY NEED TO KEEP MY ARMS LIKE THIS?
NO, ANDY. WHO TOLD YOU--
CAILLE!
WHAT? IT WAS FUNNY.
TO ME.
IN THE LAST 24 HOURS I'VE GROWN WINGS AND HORNS AND TURNED BLUE. NOW YOUR STINKY FEET ARE IN M'FACE. I'VE EARNED A CHUCKLE.
IS THE REST OF THIS NECESSARY?
I'M AFRAID SO.
JUST IN CASE.
IN CASE OF WHAT?
THE JOURNEY ON WHICH YOU WILL EMBARK IS DANGEROUS. WE ARE HERE TO BE A BEACON. TO HELP YOU FIND YOUR WAY BACK HOME.
ARE YOU SURE THIS IS WHAT YOU WANT?
I NEED TO KNOW WHO I AM, WEE. WHERE I CAME FROM. I NEED TO FIND MY PEOPLE.
THEN DRINK.

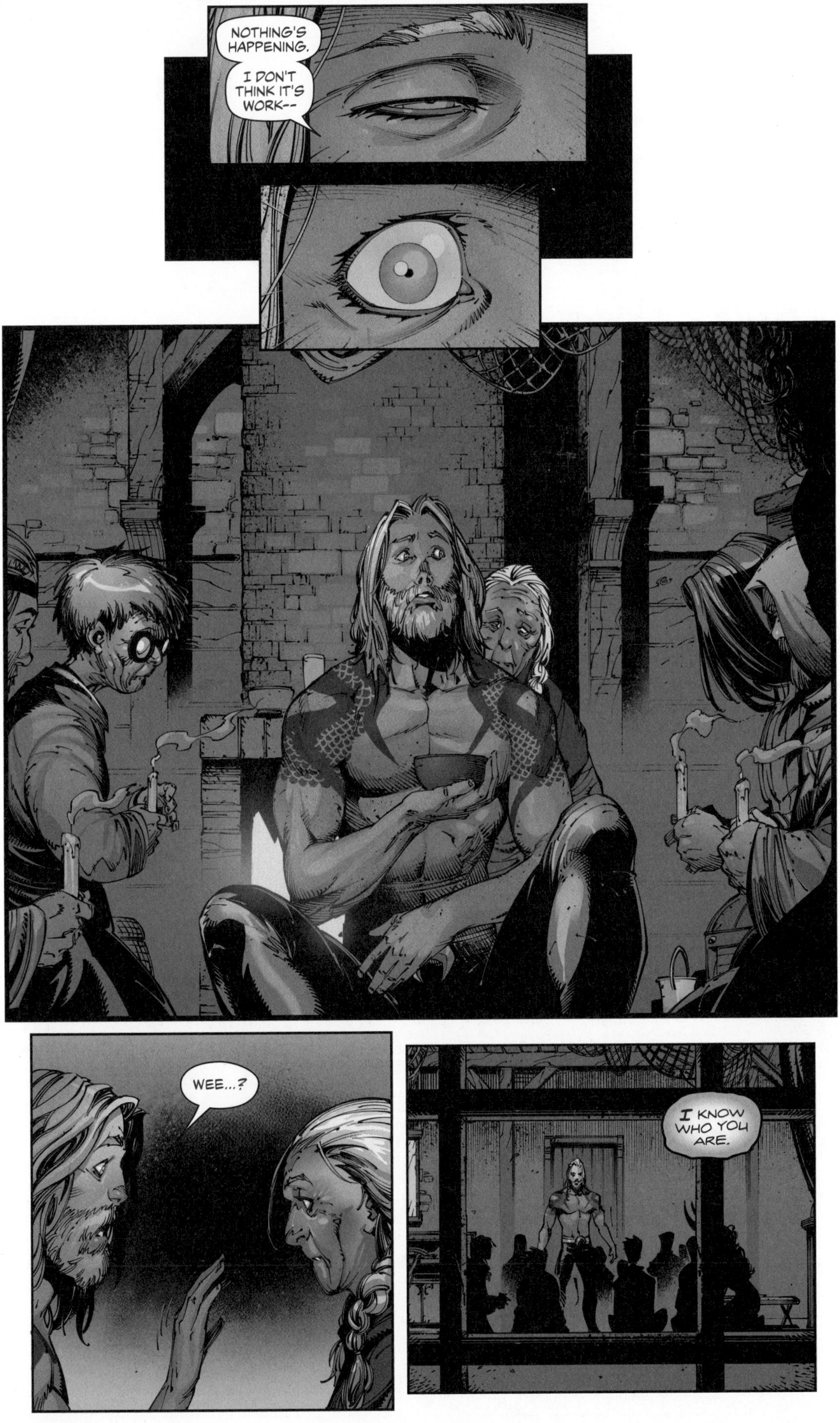
NOTHING'S HAPPENING.
I DON'T THINK IT'S WORK--
WEE...?
I KNOW WHO YOU ARE.

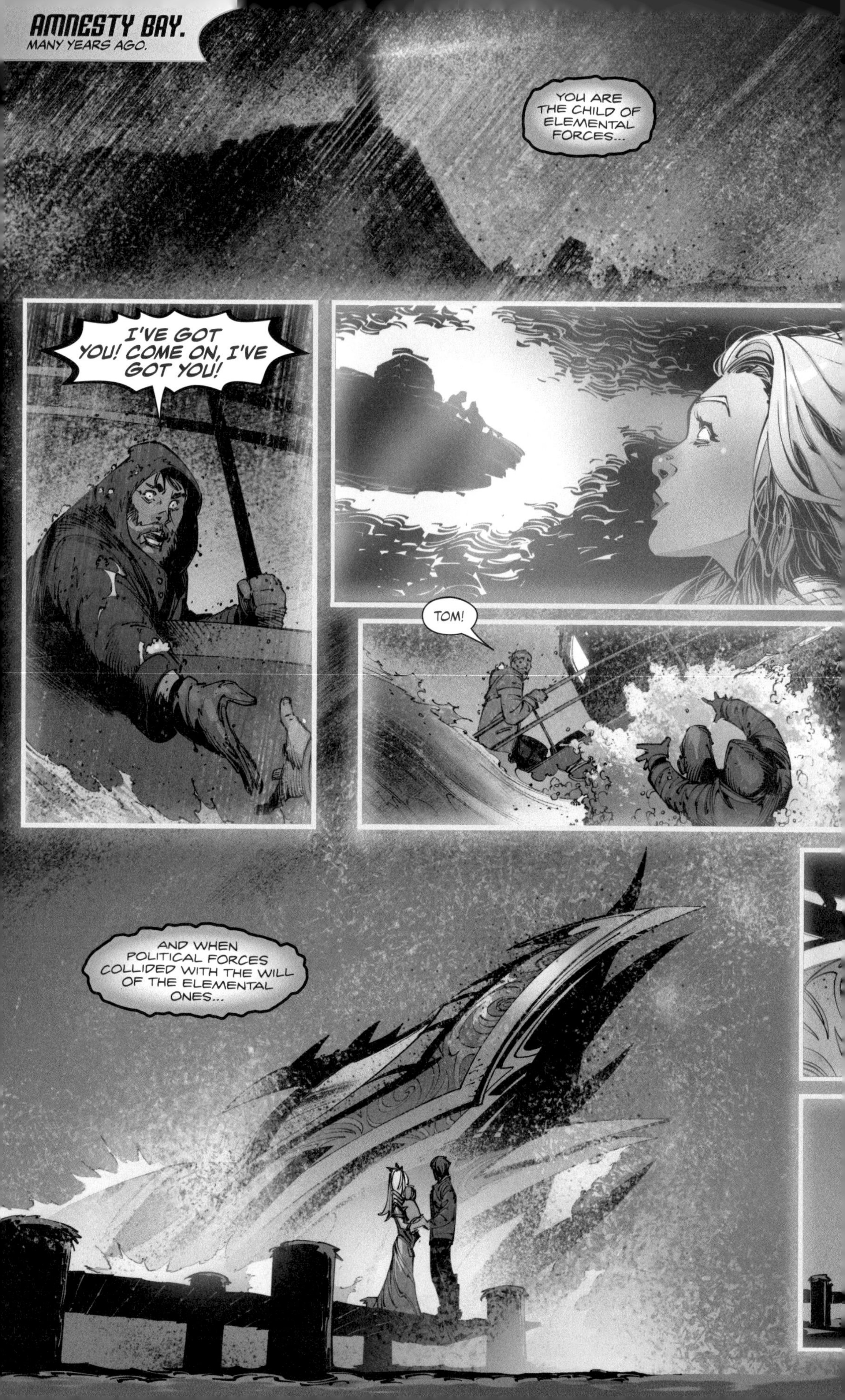
AMNESTY BAY.
MANY YEARS AGO.
YOU ARE THE CHILD OF ELEMENTAL FORCES...
I'VE GOT YOU! COME ON, I'VE GOT YOU!
TOM!
AND WHEN POLITICAL FORCES COLLIDED WITH THE WILL OF THE ELEMENTAL ONES...

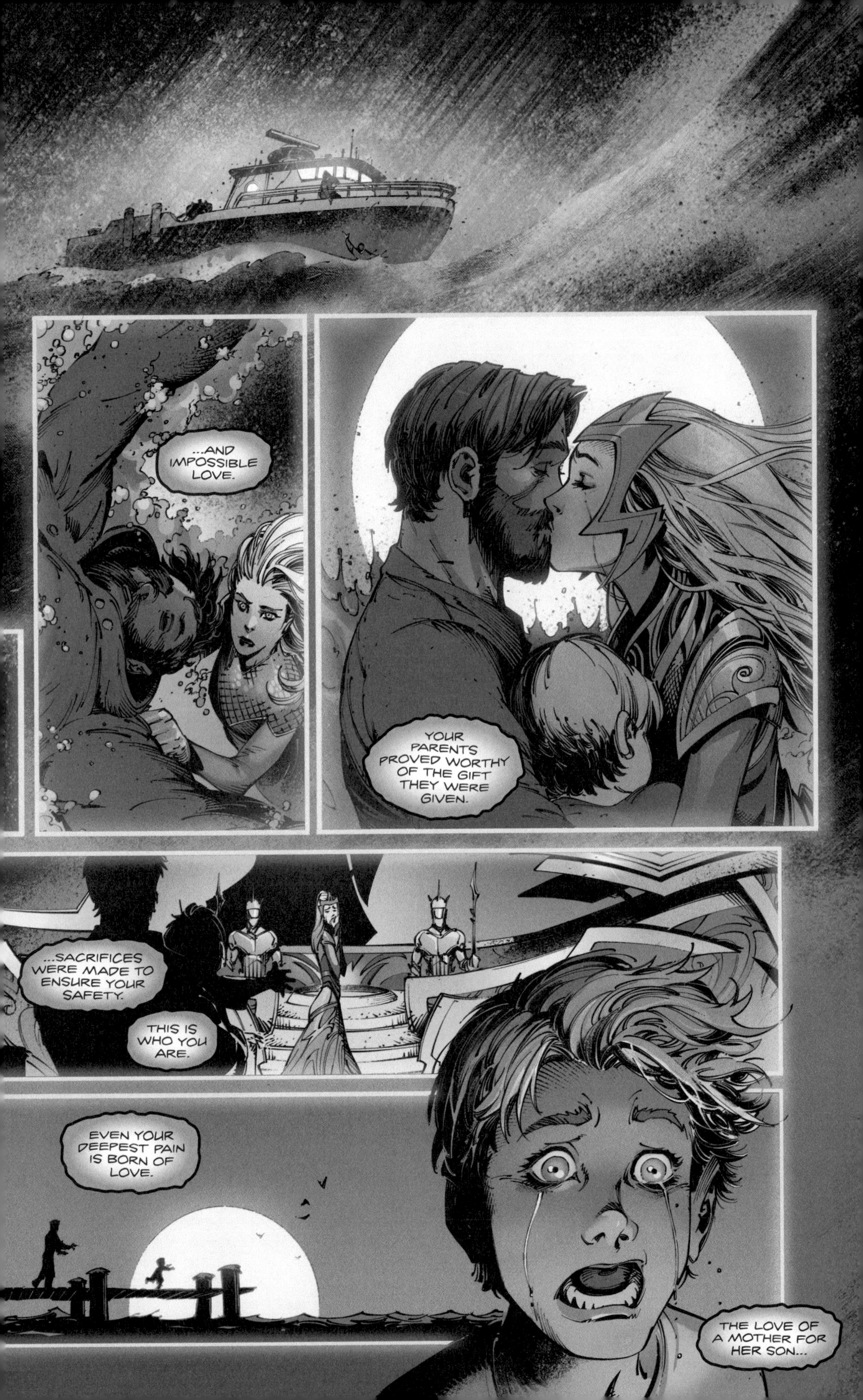
...AND IMPOSSIBLE LOVE.
YOUR PARENTS PROVED WORTHY OF THE GIFT THEY WERE GIVEN.
...SACRIFICES WERE MADE TO ENSURE YOUR SAFETY.
THIS IS WHO YOU ARE.
EVEN YOUR DEEPEST PAIN IS BORN OF LOVE.
THE LOVE OF A MOTHER FOR HER SON...

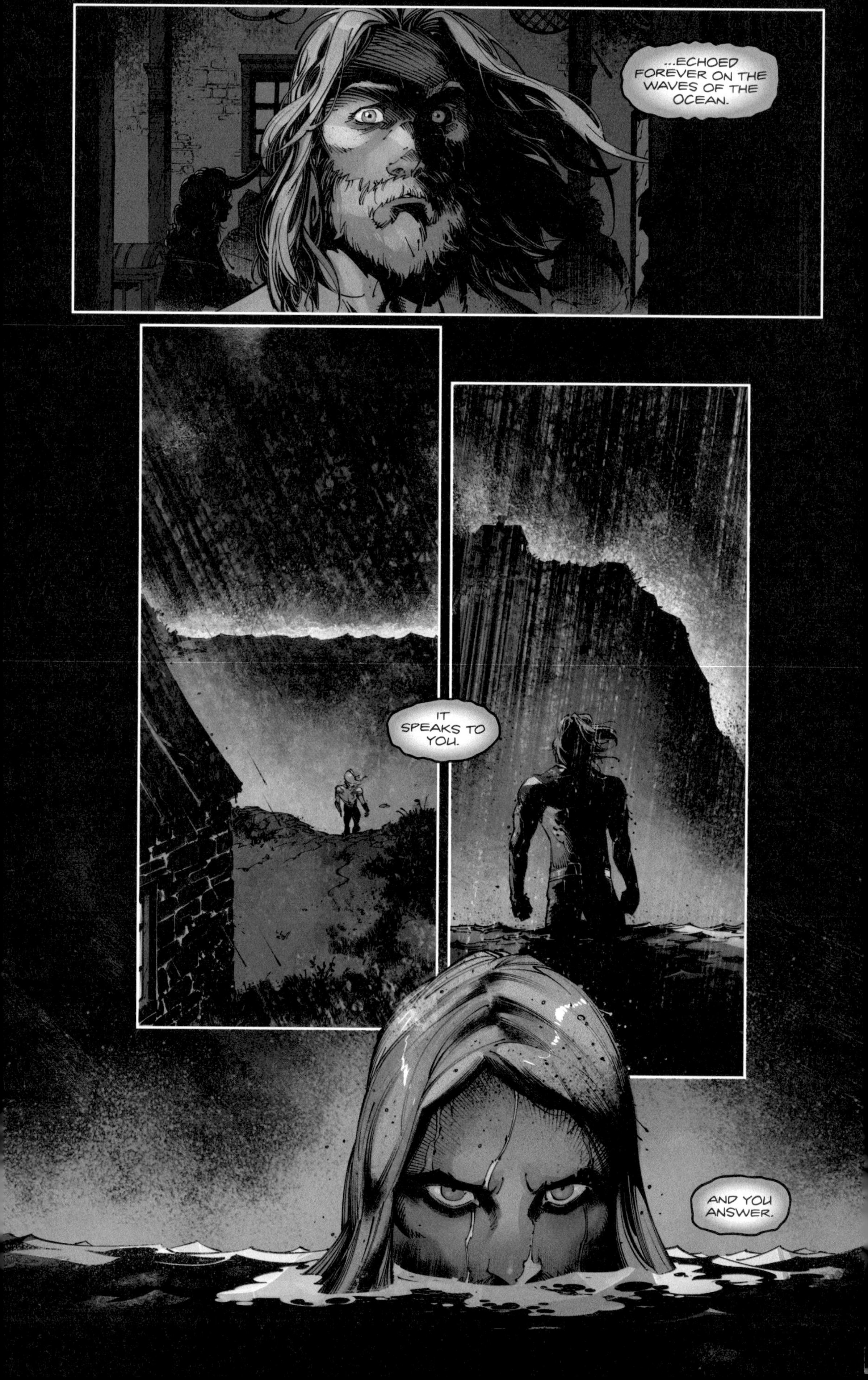
...ECHOED FOREVER ON THE WAVES OF THE OCEAN.
IT SPEAKS TO YOU.
AND YOU ANSWER.

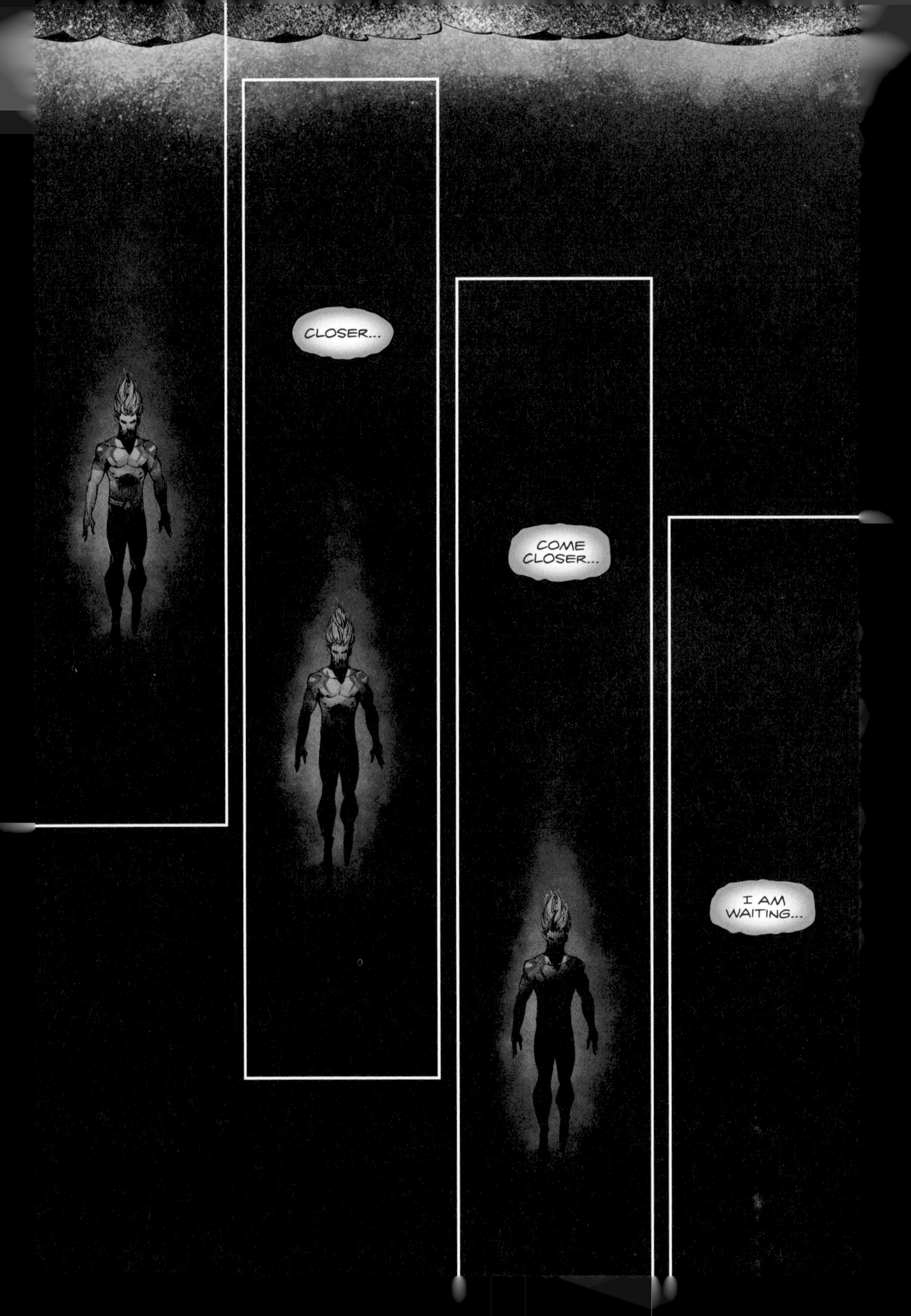
CLOSER...
COME CLOSER...
I AM WAITING...

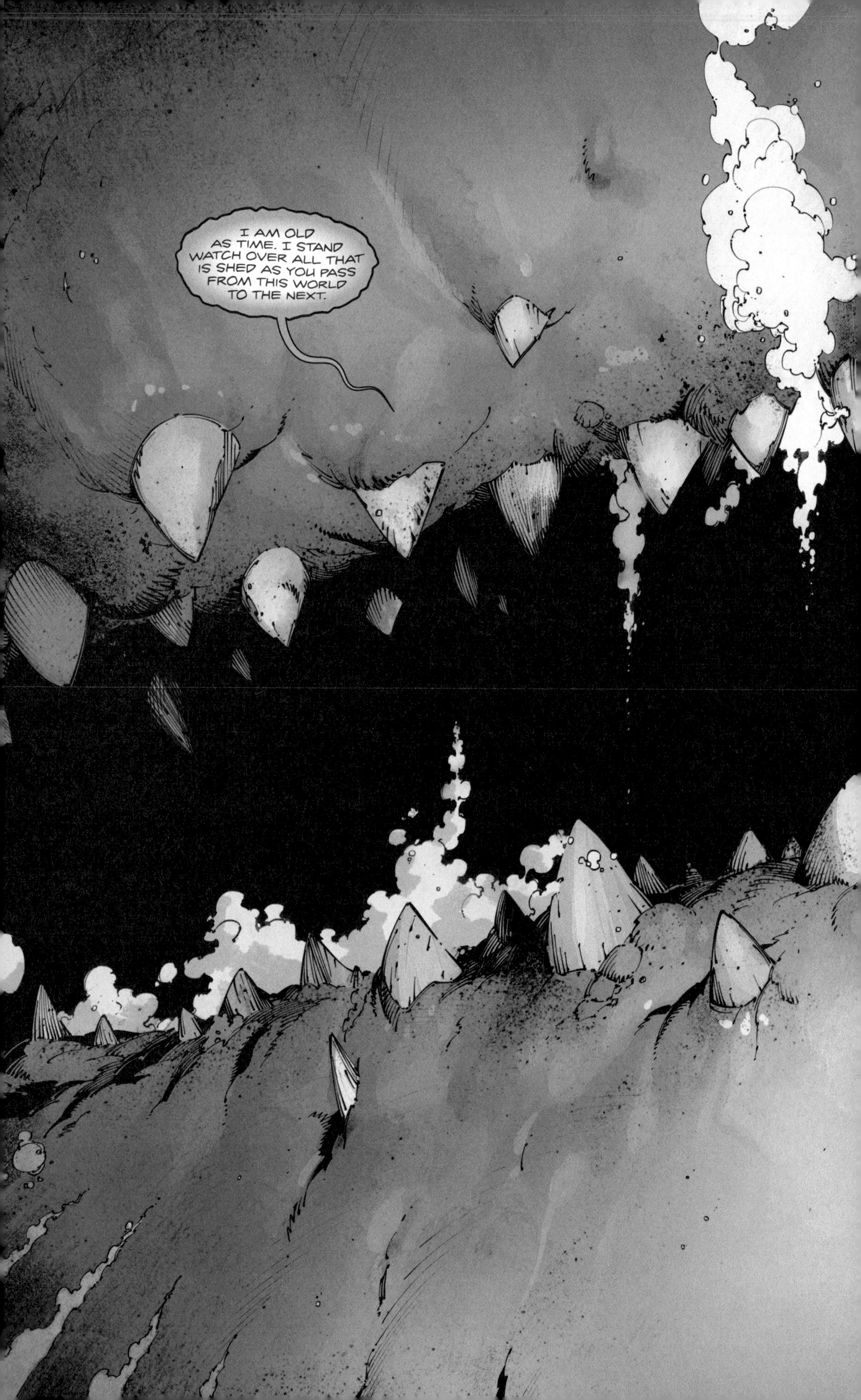
I AM OLD AS TIME. I STAND WATCH OVER ALL THAT IS SHED AS YOU PASS FROM THIS WORLD TO THE NEXT.

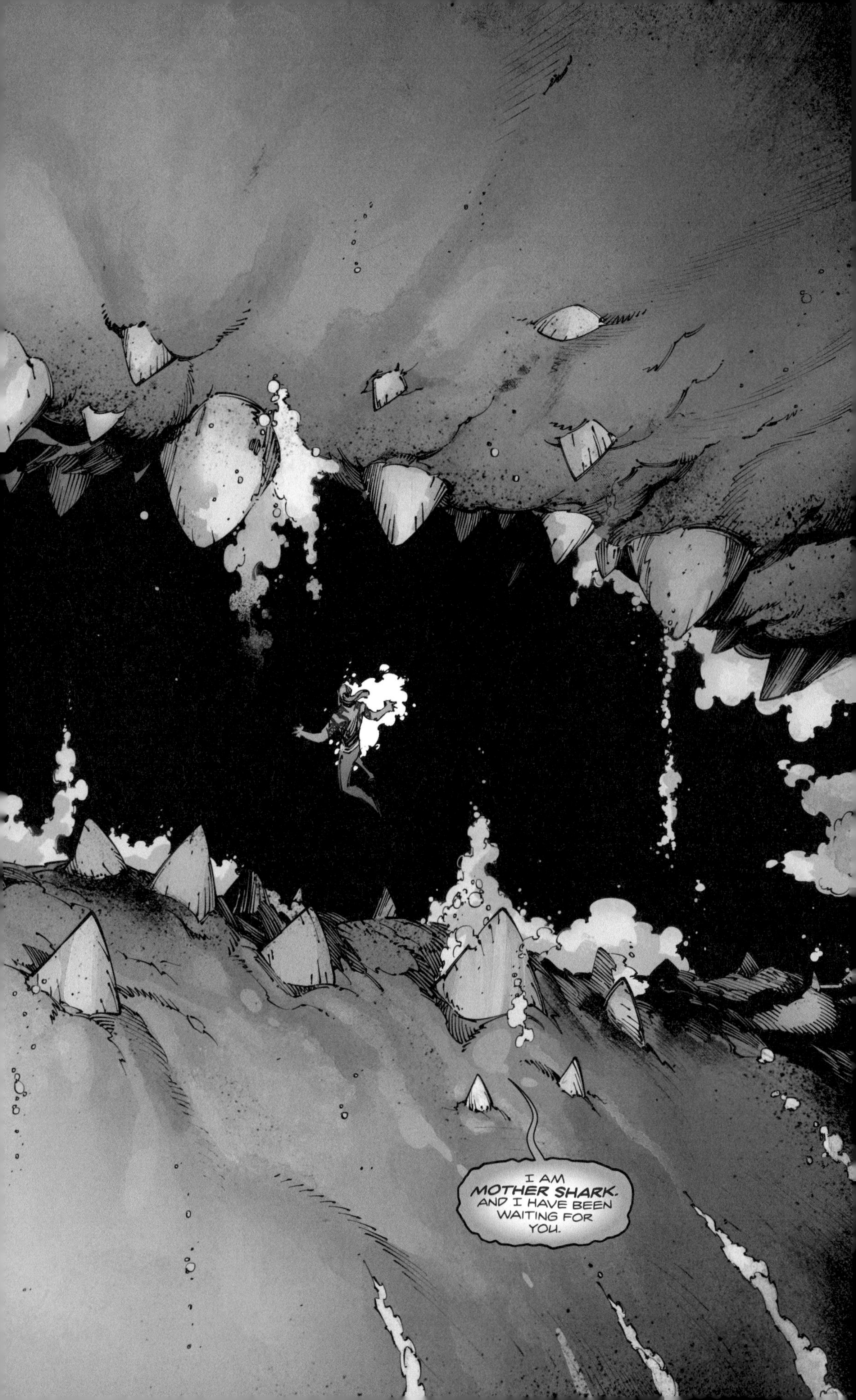
I AM
MOTHER SHARK.
AND I HAVE BEEN
WAITING FOR
YOU.

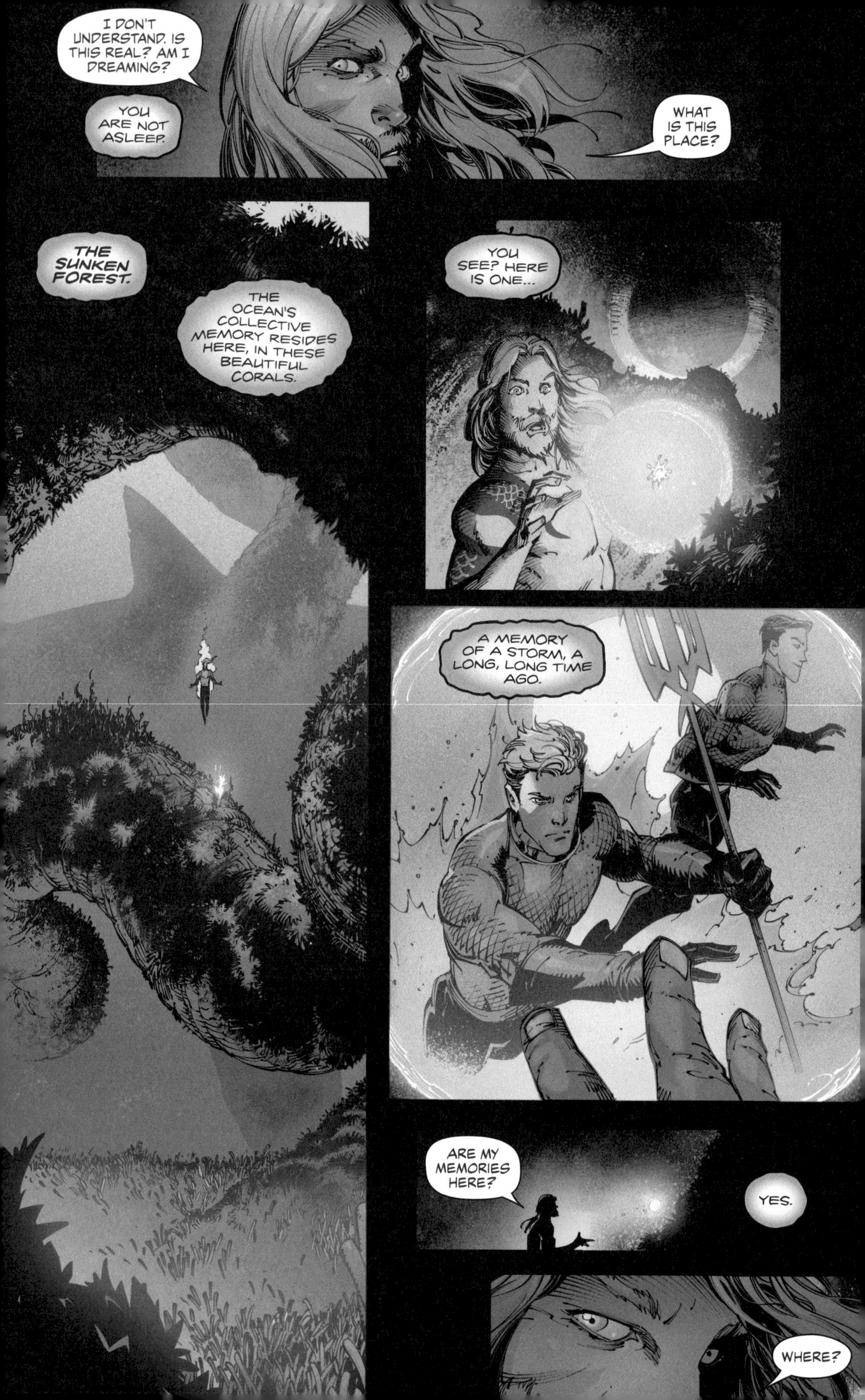
I DON'T UNDERSTAND. IS THIS REAL? AM I DREAMING?
YOU ARE NOT ASLEEP.
WHAT IS THIS PLACE?
THE SUNKEN FOREST.
THE OCEAN'S COLLECTIVE MEMORY RESIDES HERE, IN THESE BEAUTIFUL CORALS.
YOU SEE? HERE IS ONE...
A MEMORY OF A STORM, A LONG, LONG TIME AGO.
ARE MY MEMORIES HERE?
YES.
WHERE?

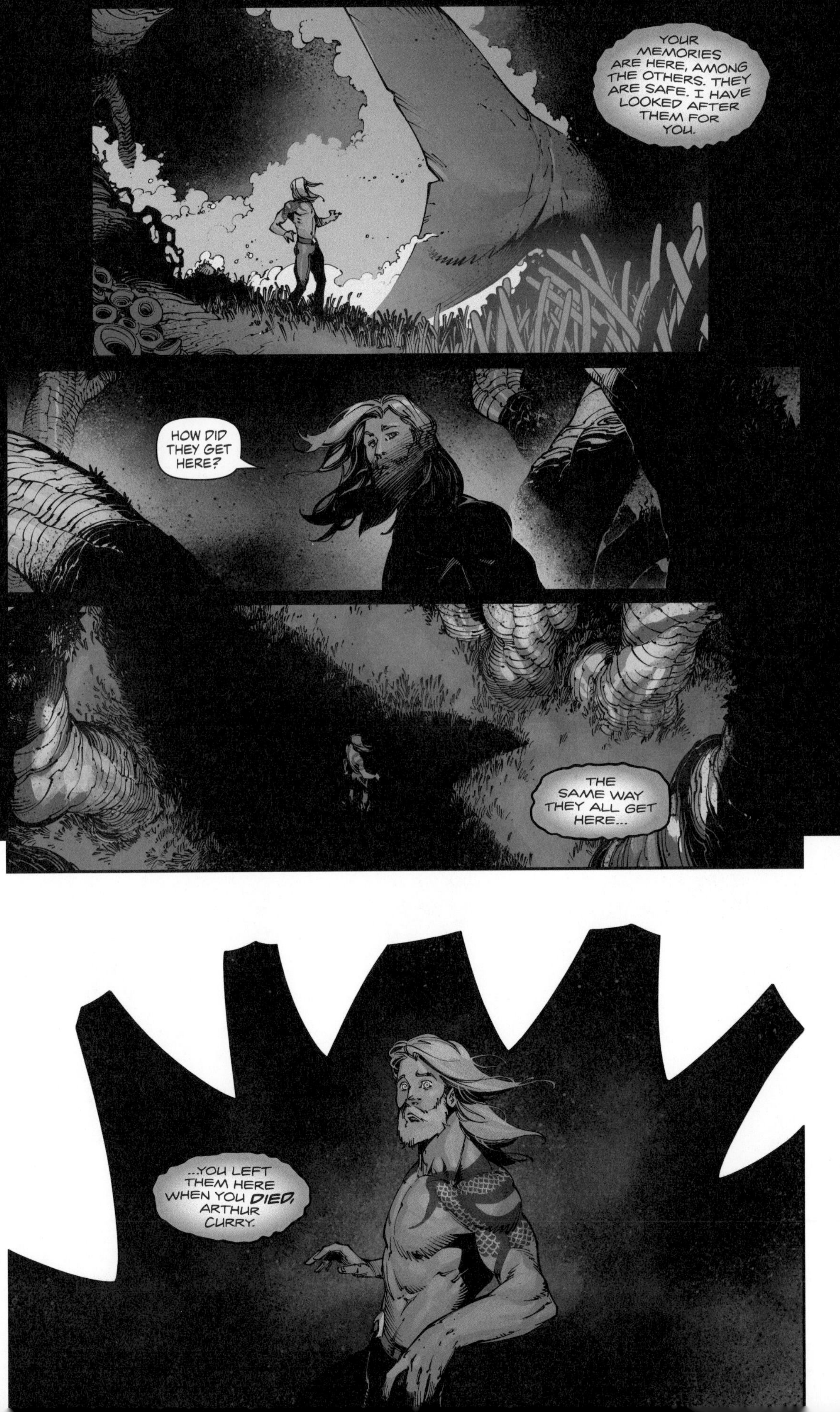
YOUR MEMORIES ARE HERE, AMONG THE OTHERS. THEY ARE SAFE. I HAVE LOOKED AFTER THEM FOR YOU.
HOW DID THEY GET HERE?
THE SAME WAY THEY ALL GET HERE...
...YOU LEFT THEM HERE WHEN YOU DIED, ARTHUR CURRY.

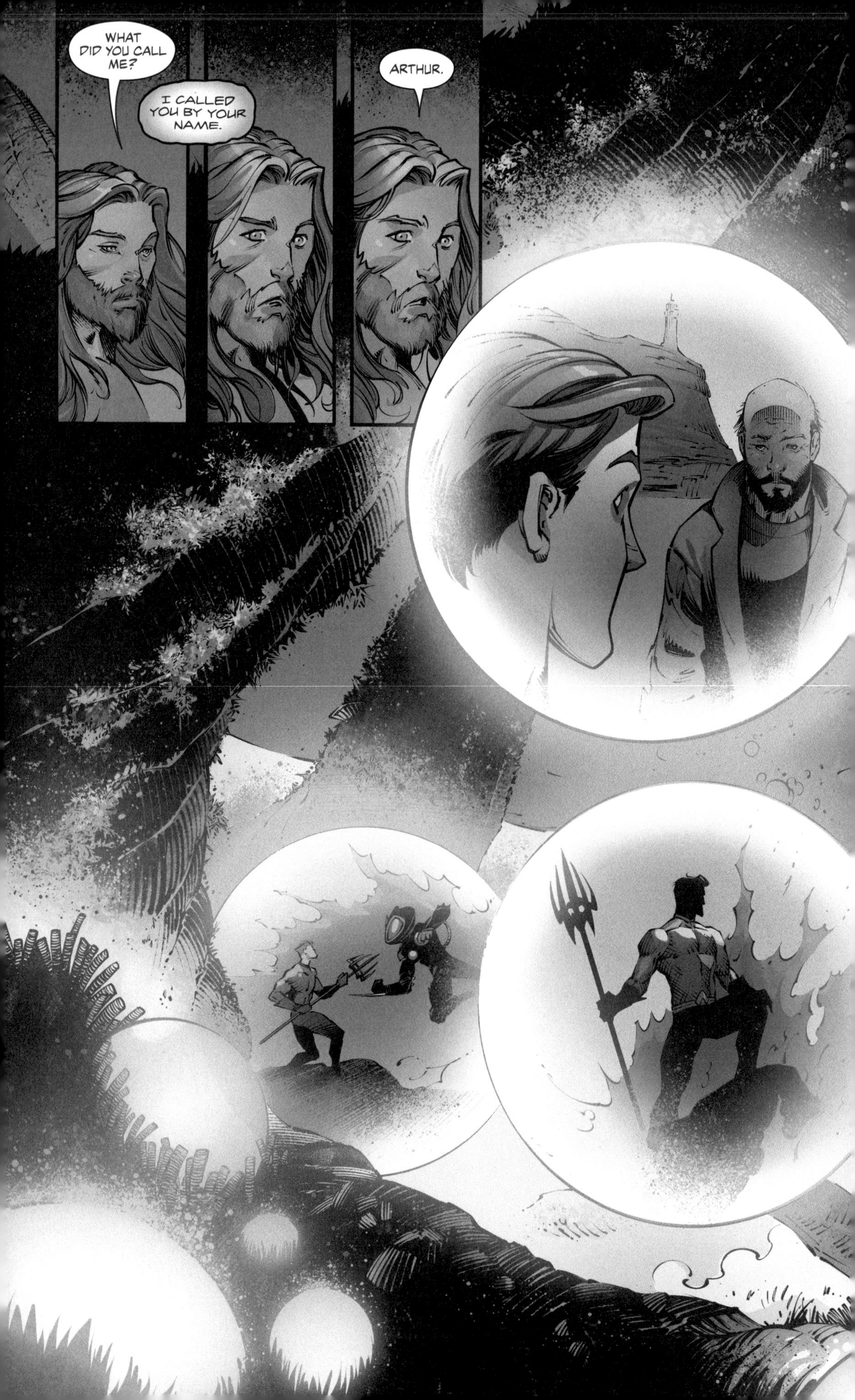
WHAT DID YOU CALL ME?
I CALLED YOU BY YOUR NAME.
ARTHUR.

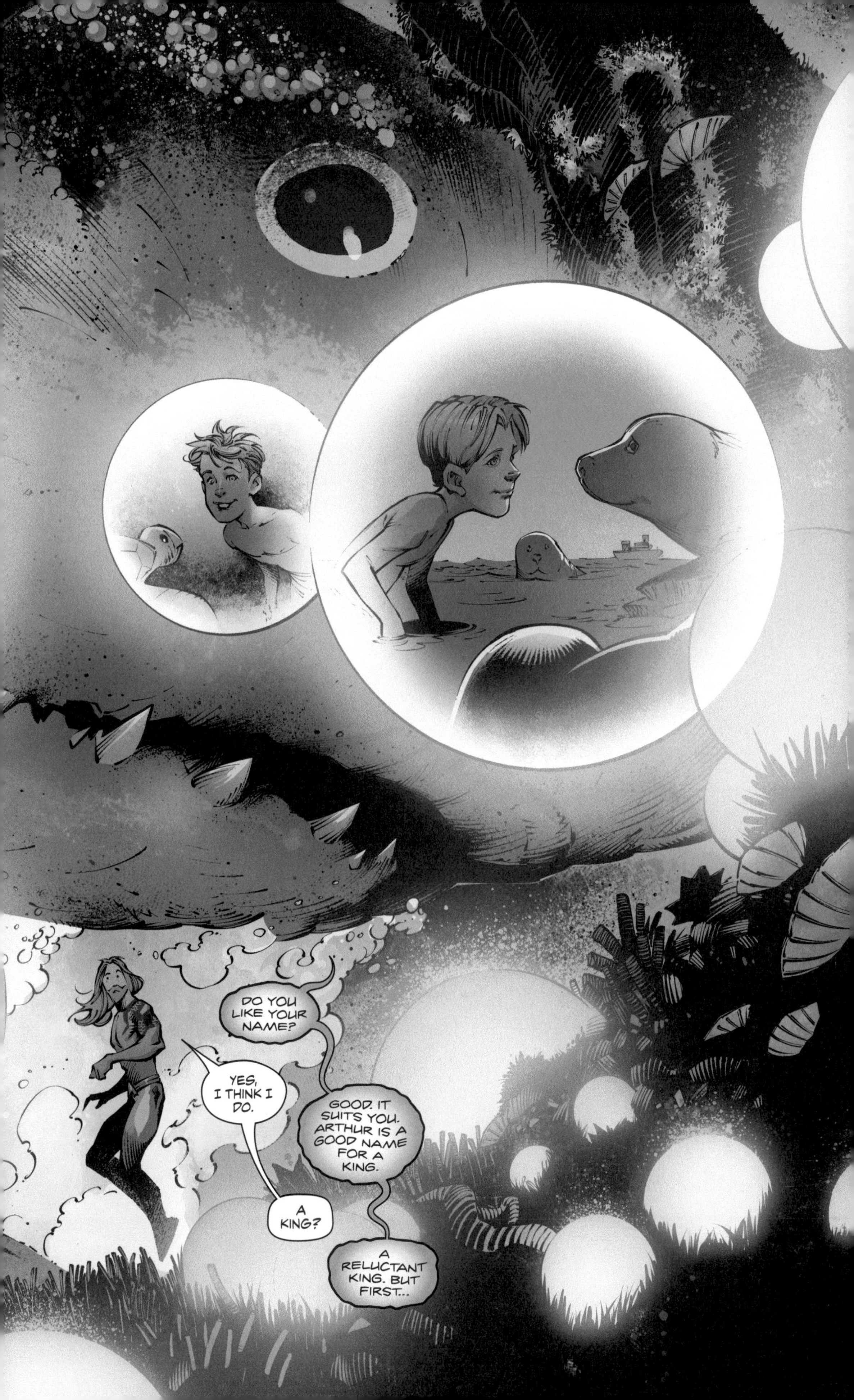
DO YOU LIKE YOUR NAME?
YES, I THINK I DO.
GOOD. IT SUITS YOU. ARTHUR IS A GOOD NAME FOR A KING.
A KING?
A RELUCTANT KING. BUT FIRST...

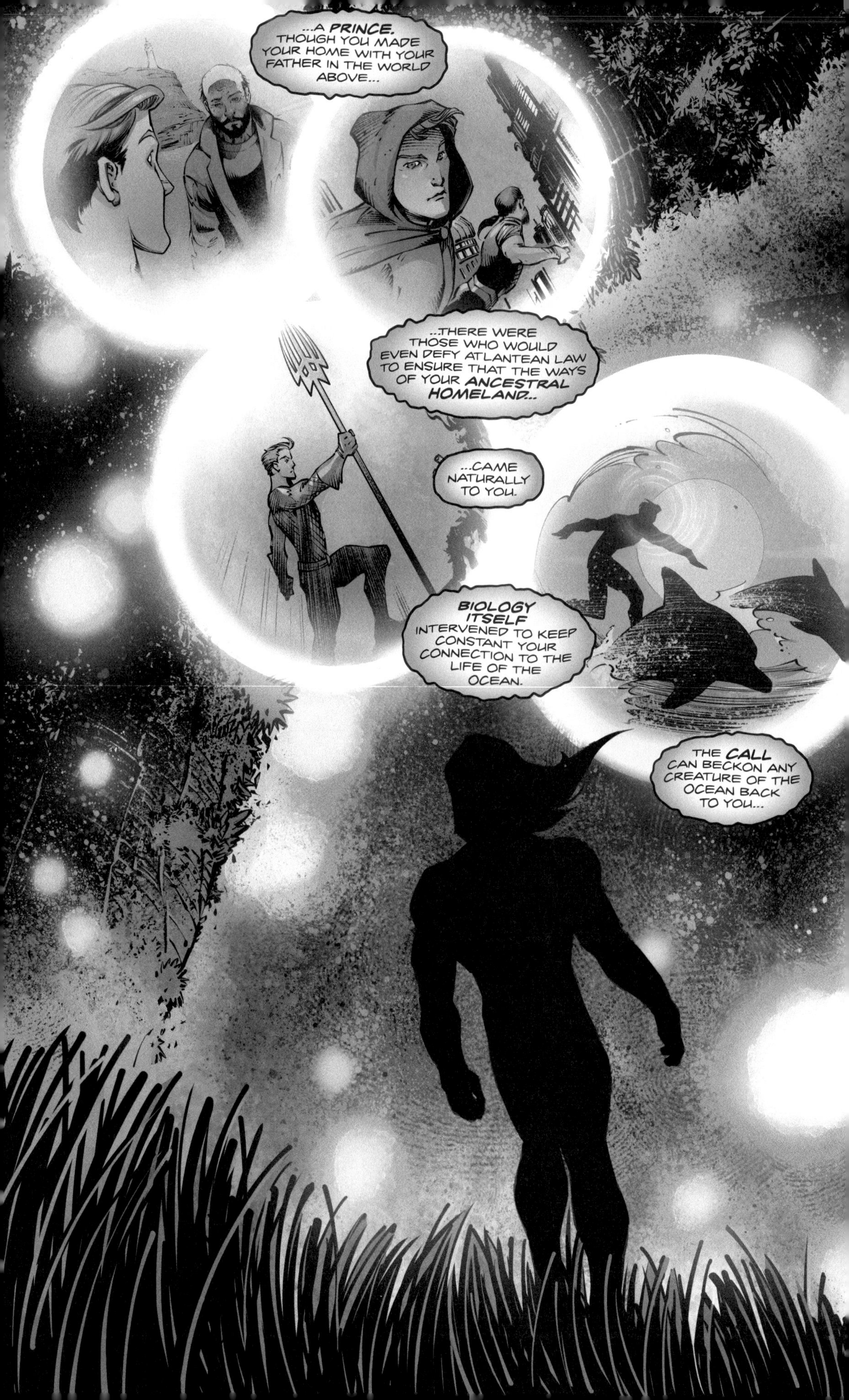
...A PRINCE. THOUGH YOU MADE YOUR HOME WITH YOUR FATHER IN THE WORLD ABOVE...
...THERE WERE THOSE WHO WOULD EVEN DEFY ATLANTEAN LAW TO ENSURE THAT THE WAYS OF YOUR ANCESTRAL HOMELAND...
...CAME NATURALLY TO YOU.
BIOLOGY ITSELF INTERVENED TO KEEP CONSTANT YOUR CONNECTION TO THE LIFE OF THE OCEAN.
THE CALL CAN BECKON ANY CREATURE OF THE OCEAN BACK TO YOU...

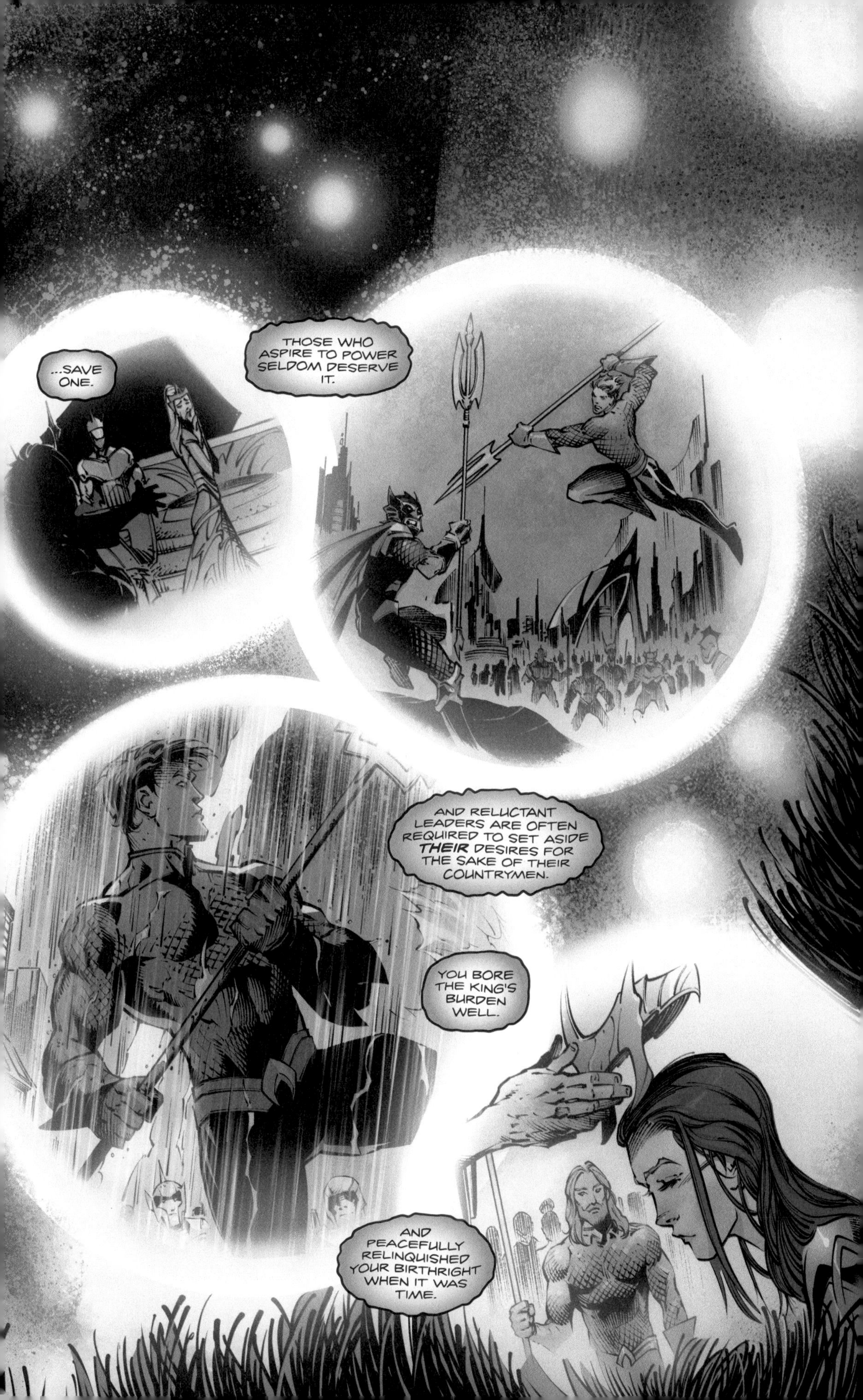
...SAVE ONE.
THOSE WHO ASPIRE TO POWER SELDOM DESERVE IT.
AND RELUCTANT LEADERS ARE OFTEN REQUIRED TO SET ASIDE *THEIR* DESIRES FOR THE SAKE OF THEIR COUNTRYMEN.
YOU BORE THE KING'S BURDEN WELL.
AND PEACEFULLY RELINQUISHED YOUR BIRTHRIGHT WHEN IT WAS TIME.

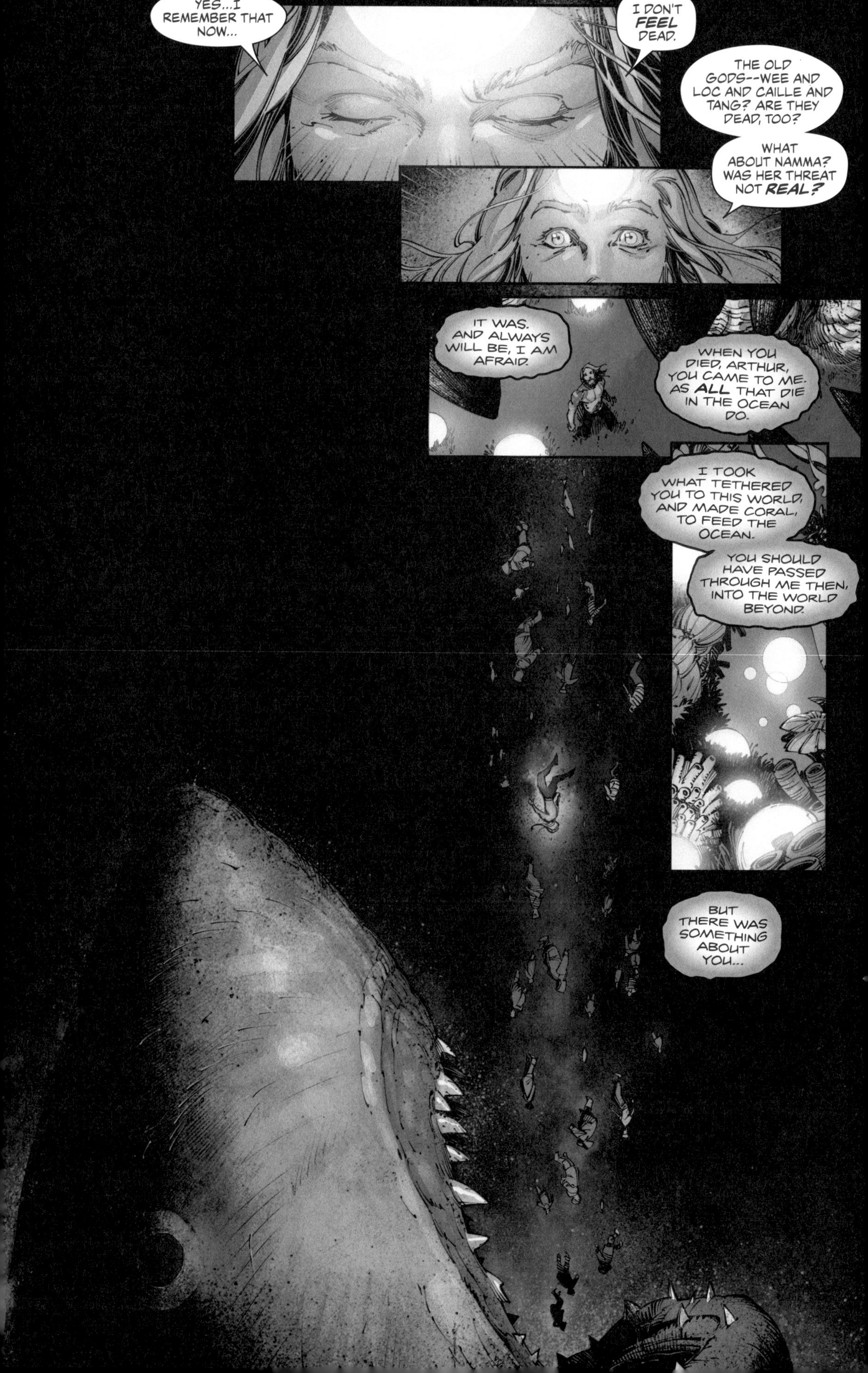
YES...I REMEMBER THAT NOW...
I DON'T FEEL DEAD.
THE OLD GODS--WEE AND LOC AND CAILLE AND TANG? ARE THEY DEAD, TOO?
WHAT ABOUT NAMMA? WAS HER THREAT NOT REAL?
IT WAS. AND ALWAYS WILL BE, I AM AFRAID.
WHEN YOU DIED, ARTHUR, YOU CAME TO ME. AS ALL THAT DIE IN THE OCEAN DO.
I TOOK WHAT TETHERED YOU TO THIS WORLD, AND MADE CORAL, TO FEED THE OCEAN.
YOU SHOULD HAVE PASSED THROUGH ME THEN, INTO THE WORLD BEYOND.
BUT THERE WAS SOMETHING ABOUT YOU...

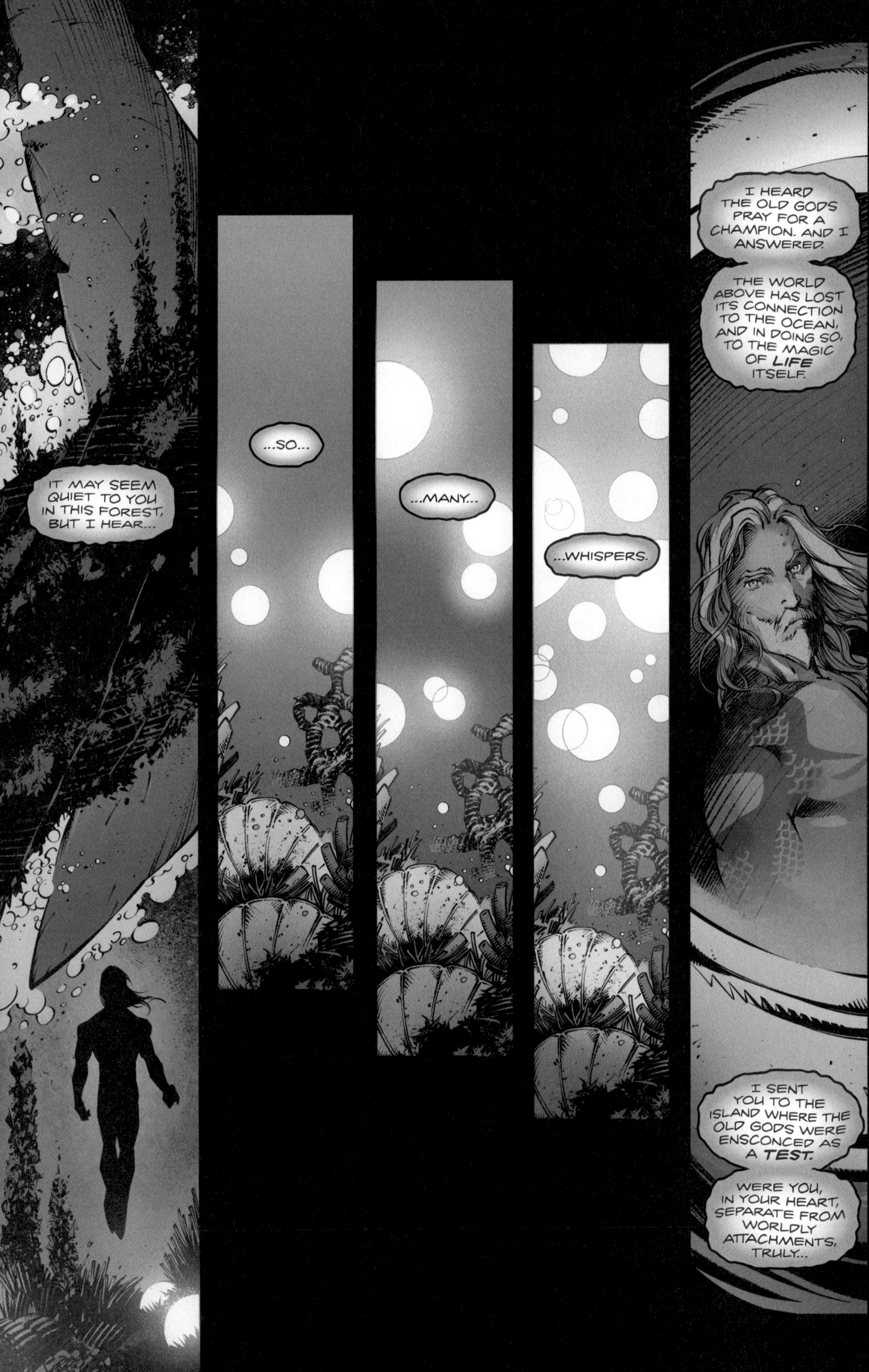
IT MAY SEEM QUIET TO YOU IN THIS FOREST, BUT I HEAR...
...SO...
...MANY...
...WHISPERS.
I HEARD THE OLD GODS PRAY FOR A CHAMPION. AND I ANSWERED.
THE WORLD ABOVE HAS LOST ITS CONNECTION TO THE OCEAN, AND IN DOING SO, TO THE MAGIC OF LIFE ITSELF.
I SENT YOU TO THE ISLAND WHERE THE OLD GODS WERE ENSCONCED AS A TEST.
WERE YOU, IN YOUR HEART, SEPARATE FROM WORLDLY ATTACHMENTS, TRULY...

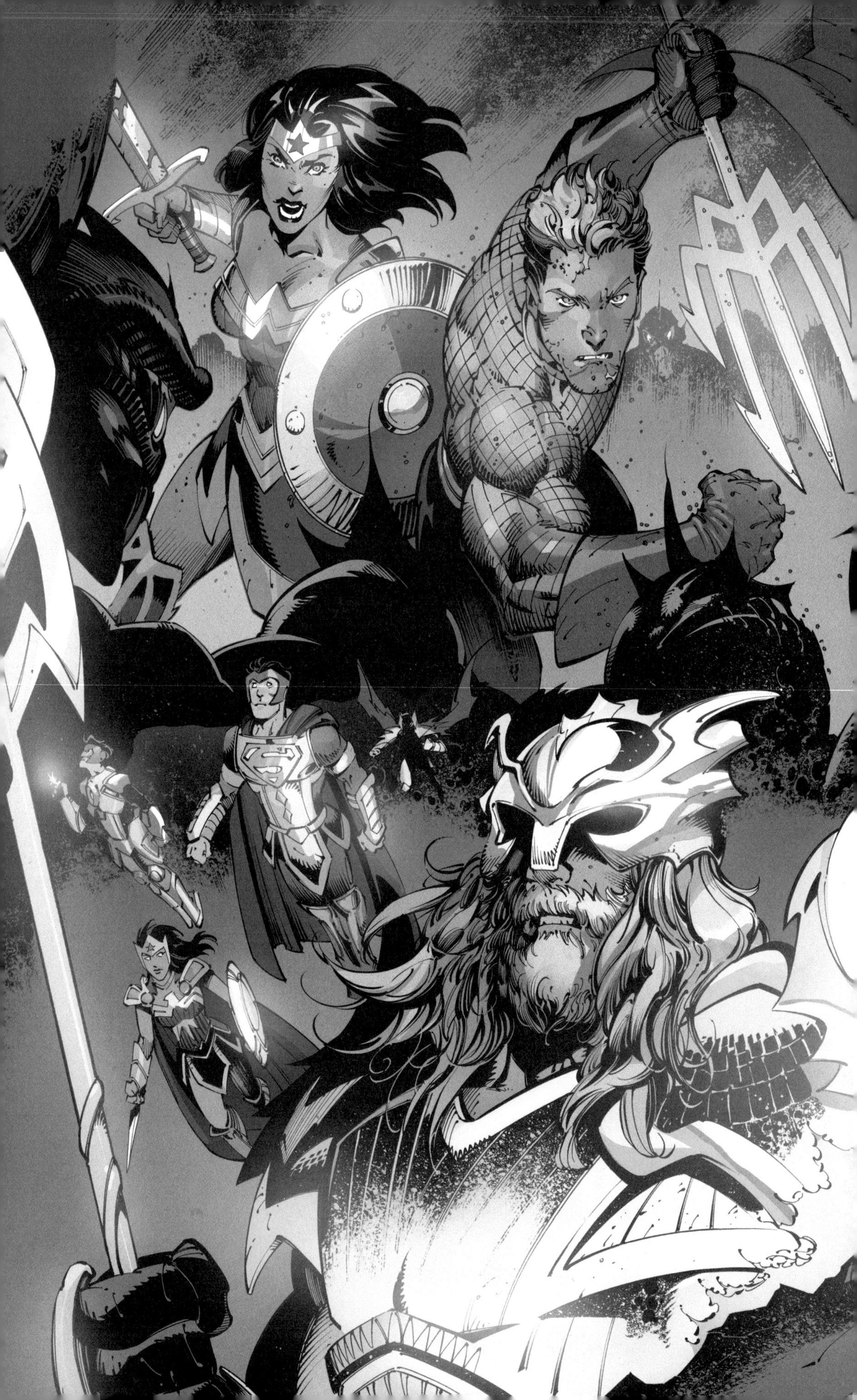

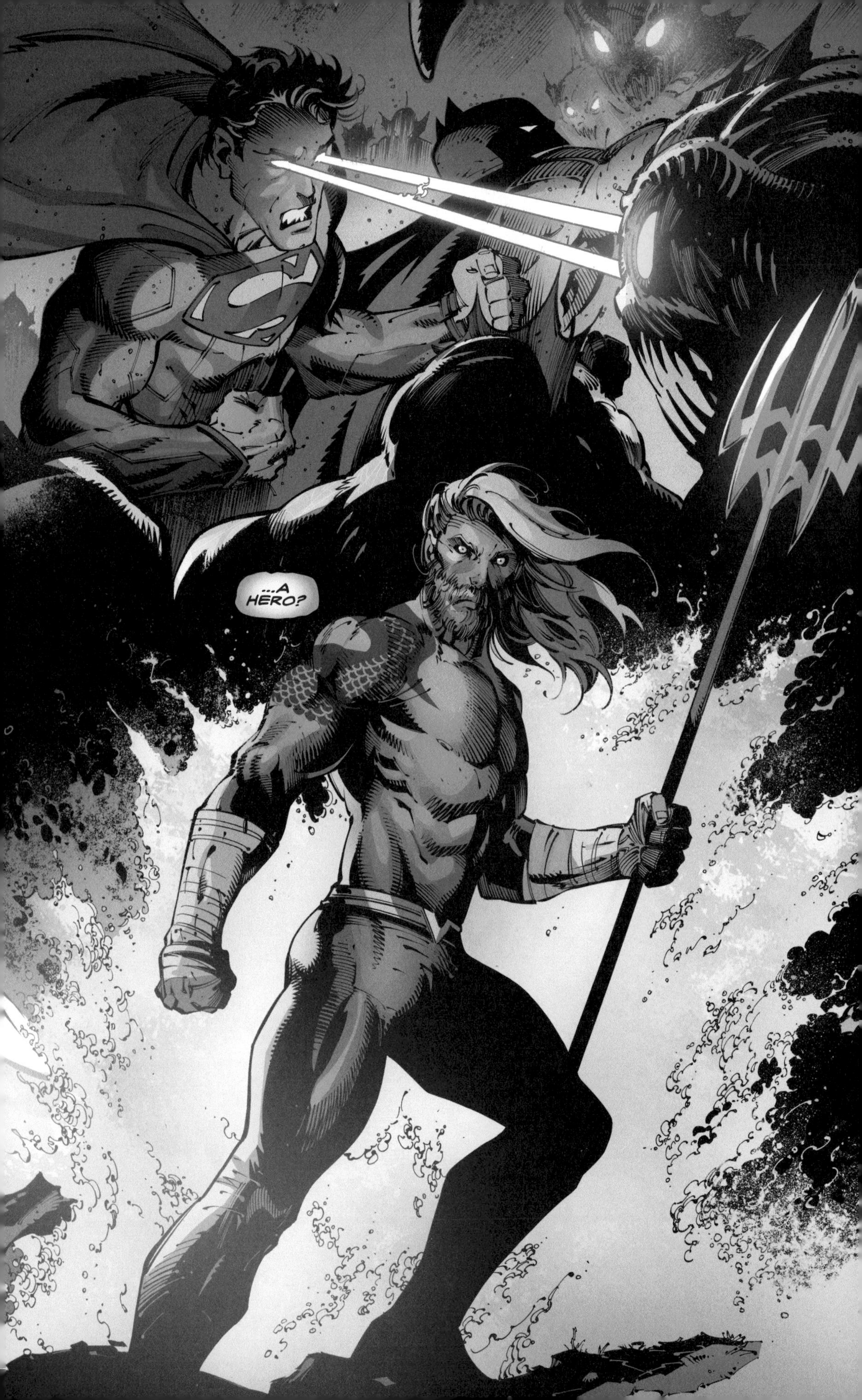
...A HERO?

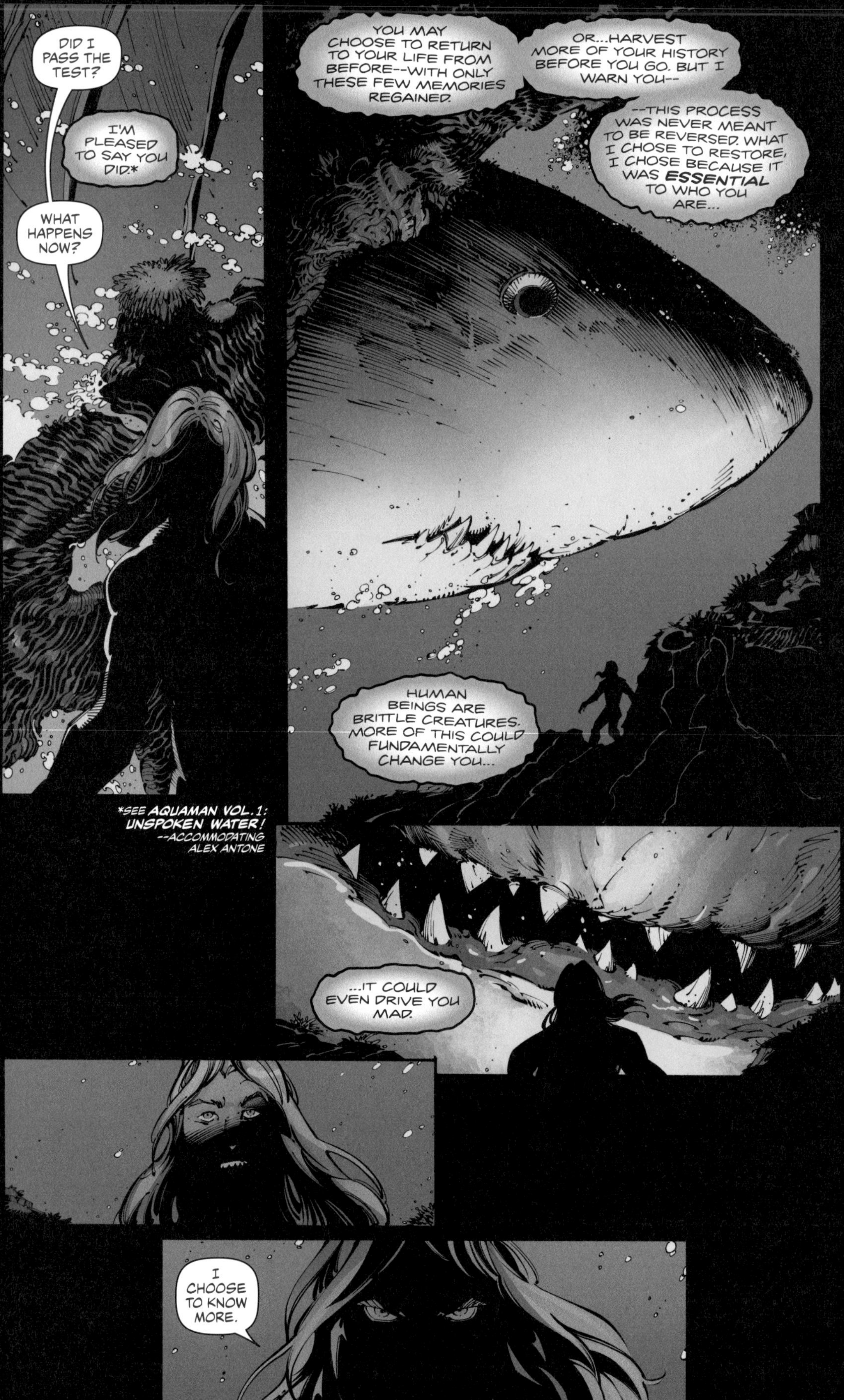
DID I PASS THE TEST?
I'M PLEASED TO SAY YOU DID.*
WHAT HAPPENS NOW?
*SEE AQUAMAN VOL.1: UNSPOKEN WATER! --ACCOMMODATING ALEX ANTONE
YOU MAY CHOOSE TO RETURN TO YOUR LIFE FROM BEFORE--WITH ONLY THESE FEW MEMORIES REGAINED.
OR...HARVEST MORE OF YOUR HISTORY BEFORE YOU GO. BUT I WARN YOU--
--THIS PROCESS WAS NEVER MEANT TO BE REVERSED. WHAT I CHOSE TO RESTORE, I CHOSE BECAUSE IT WAS ESSENTIAL TO WHO YOU ARE...
HUMAN BEINGS ARE BRITTLE CREATURES. MORE OF THIS COULD FUNDAMENTALLY CHANGE YOU...
...IT COULD EVEN DRIVE YOU MAD.
I CHOOSE TO KNOW MORE.

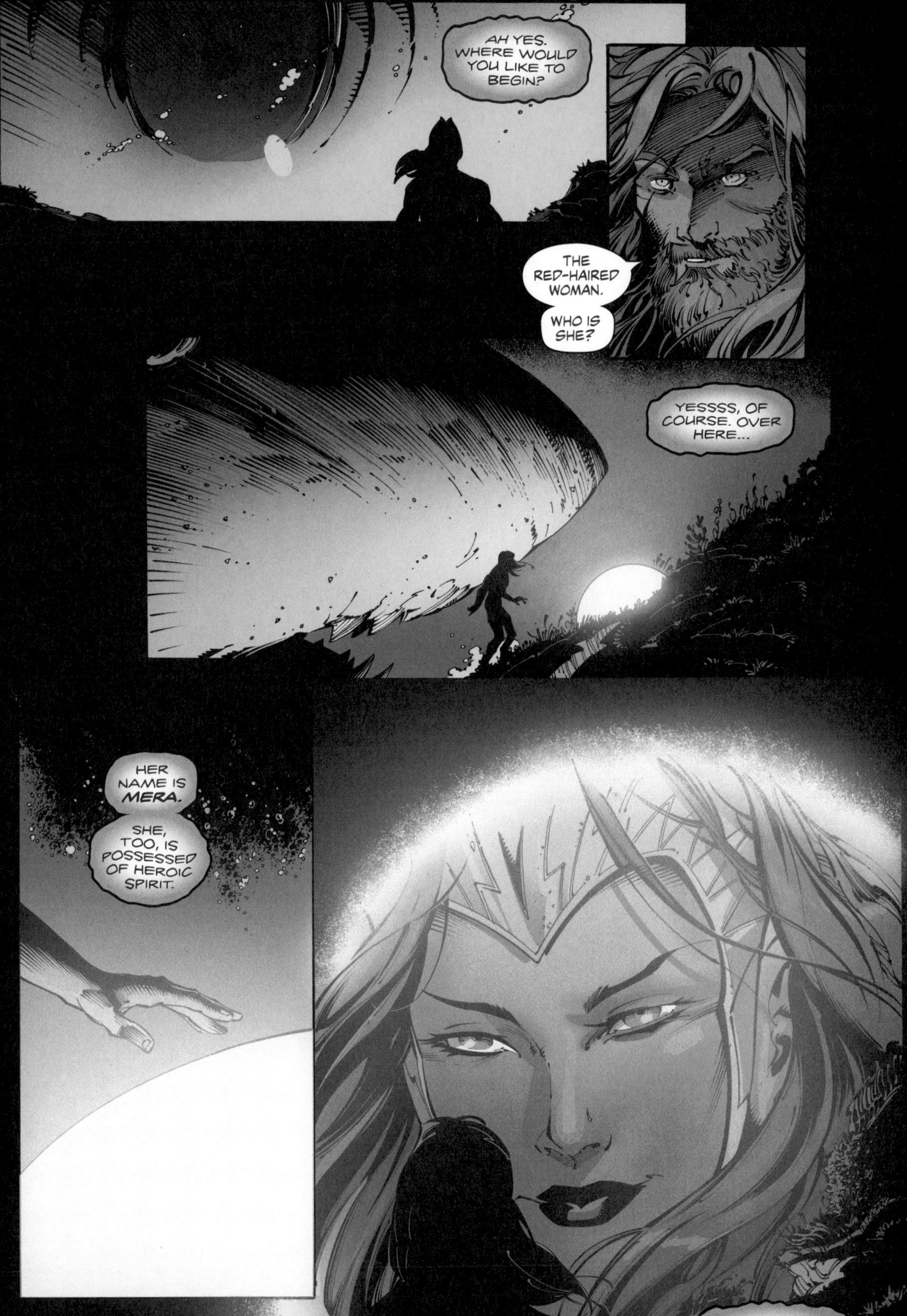
AH YES. WHERE WOULD YOU LIKE TO BEGIN?
THE RED-HAIRED WOMAN.
WHO IS SHE?
YESSSS, OF COURSE. OVER HERE...
HER NAME IS **MERA.**
SHE, TOO, IS POSSESSED OF HEROIC SPIRIT.

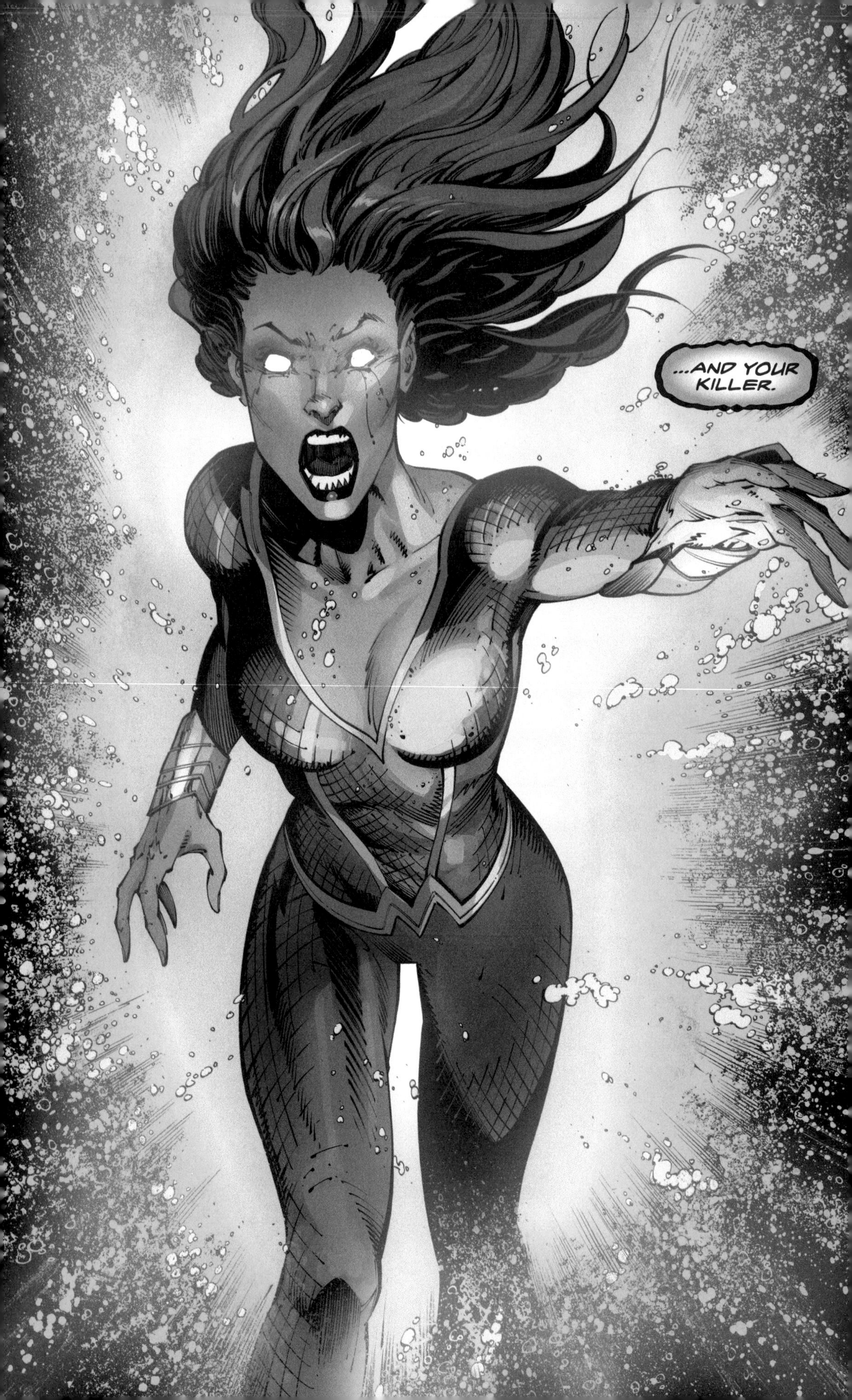
...AND YOUR KILLER.

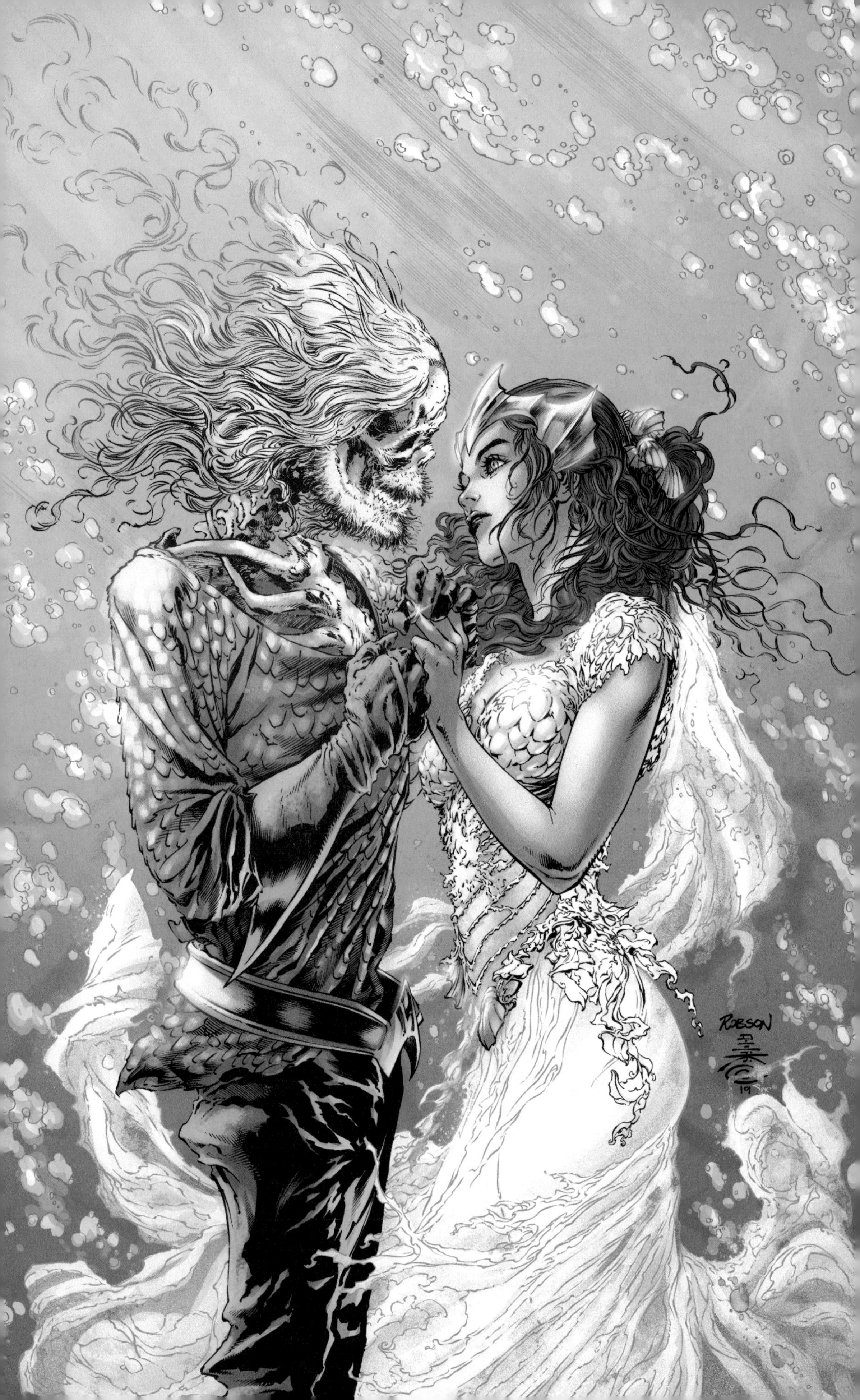
ROBSON

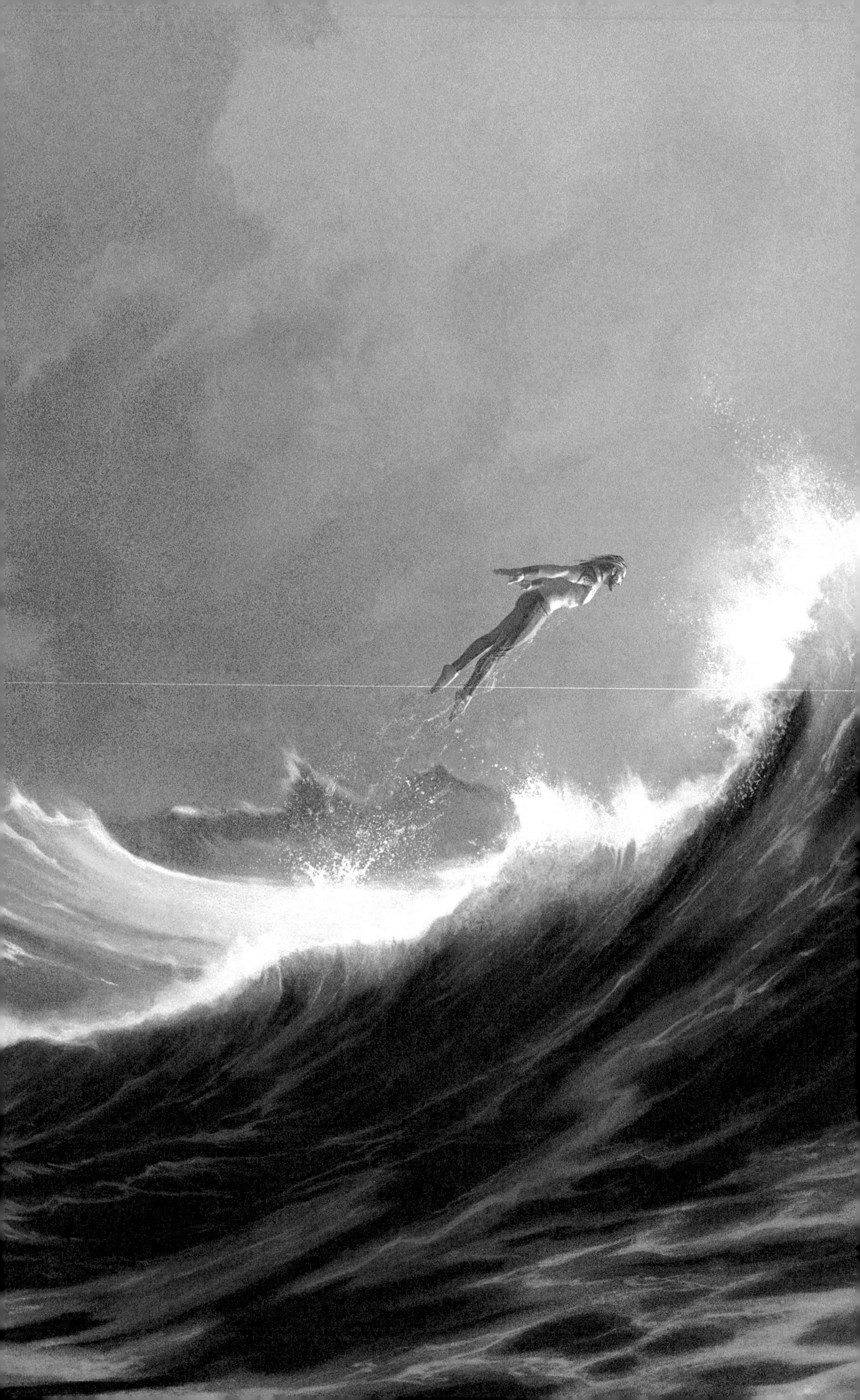

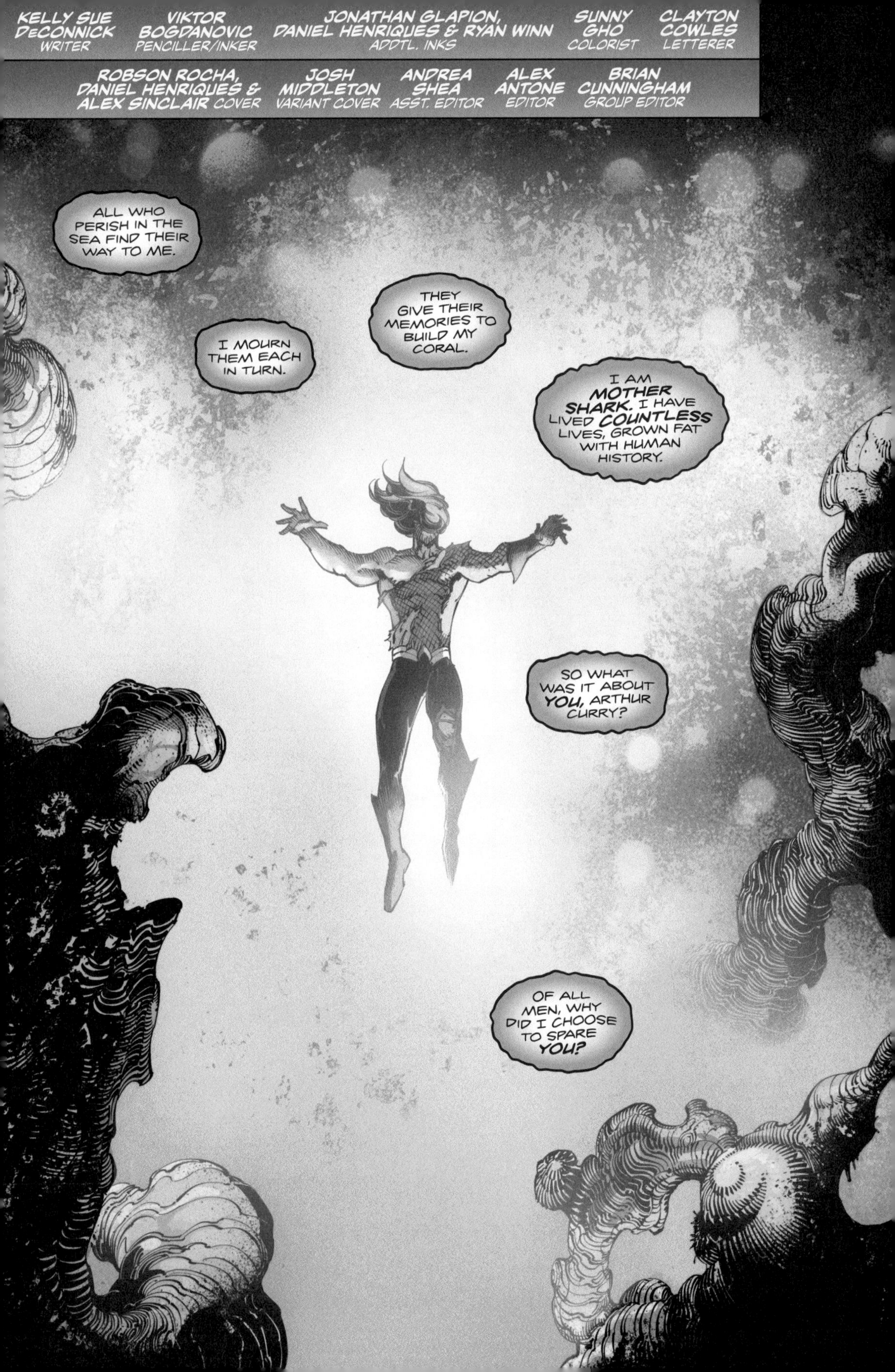
KELLY SUE DeCONNICK WRITER
VIKTOR BOGDANOVIC PENCILLER/INKER
JONATHAN GLAPION, DANIEL HENRIQUES & RYAN WINN ADDTL. INKS
SUNNY GHO COLORIST
CLAYTON COWLES LETTERER
ROBSON ROCHA, DANIEL HENRIQUES & ALEX SINCLAIR COVER
JOSH MIDDLETON VARIANT COVER
ANDREA SHEA ASST. EDITOR
ALEX ANTONE EDITOR
BRIAN CUNNINGHAM GROUP EDITOR
ALL WHO PERISH IN THE SEA FIND THEIR WAY TO ME.
I MOURN THEM EACH IN TURN.
THEY GIVE THEIR MEMORIES TO BUILD MY CORAL.
I AM MOTHER SHARK. I HAVE LIVED COUNTLESS LIVES, GROWN FAT WITH HUMAN HISTORY.
SO WHAT WAS IT ABOUT YOU, ARTHUR CURRY?
OF ALL MEN, WHY DID I CHOOSE TO SPARE YOU?

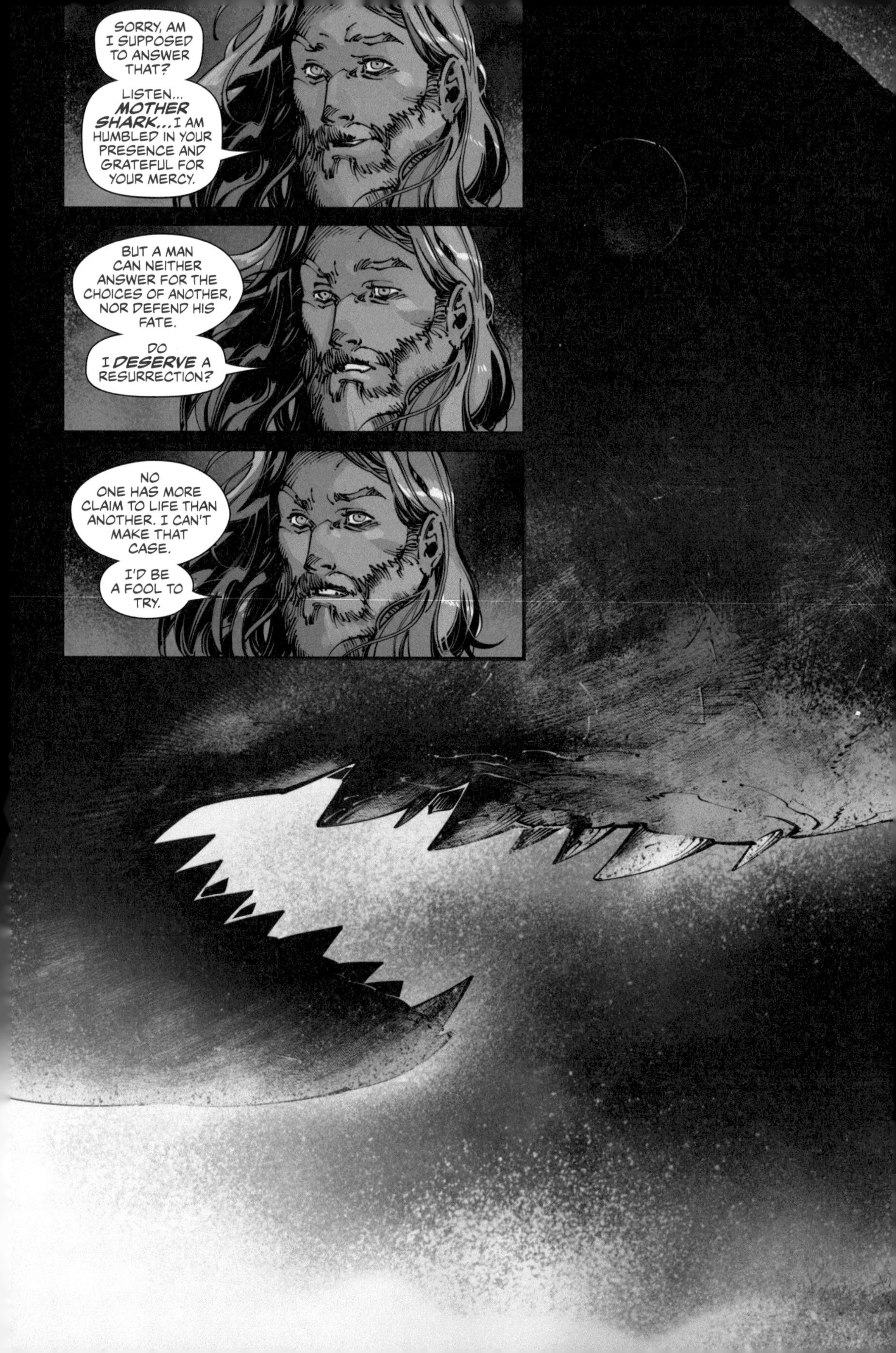
SORRY, AM I SUPPOSED TO ANSWER THAT?
LISTEN... MOTHER SHARK... I AM HUMBLED IN YOUR PRESENCE AND GRATEFUL FOR YOUR MERCY.
BUT A MAN CAN NEITHER ANSWER FOR THE CHOICES OF ANOTHER, NOR DEFEND HIS FATE.
DO I DESERVE A RESURRECTION?
NO ONE HAS MORE CLAIM TO LIFE THAN ANOTHER. I CAN'T MAKE THAT CASE.
I'D BE A FOOL TO TRY.

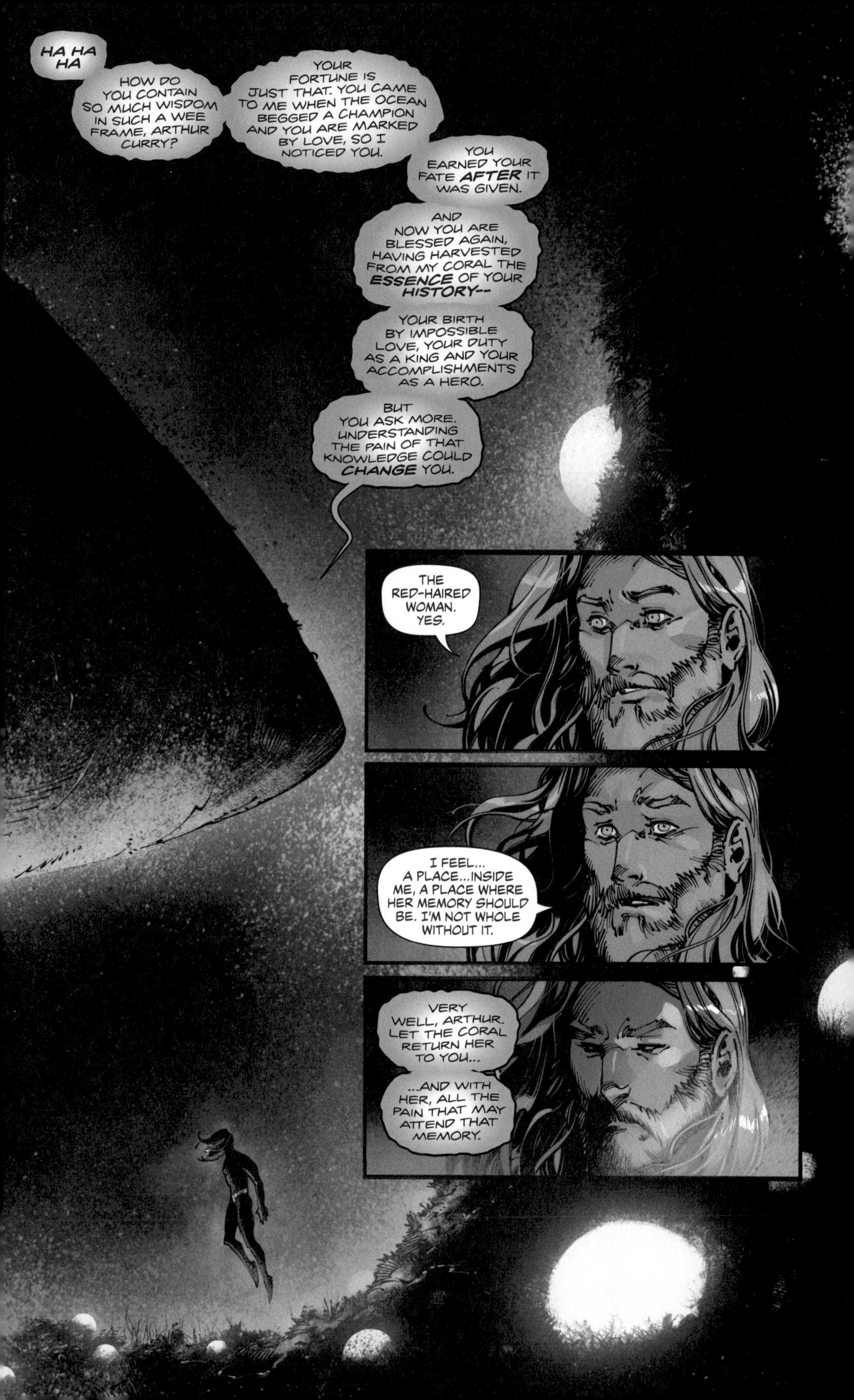
HA HA HA
HOW DO YOU CONTAIN SO MUCH WISDOM IN SUCH A WEE FRAME, ARTHUR CURRY?
YOUR FORTUNE IS JUST THAT. YOU CAME TO ME WHEN THE OCEAN BEGGED A CHAMPION AND YOU ARE MARKED BY LOVE, SO I NOTICED YOU.
YOU EARNED YOUR FATE AFTER IT WAS GIVEN.
AND NOW YOU ARE BLESSED AGAIN, HAVING HARVESTED FROM MY CORAL THE ESSENCE OF YOUR HISTORY--
YOUR BIRTH BY IMPOSSIBLE LOVE, YOUR DUTY AS A KING AND YOUR ACCOMPLISHMENTS AS A HERO.
BUT YOU ASK MORE. UNDERSTANDING THE PAIN OF THAT KNOWLEDGE COULD CHANGE YOU.
THE RED-HAIRED WOMAN. YES.
I FEEL... A PLACE...INSIDE ME, A PLACE WHERE HER MEMORY SHOULD BE. I'M NOT WHOLE WITHOUT IT.
VERY WELL, ARTHUR. LET THE CORAL RETURN HER TO YOU...
...AND WITH HER, ALL THE PAIN THAT MAY ATTEND THAT MEMORY.

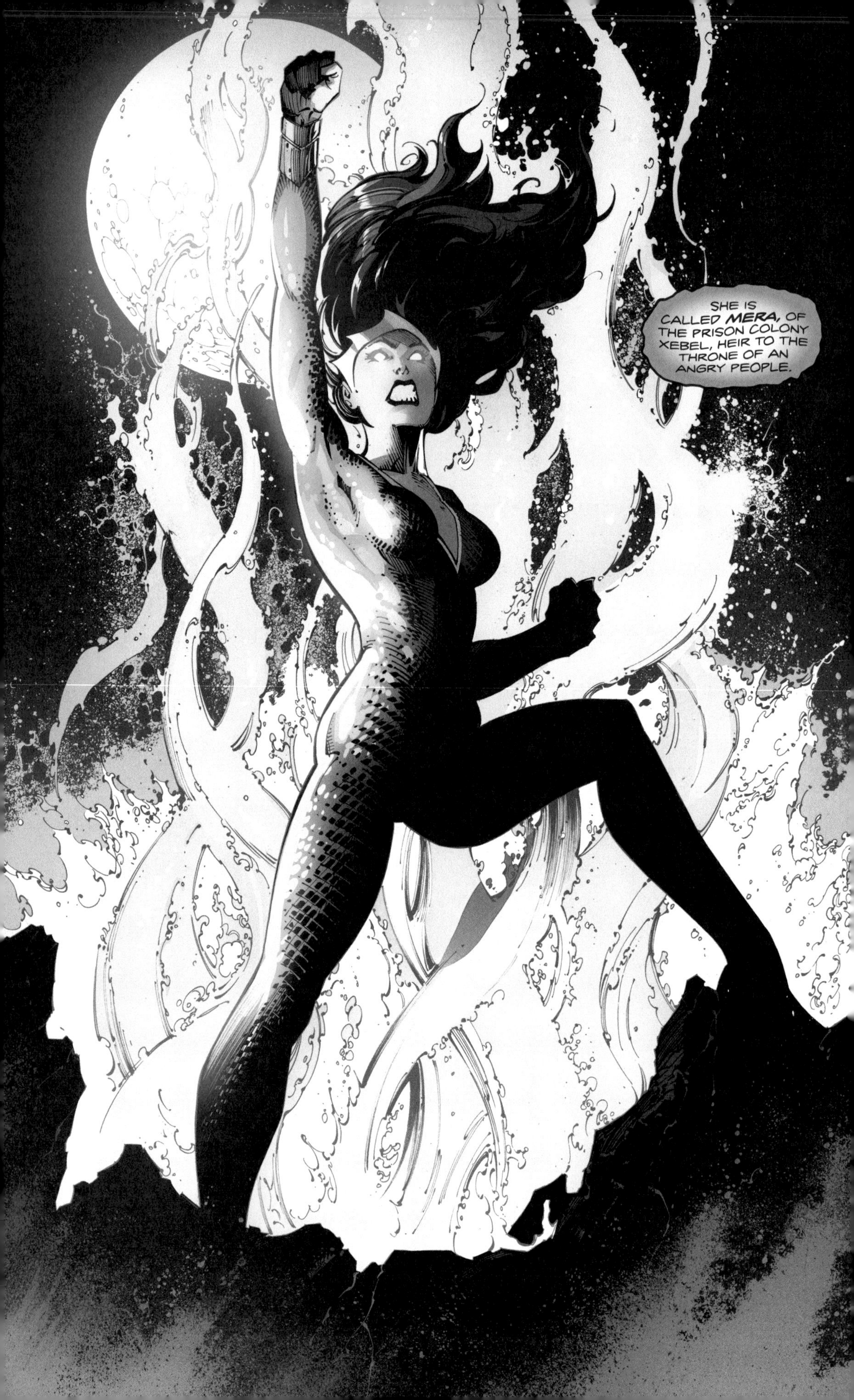
SHE IS CALLED MERA, OF THE PRISON COLONY XEBEL, HEIR TO THE THRONE OF AN ANGRY PEOPLE.

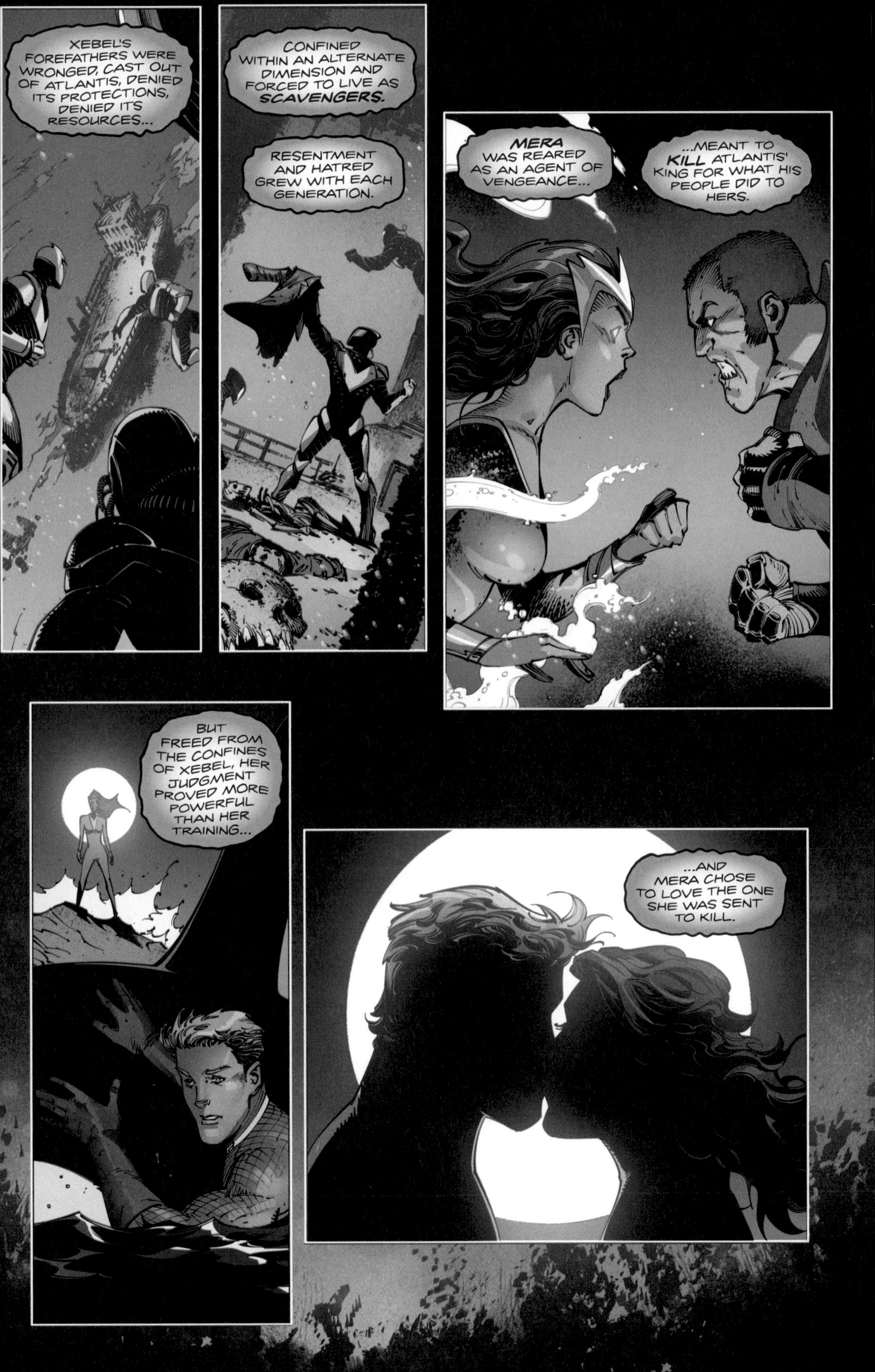
XEBEL'S FOREFATHERS WERE WRONGED, CAST OUT OF ATLANTIS, DENIED ITS PROTECTIONS, DENIED ITS RESOURCES...
CONFINED WITHIN AN ALTERNATE DIMENSION AND FORCED TO LIVE AS SCAVENGERS.
RESENTMENT AND HATRED GREW WITH EACH GENERATION.
MERA WAS REARED AS AN AGENT OF VENGEANCE...
...MEANT TO KILL ATLANTIS' KING FOR WHAT HIS PEOPLE DID TO HERS.
BUT FREED FROM THE CONFINES OF XEBEL, HER JUDGMENT PROVED MORE POWERFUL THAN HER TRAINING...
...AND MERA CHOSE TO LOVE THE ONE SHE WAS SENT TO KILL.

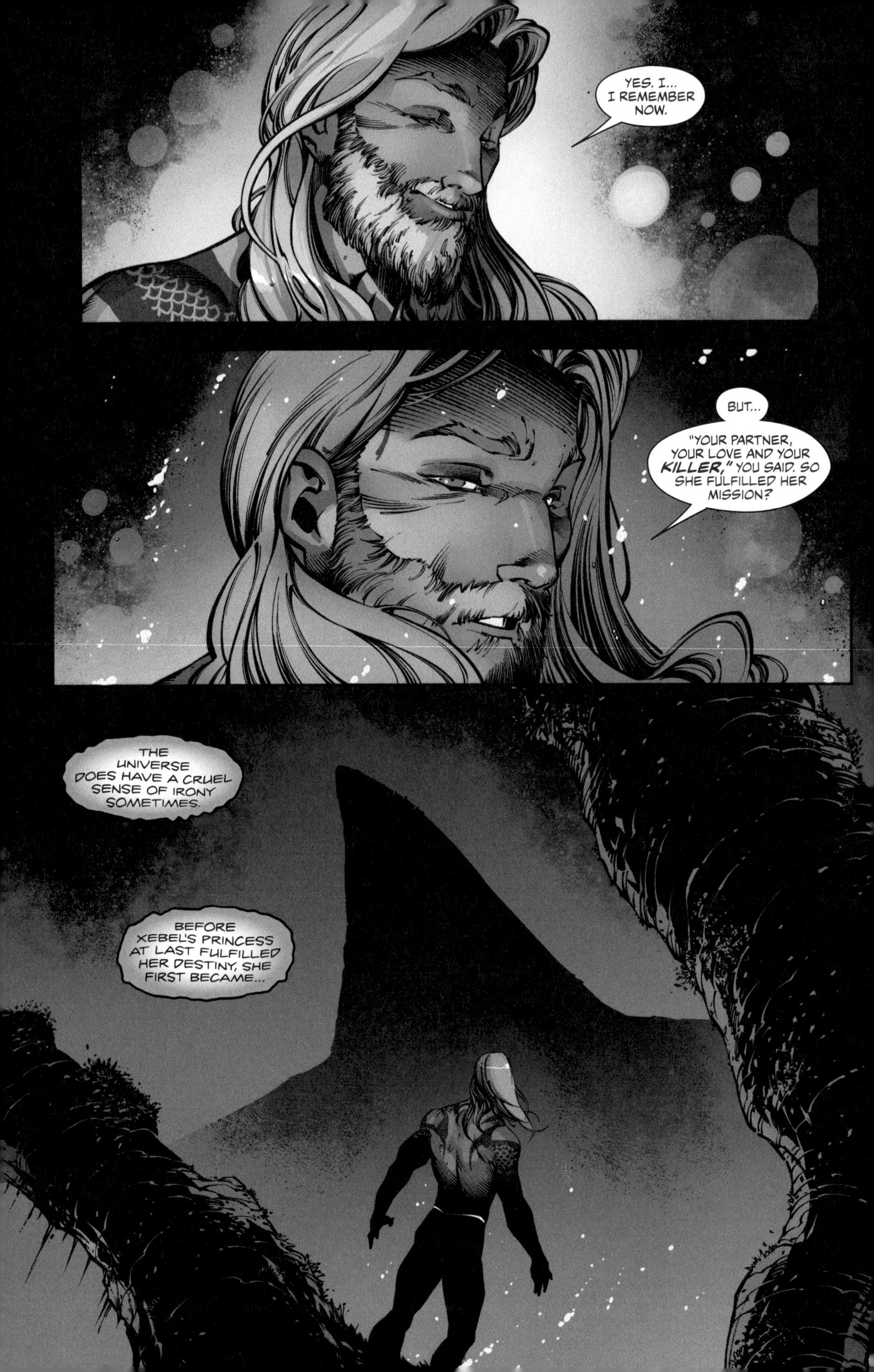
YES. I... I REMEMBER NOW.
BUT...
"YOUR PARTNER, YOUR LOVE AND YOUR KILLER," YOU SAID. SO SHE FULFILLED HER MISSION?
THE UNIVERSE DOES HAVE A CRUEL SENSE OF IRONY SOMETIMES.
BEFORE XEBEL'S PRINCESS AT LAST FULFILLED HER DESTINY, SHE FIRST BECAME...

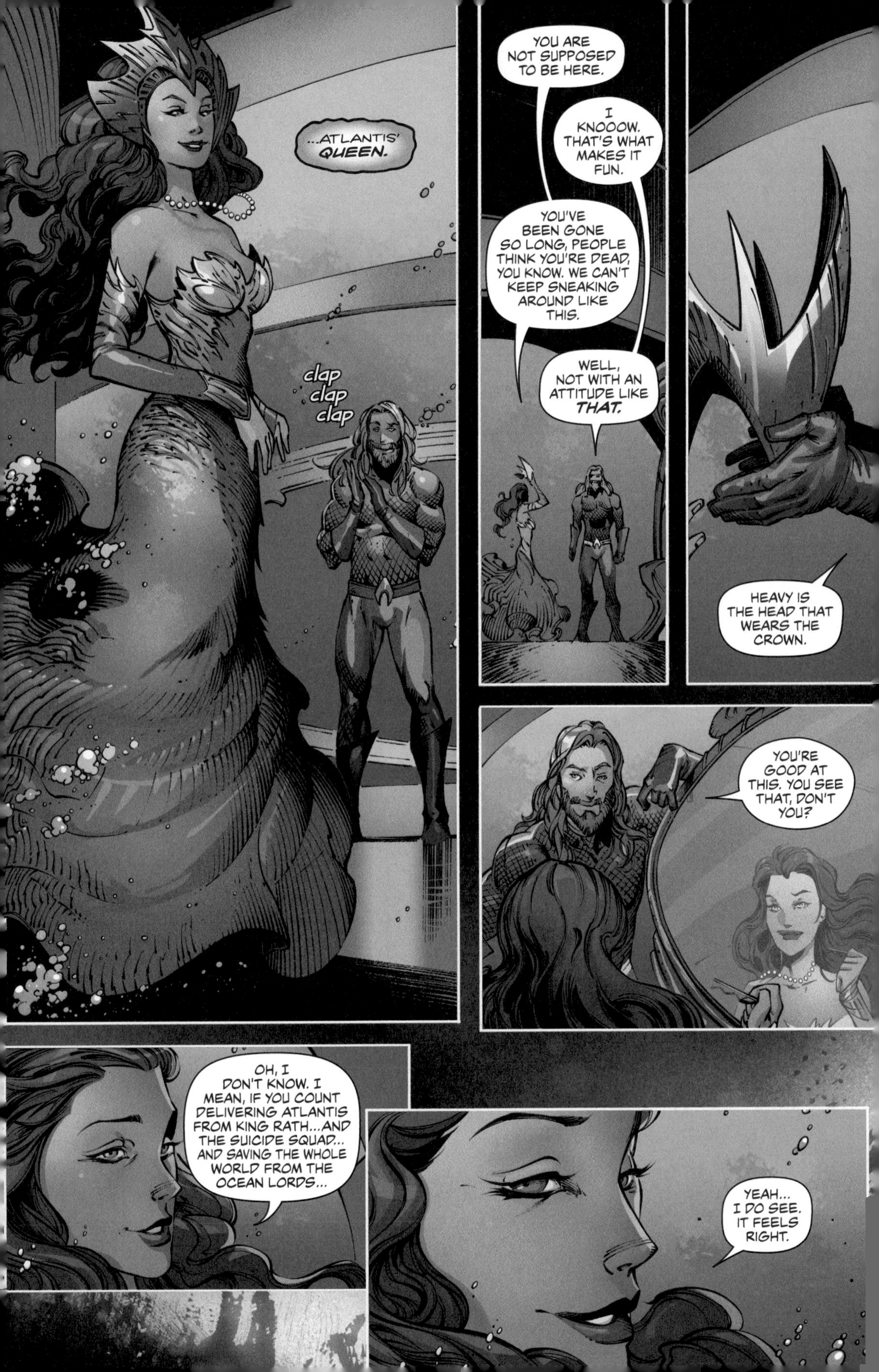

...ATLANTIS' QUEEN.
clap clap clap
YOU ARE NOT SUPPOSED TO BE HERE.
I KNOOOW. THAT'S WHAT MAKES IT FUN.
YOU'VE BEEN GONE SO LONG, PEOPLE THINK YOU'RE DEAD, YOU KNOW. WE CAN'T KEEP SNEAKING AROUND LIKE THIS.
WELL, NOT WITH AN ATTITUDE LIKE THAT.
HEAVY IS THE HEAD THAT WEARS THE CROWN.
YOU'RE GOOD AT THIS. YOU SEE THAT, DON'T YOU?
OH, I DON'T KNOW. I MEAN, IF YOU COUNT DELIVERING ATLANTIS FROM KING RATH...AND THE SUICIDE SQUAD... AND SAVING THE WHOLE WORLD FROM THE OCEAN LORDS...
YEAH... I DO SEE. IT FEELS RIGHT.

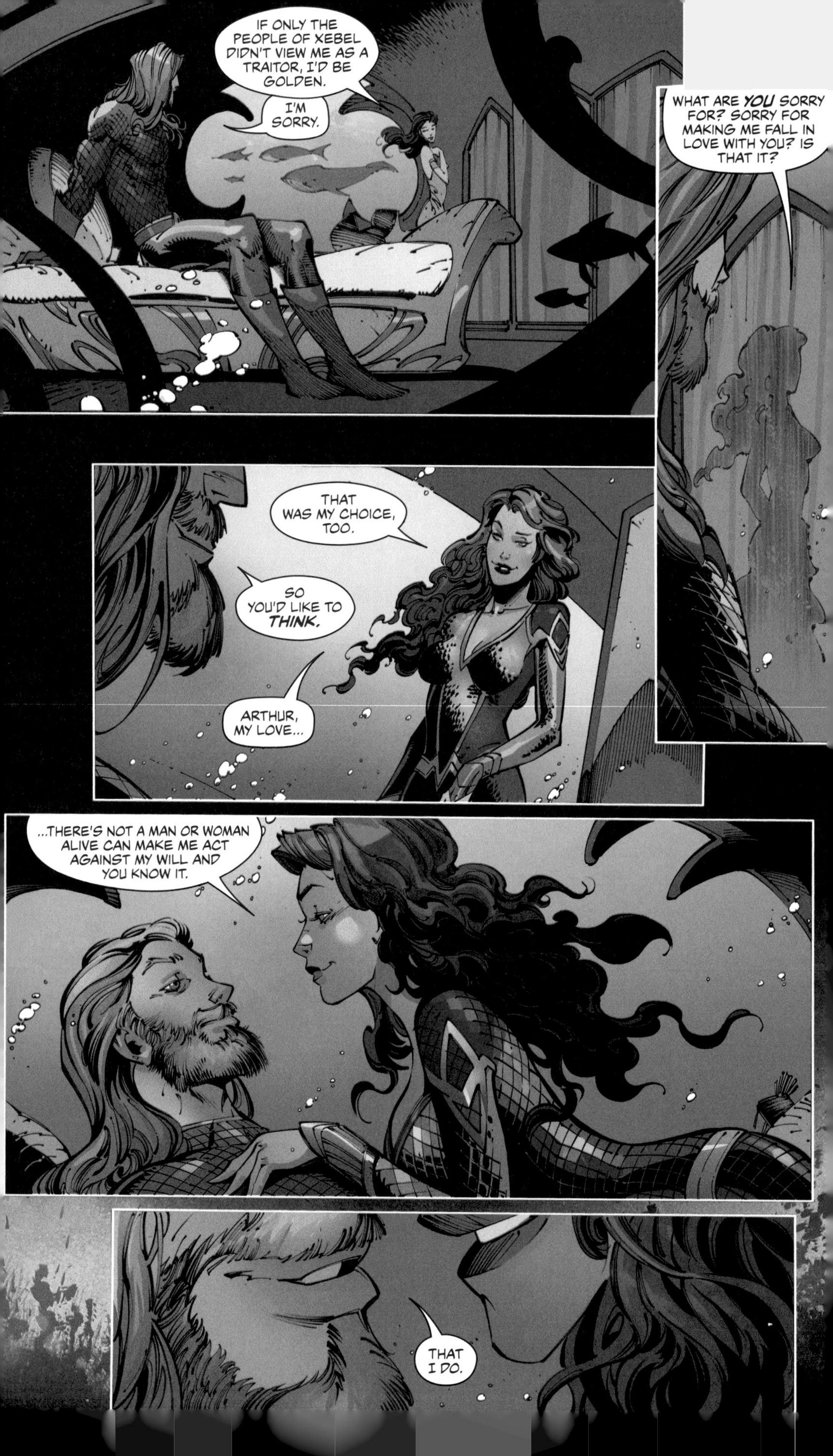
IF ONLY THE PEOPLE OF XEBEL DIDN'T VIEW ME AS A TRAITOR, I'D BE GOLDEN.
I'M SORRY.
WHAT ARE YOU SORRY FOR? SORRY FOR MAKING ME FALL IN LOVE WITH YOU? IS THAT IT?
THAT WAS MY CHOICE, TOO.
SO YOU'D LIKE TO THINK.
ARTHUR, MY LOVE...
...THERE'S NOT A MAN OR WOMAN ALIVE CAN MAKE ME ACT AGAINST MY WILL AND YOU KNOW IT.
THAT I DO.

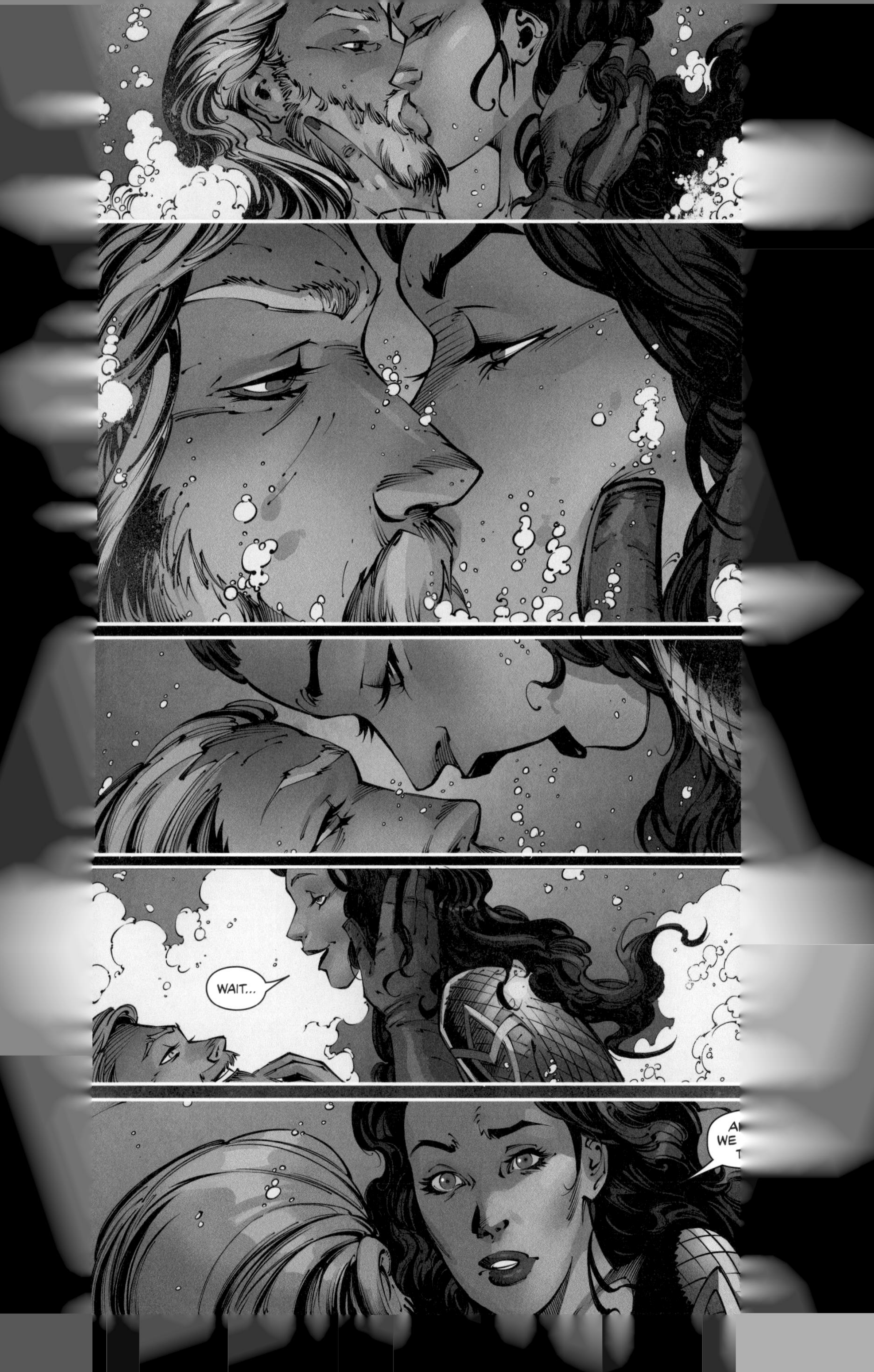
WAIT...

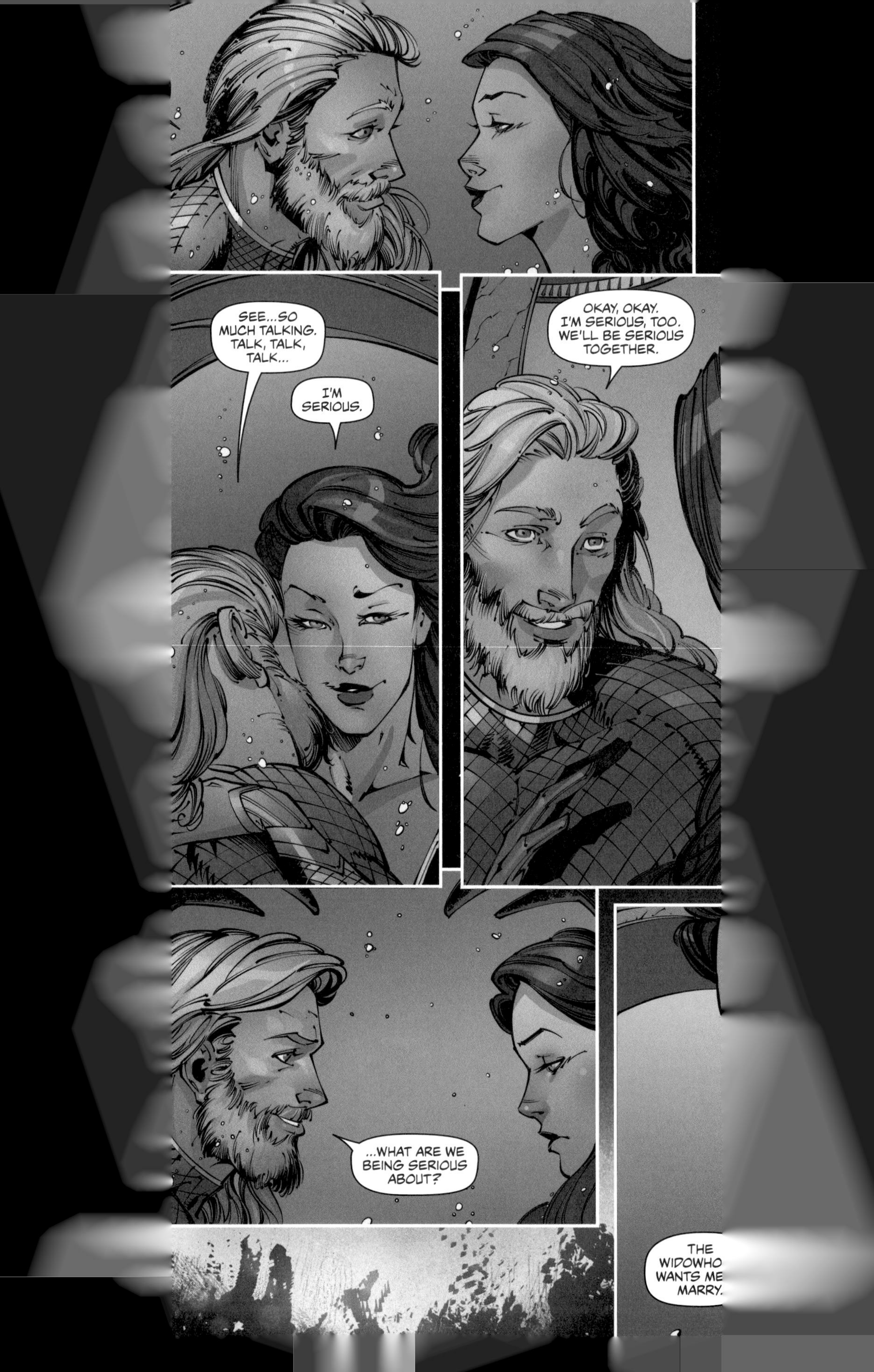
SEE...SO MUCH TALKING. TALK, TALK, TALK...
I'M SERIOUS.
OKAY, OKAY. I'M SERIOUS, TOO. WE'LL BE SERIOUS TOGETHER.
...WHAT ARE WE BEING SERIOUS ABOUT?
THE WIDOWHO WANTS ME MARRY.

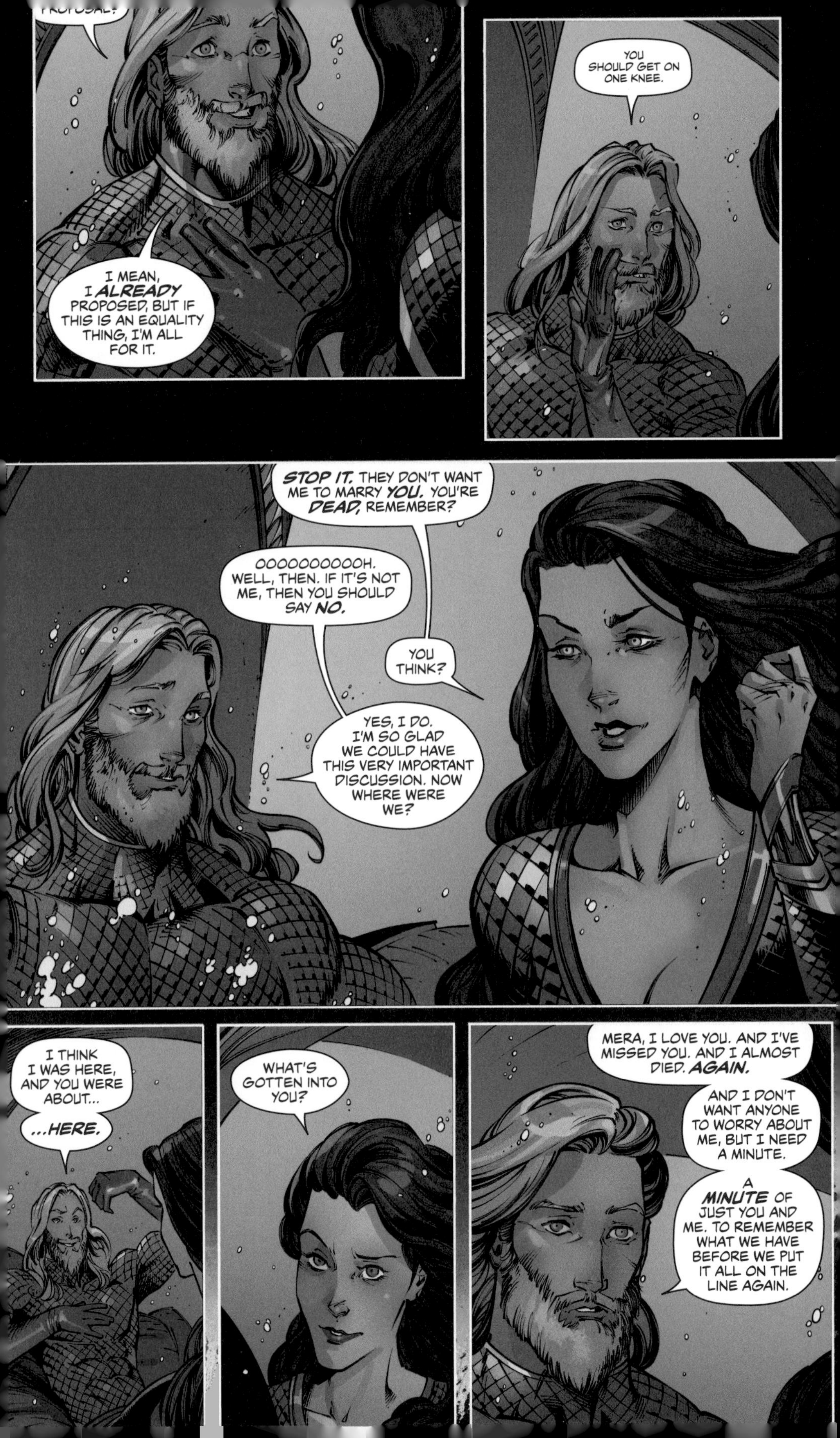
I MEAN, I ALREADY PROPOSED, BUT IF THIS IS AN EQUALITY THING, I'M ALL FOR IT.
YOU SHOULD GET ON ONE KNEE.
STOP IT. THEY DON'T WANT ME TO MARRY YOU. YOU'RE DEAD, REMEMBER?
OOOOOOOOOOH. WELL, THEN. IF IT'S NOT ME, THEN YOU SHOULD SAY NO.
YOU THINK?
YES, I DO. I'M SO GLAD WE COULD HAVE THIS VERY IMPORTANT DISCUSSION. NOW WHERE WERE WE?
I THINK I WAS HERE, AND YOU WERE ABOUT...
...HERE.
WHAT'S GOTTEN INTO YOU?
MERA, I LOVE YOU. AND I'VE MISSED YOU. AND I ALMOST DIED. AGAIN.
AND I DON'T WANT ANYONE TO WORRY ABOUT ME, BUT I NEED A MINUTE.
A MINUTE OF JUST YOU AND ME. TO REMEMBER WHAT WE HAVE BEFORE WE PUT IT ALL ON THE LINE AGAIN.

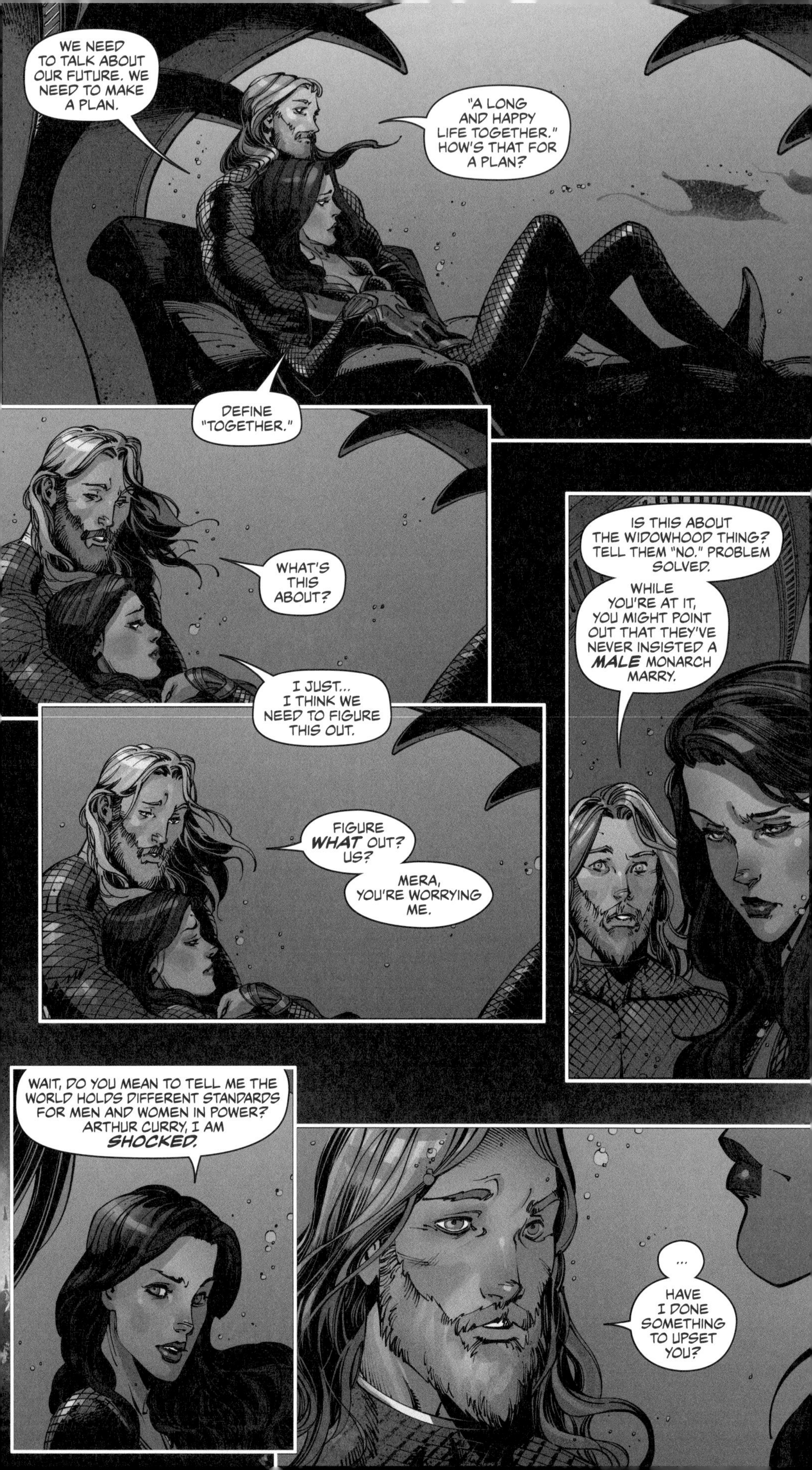
WE NEED TO TALK ABOUT OUR FUTURE. WE NEED TO MAKE A PLAN.
"A LONG AND HAPPY LIFE TOGETHER." HOW'S THAT FOR A PLAN?
DEFINE "TOGETHER."
WHAT'S THIS ABOUT?
I JUST... I THINK WE NEED TO FIGURE THIS OUT.
FIGURE WHAT OUT? US?
MERA, YOU'RE WORRYING ME.
IS THIS ABOUT THE WIDOWHOOD THING? TELL THEM "NO." PROBLEM SOLVED.
WHILE YOU'RE AT IT, YOU MIGHT POINT OUT THAT THEY'VE NEVER INSISTED A MALE MONARCH MARRY.
WAIT, DO YOU MEAN TO TELL ME THE WORLD HOLDS DIFFERENT STANDARDS FOR MEN AND WOMEN IN POWER? ARTHUR CURRY, I AM SHOCKED.
...
HAVE I DONE SOMETHING TO UPSET YOU?

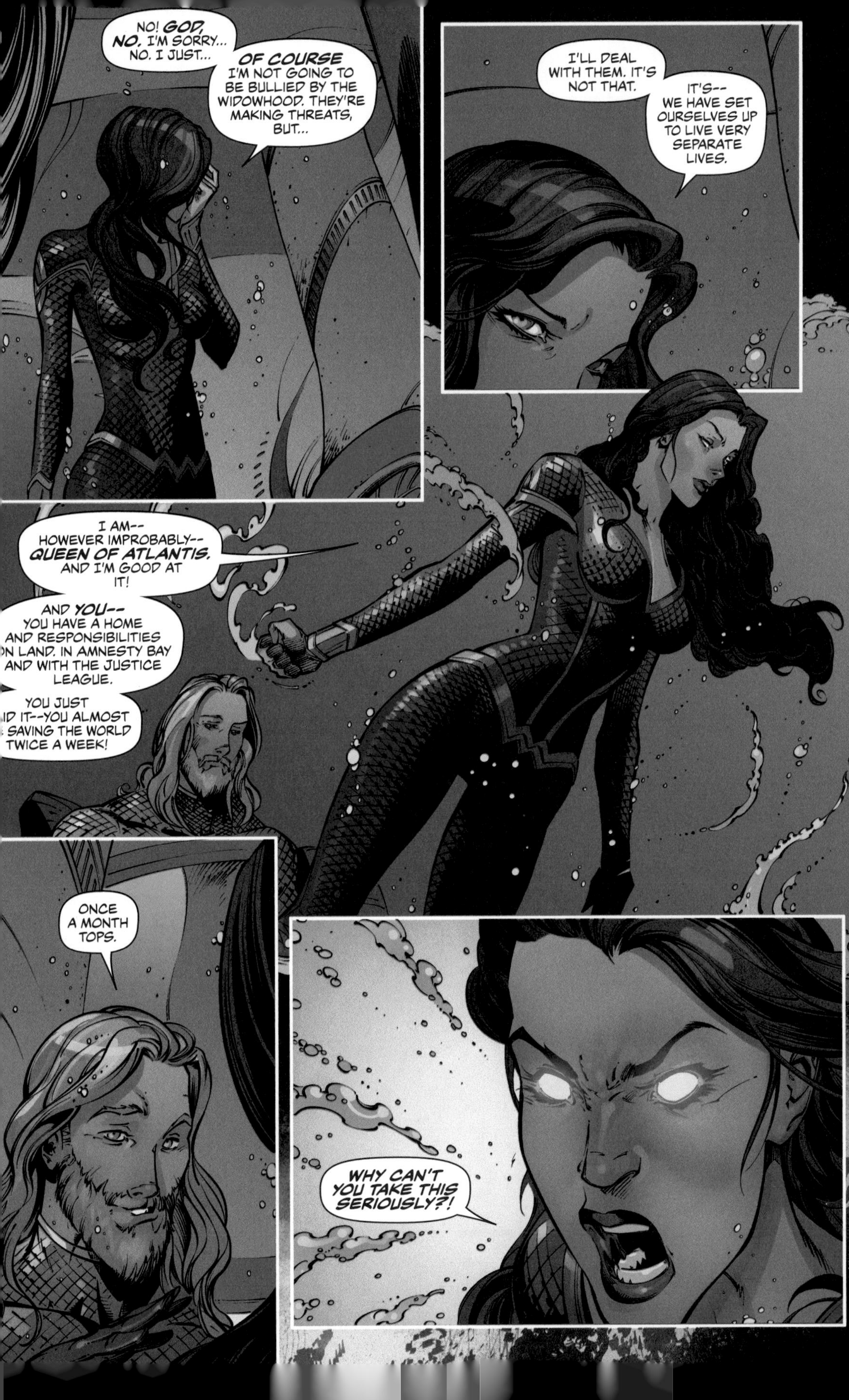
NO! GOD, NO. I'M SORRY... NO. I JUST...
OF COURSE I'M NOT GOING TO BE BULLIED BY THE WIDOWHOOD. THEY'RE MAKING THREATS, BUT...
I'LL DEAL WITH THEM. IT'S NOT THAT.
IT'S-- WE HAVE SET OURSELVES UP TO LIVE VERY SEPARATE LIVES.
I AM-- HOWEVER IMPROBABLY-- QUEEN OF ATLANTIS. AND I'M GOOD AT IT!
AND YOU-- YOU HAVE A HOME AND RESPONSIBILITIES ON LAND. IN AMNESTY BAY AND WITH THE JUSTICE LEAGUE.
YOU JUST ID IT--YOU ALMOST SAVING THE WORLD TWICE A WEEK!
ONCE A MONTH TOPS.
WHY CAN'T YOU TAKE THIS SERIOUSLY?!

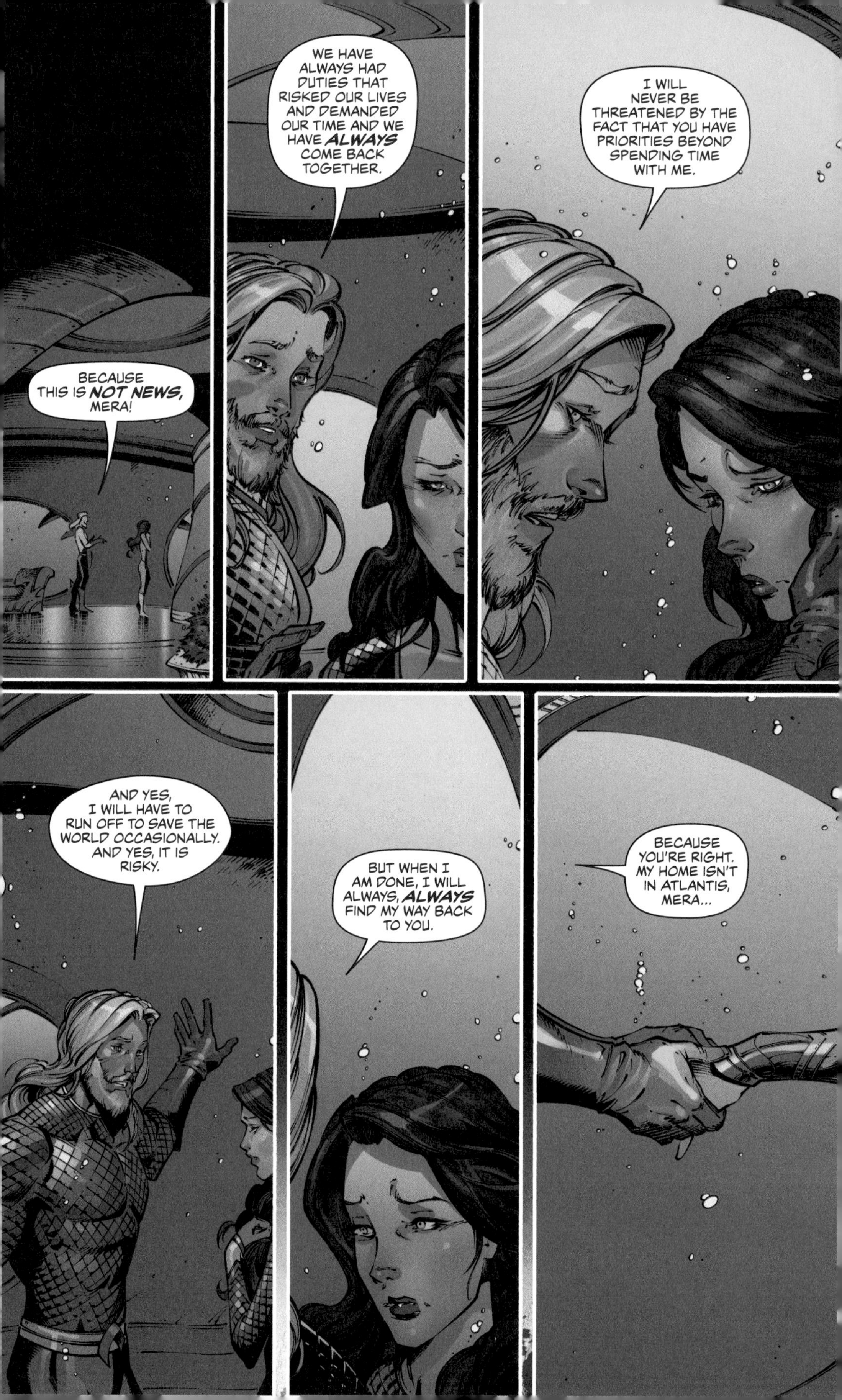
BECAUSE THIS IS NOT NEWS, MERA!
WE HAVE ALWAYS HAD DUTIES THAT RISKED OUR LIVES AND DEMANDED OUR TIME AND WE HAVE ALWAYS COME BACK TOGETHER.
I WILL NEVER BE THREATENED BY THE FACT THAT YOU HAVE PRIORITIES BEYOND SPENDING TIME WITH ME.
AND YES, I WILL HAVE TO RUN OFF TO SAVE THE WORLD OCCASIONALLY. AND YES, IT IS RISKY.
BUT WHEN I AM DONE, I WILL ALWAYS, ALWAYS FIND MY WAY BACK TO YOU.
BECAUSE YOU'RE RIGHT. MY HOME ISN'T IN ATLANTIS, MERA...

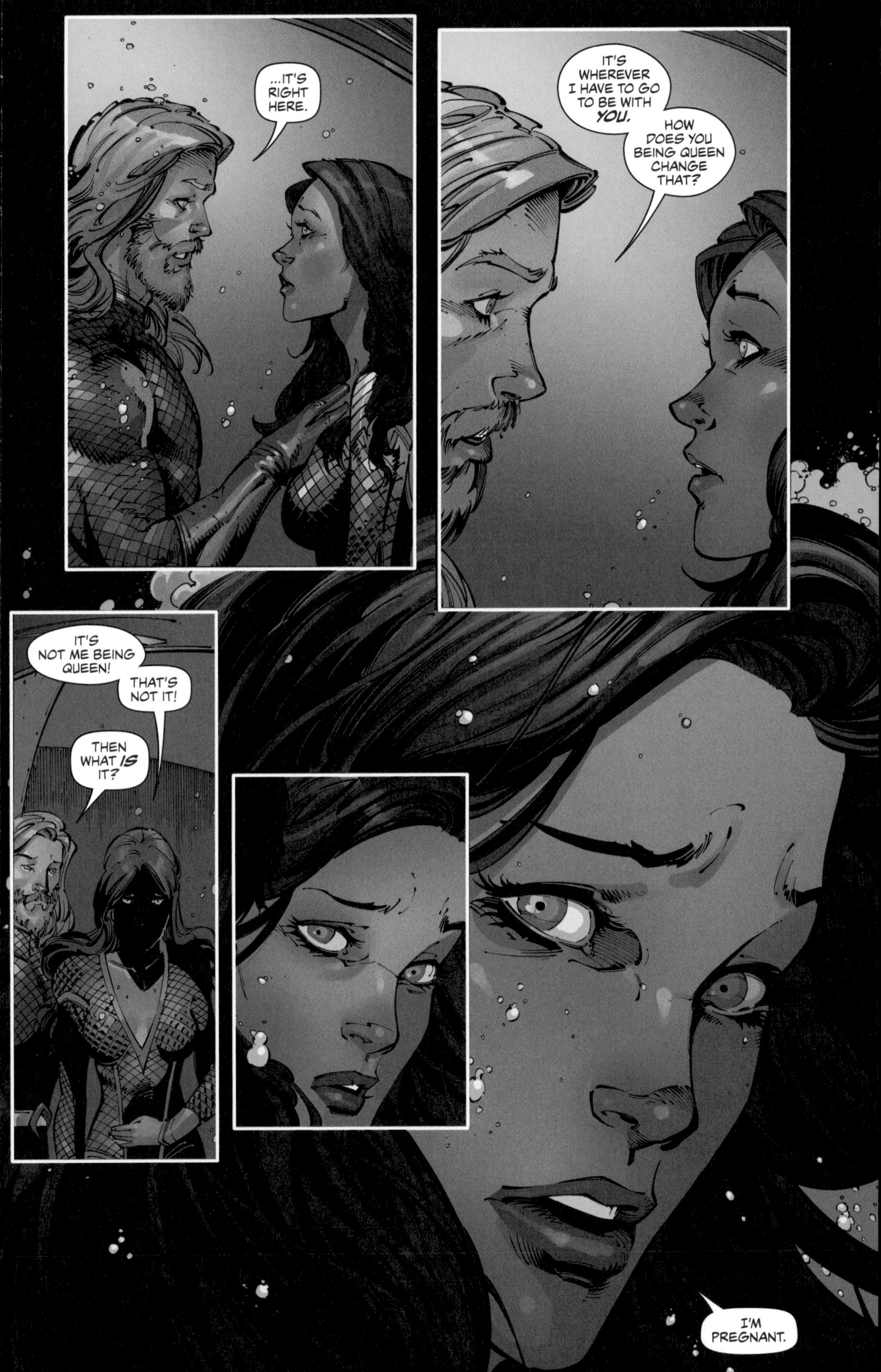

...IT'S RIGHT HERE.
IT'S WHEREVER I HAVE TO GO TO BE WITH *YOU.*
HOW DOES YOU BEING QUEEN CHANGE THAT?
IT'S NOT ME BEING QUEEN!
THAT'S NOT IT!
THEN WHAT *IS* IT?
I'M PREGNANT.

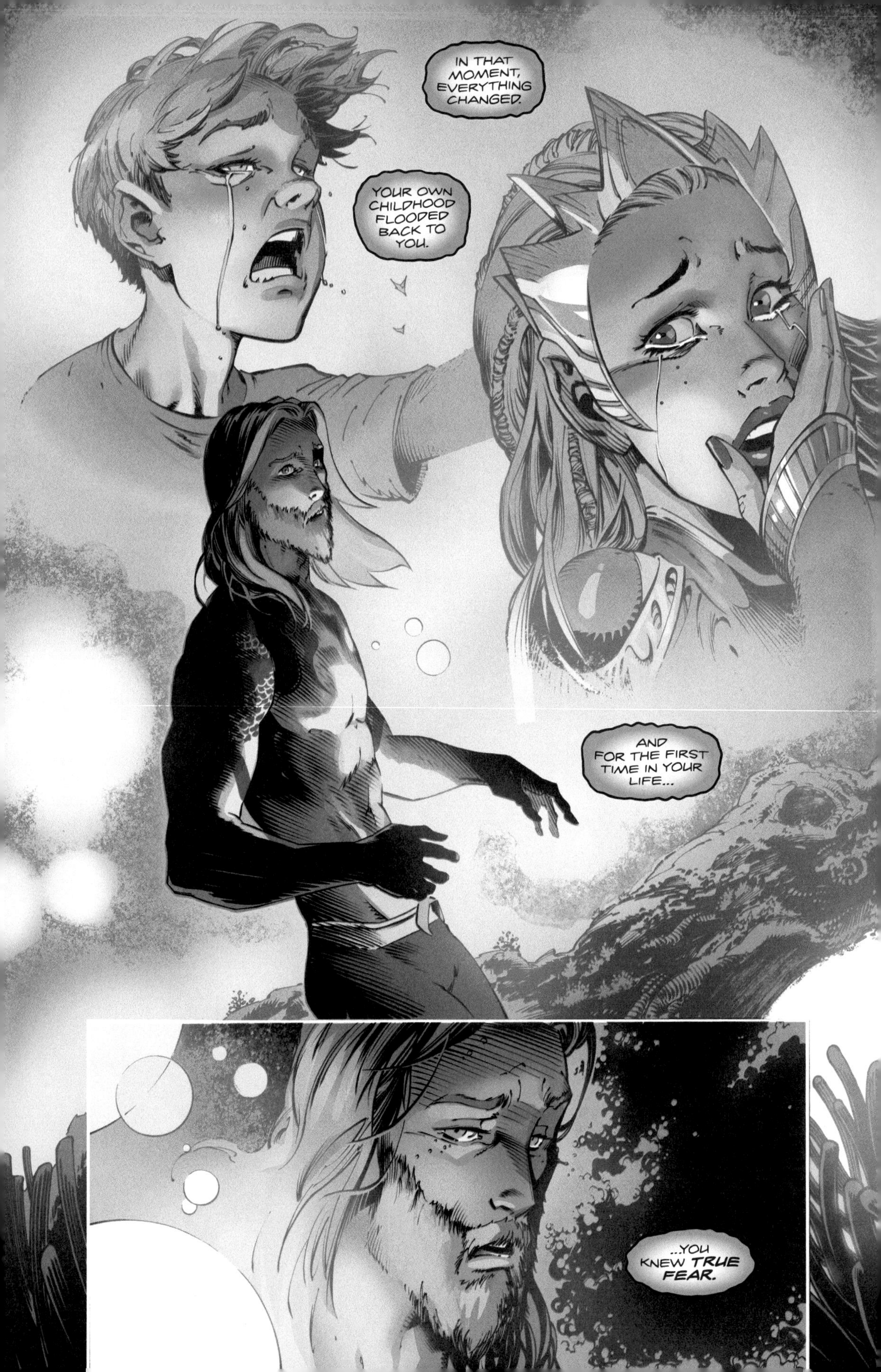
IN THAT MOMENT, EVERYTHING CHANGED.
YOUR OWN CHILDHOOD FLOODED BACK TO YOU.
AND FOR THE FIRST TIME IN YOUR LIFE...
...YOU KNEW TRUE FEAR.

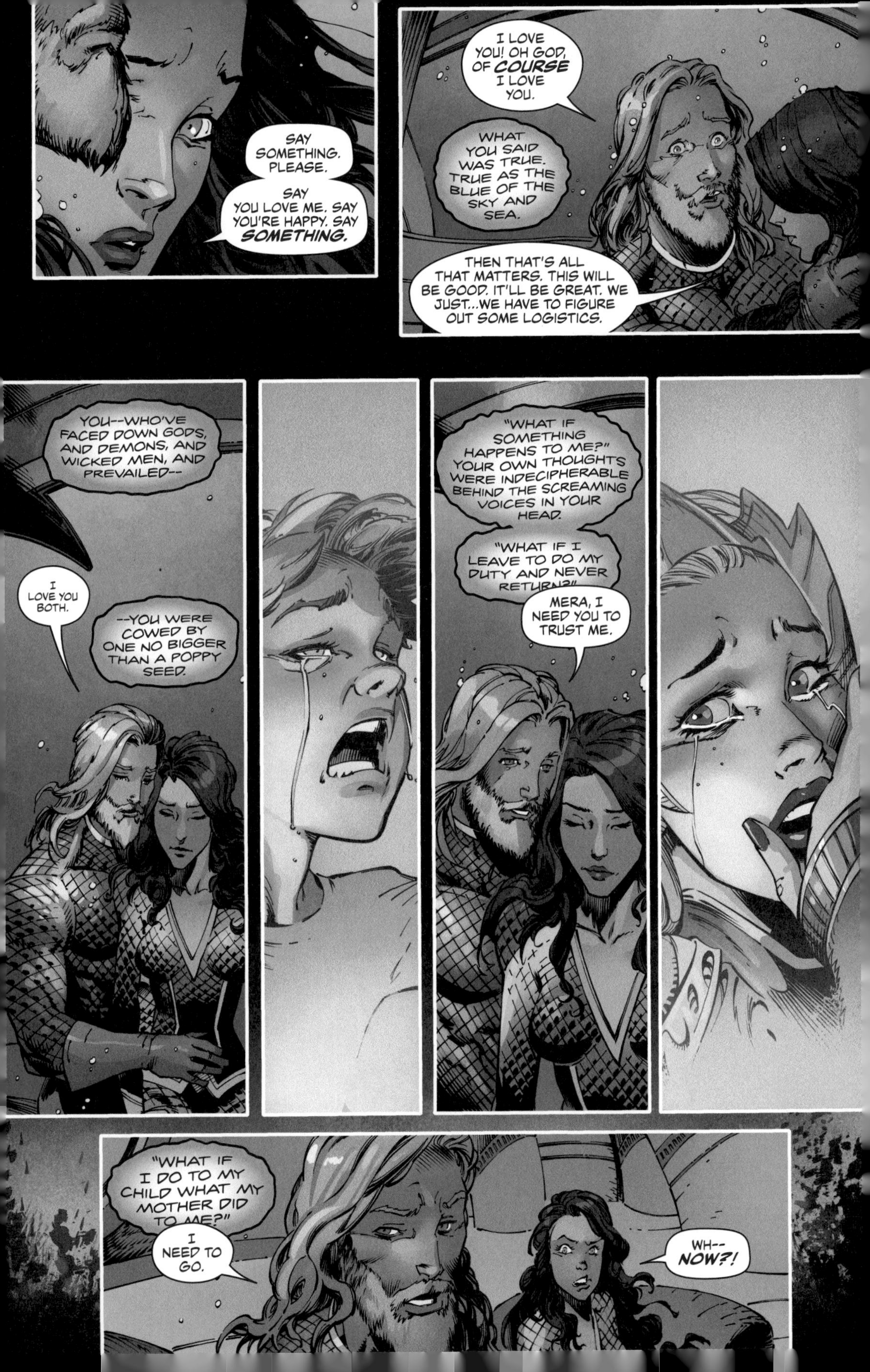
SAY SOMETHING. PLEASE.
SAY YOU LOVE ME. SAY YOU'RE HAPPY. SAY SOMETHING.
I LOVE YOU! OH GOD, OF COURSE I LOVE YOU.
WHAT YOU SAID WAS TRUE. TRUE AS THE BLUE OF THE SKY AND SEA.
THEN THAT'S ALL THAT MATTERS. THIS WILL BE GOOD. IT'LL BE GREAT. WE JUST...WE HAVE TO FIGURE OUT SOME LOGISTICS.
YOU--WHO'VE FACED DOWN GODS, AND DEMONS, AND WICKED MEN, AND PREVAILED--
I LOVE YOU BOTH.
--YOU WERE COWED BY ONE NO BIGGER THAN A POPPY SEED.
"WHAT IF SOMETHING HAPPENS TO ME?" YOUR OWN THOUGHTS WERE INDECIPHERABLE BEHIND THE SCREAMING VOICES IN YOUR HEAD.
"WHAT IF I LEAVE TO DO MY DUTY AND NEVER RETURN?"
MERA, I NEED YOU TO TRUST ME.
"WHAT IF I DO TO MY CHILD WHAT MY MOTHER DID TO ME?"
I NEED TO GO.
WH-- NOW?!

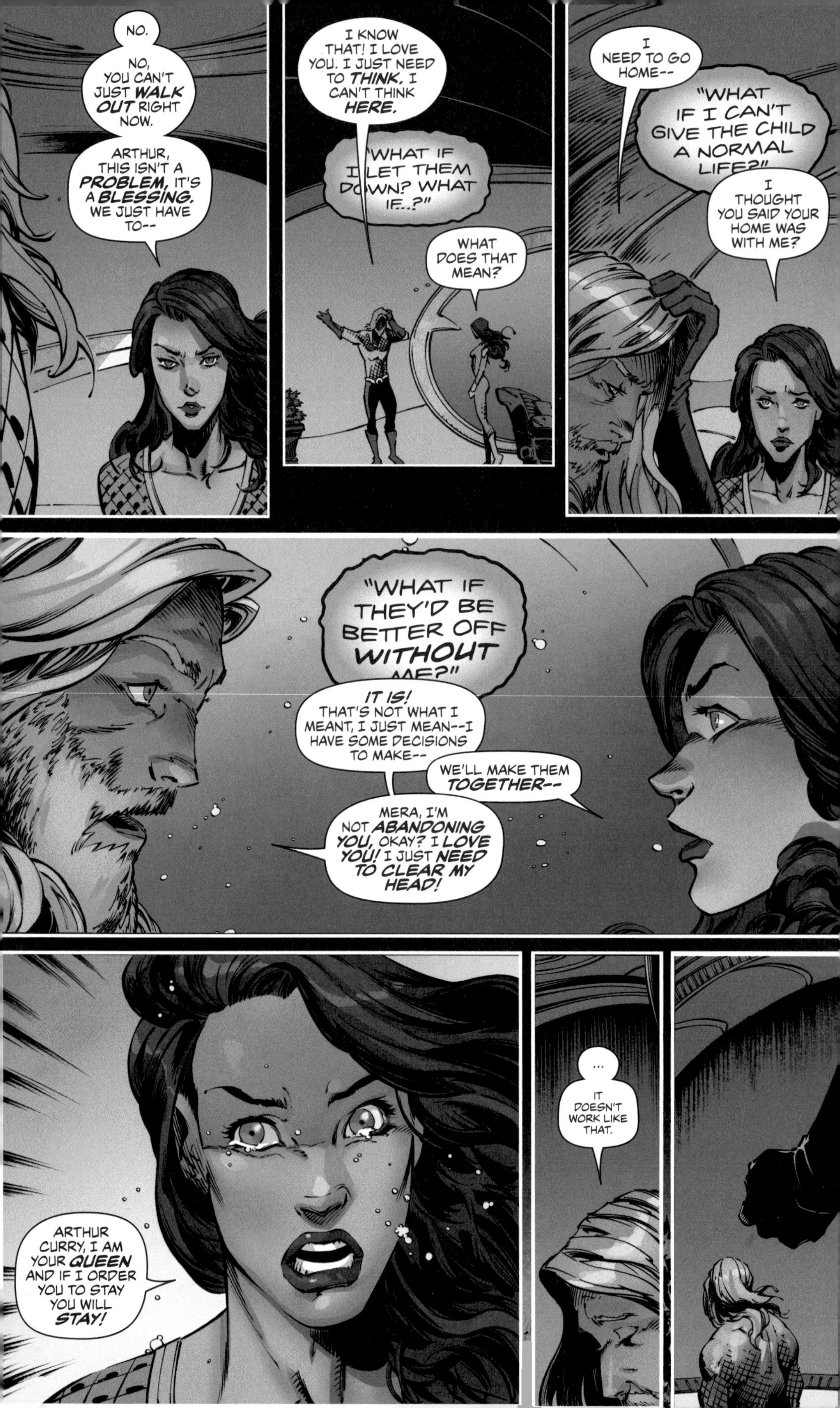
NO.
NO, YOU CAN'T JUST WALK OUT RIGHT NOW.
ARTHUR, THIS ISN'T A PROBLEM, IT'S A BLESSING. WE JUST HAVE TO--
I KNOW THAT! I LOVE YOU. I JUST NEED TO THINK. I CAN'T THINK HERE.
"WHAT IF I LET THEM DOWN? WHAT IF..?"
WHAT DOES THAT MEAN?
I NEED TO GO HOME--
"WHAT IF I CAN'T GIVE THE CHILD A NORMAL LIFE?"
I THOUGHT YOU SAID YOUR HOME WAS WITH ME?
"WHAT IF THEY'D BE BETTER OFF WITHOUT ME?"
IT IS! THAT'S NOT WHAT I MEANT, I JUST MEAN--I HAVE SOME DECISIONS TO MAKE--
WE'LL MAKE THEM TOGETHER--
MERA, I'M NOT ABANDONING YOU, OKAY? I LOVE YOU! I JUST NEED TO CLEAR MY HEAD!
ARTHUR CURRY, I AM YOUR QUEEN AND IF I ORDER YOU TO STAY YOU WILL STAY!
...
IT DOESN'T WORK LIKE THAT.

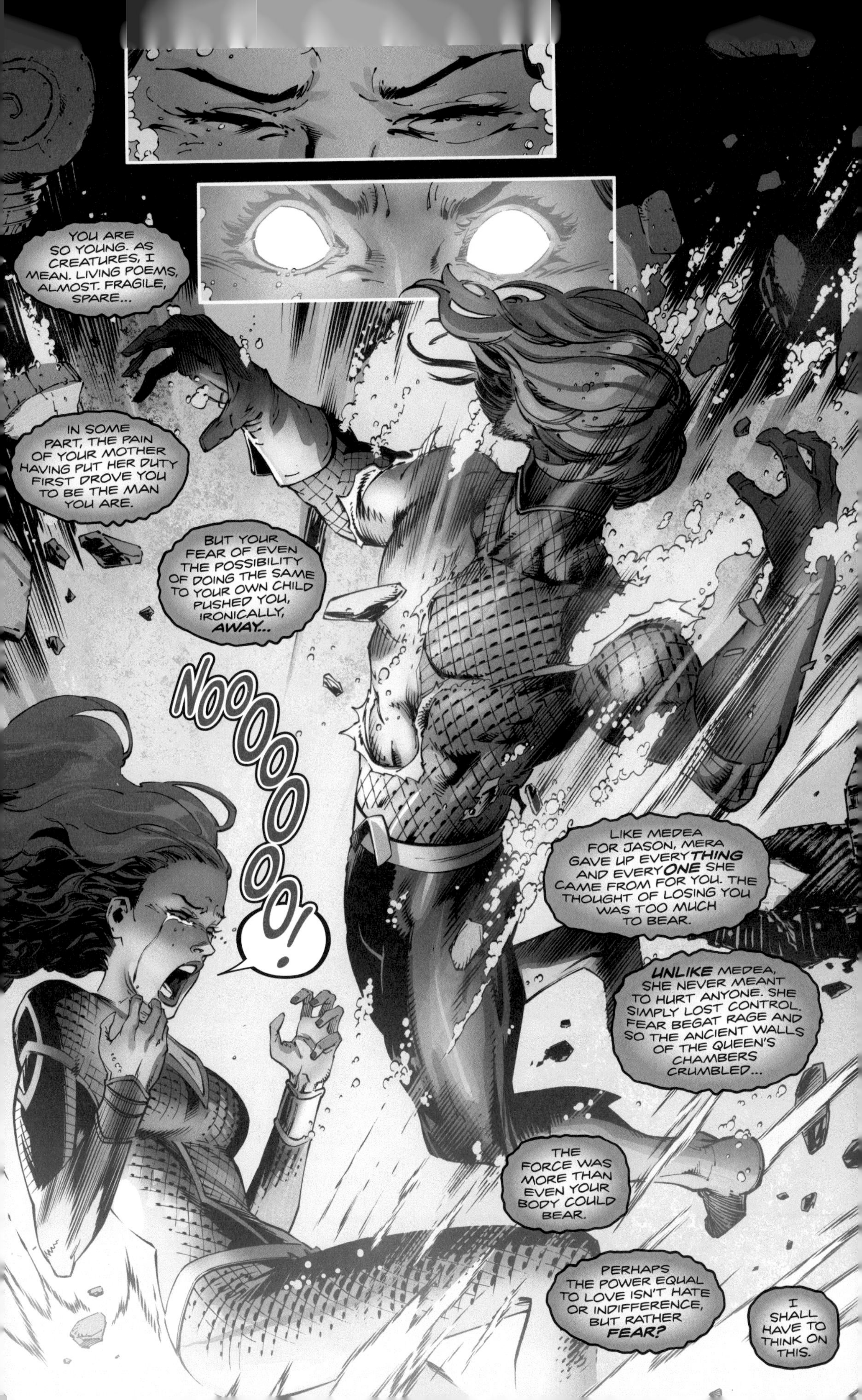
YOU ARE SO YOUNG. AS CREATURES, I MEAN. LIVING POEMS, ALMOST. FRAGILE, SPARE...
IN SOME PART, THE PAIN OF YOUR MOTHER HAVING PUT HER DUTY FIRST DROVE YOU TO BE THE MAN YOU ARE.
BUT YOUR FEAR OF EVEN THE POSSIBILITY OF DOING THE SAME TO YOUR OWN CHILD PUSHED YOU, IRONICALLY, AWAY...
NOOOOOOOOO!
LIKE MEDEA FOR JASON, MERA GAVE UP EVERYTHING AND EVERYONE SHE CAME FROM FOR YOU. THE THOUGHT OF LOSING YOU WAS TOO MUCH TO BEAR.
UNLIKE MEDEA, SHE NEVER MEANT TO HURT ANYONE. SHE SIMPLY LOST CONTROL. FEAR BEGAT RAGE AND SO THE ANCIENT WALLS OF THE QUEEN'S CHAMBERS CRUMBLED...
THE FORCE WAS MORE THAN EVEN YOUR BODY COULD BEAR.
PERHAPS THE POWER EQUAL TO LOVE ISN'T HATE OR INDIFFERENCE, BUT RATHER FEAR?
I SHALL HAVE TO THINK ON THIS.

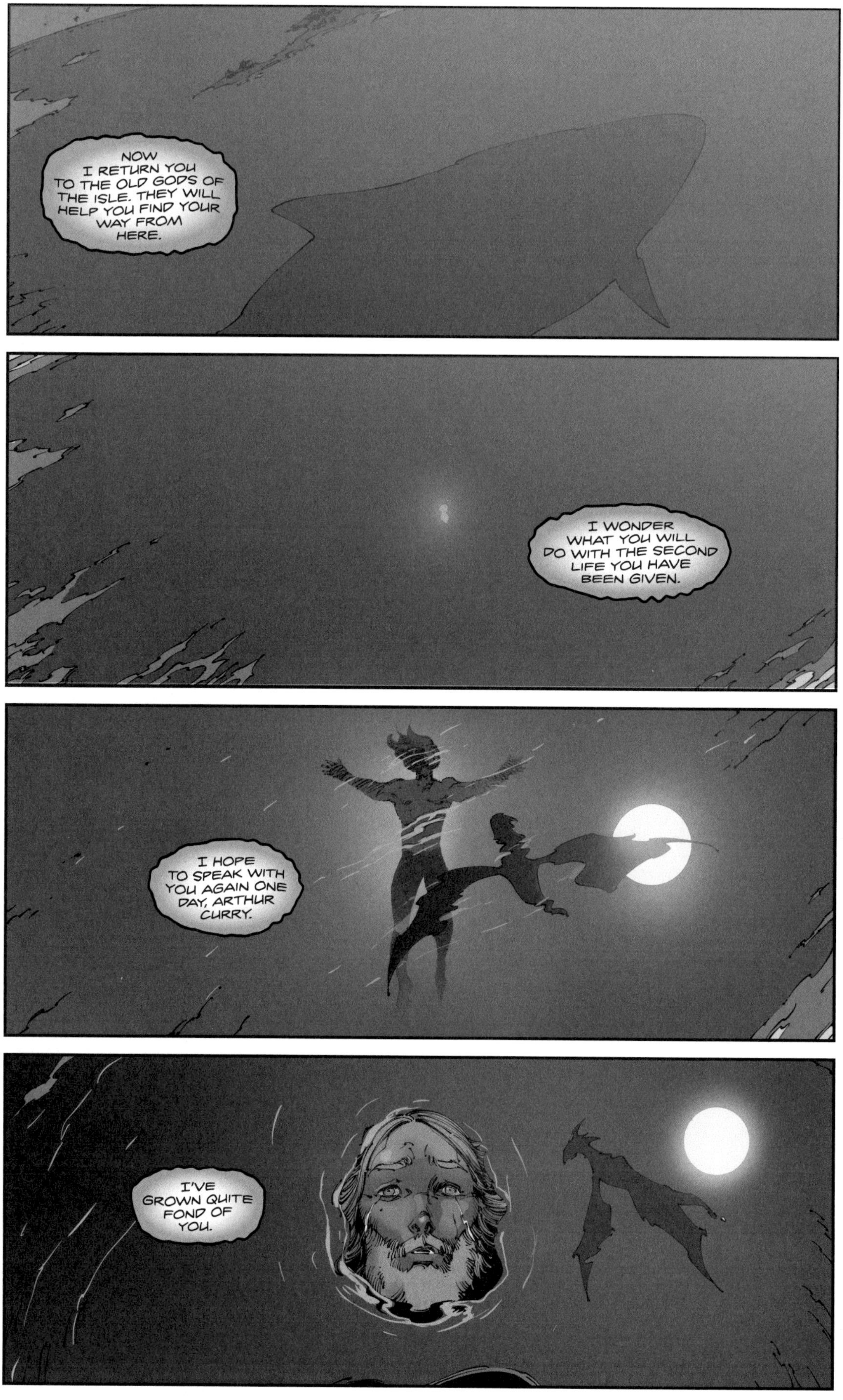
NOW I RETURN YOU TO THE OLD GODS OF THE ISLE. THEY WILL HELP YOU FIND YOUR WAY FROM HERE.
I WONDER WHAT YOU WILL DO WITH THE SECOND LIFE YOU HAVE BEEN GIVEN.
I HOPE TO SPEAK WITH YOU AGAIN ONE DAY, ARTHUR CURRY.
I'VE GROWN QUITE FOND OF YOU.

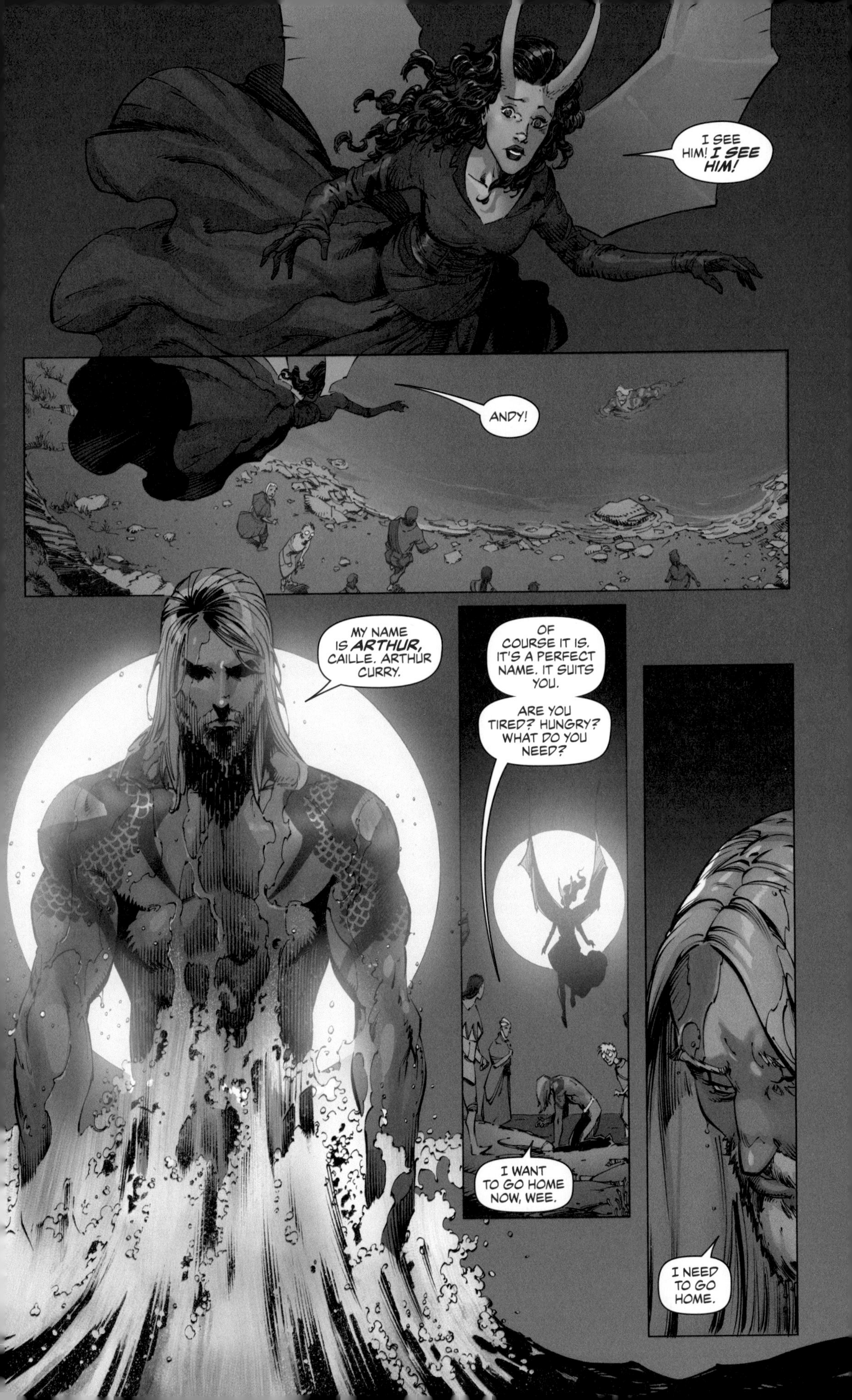
I SEE HIM! I SEE HIM!
ANDY!
MY NAME IS ARTHUR, CAILLE. ARTHUR CURRY.
OF COURSE IT IS. IT'S A PERFECT NAME. IT SUITS YOU.
ARE YOU TIRED? HUNGRY? WHAT DO YOU NEED?
I WANT TO GO HOME NOW, WEE.
I NEED TO GO HOME.

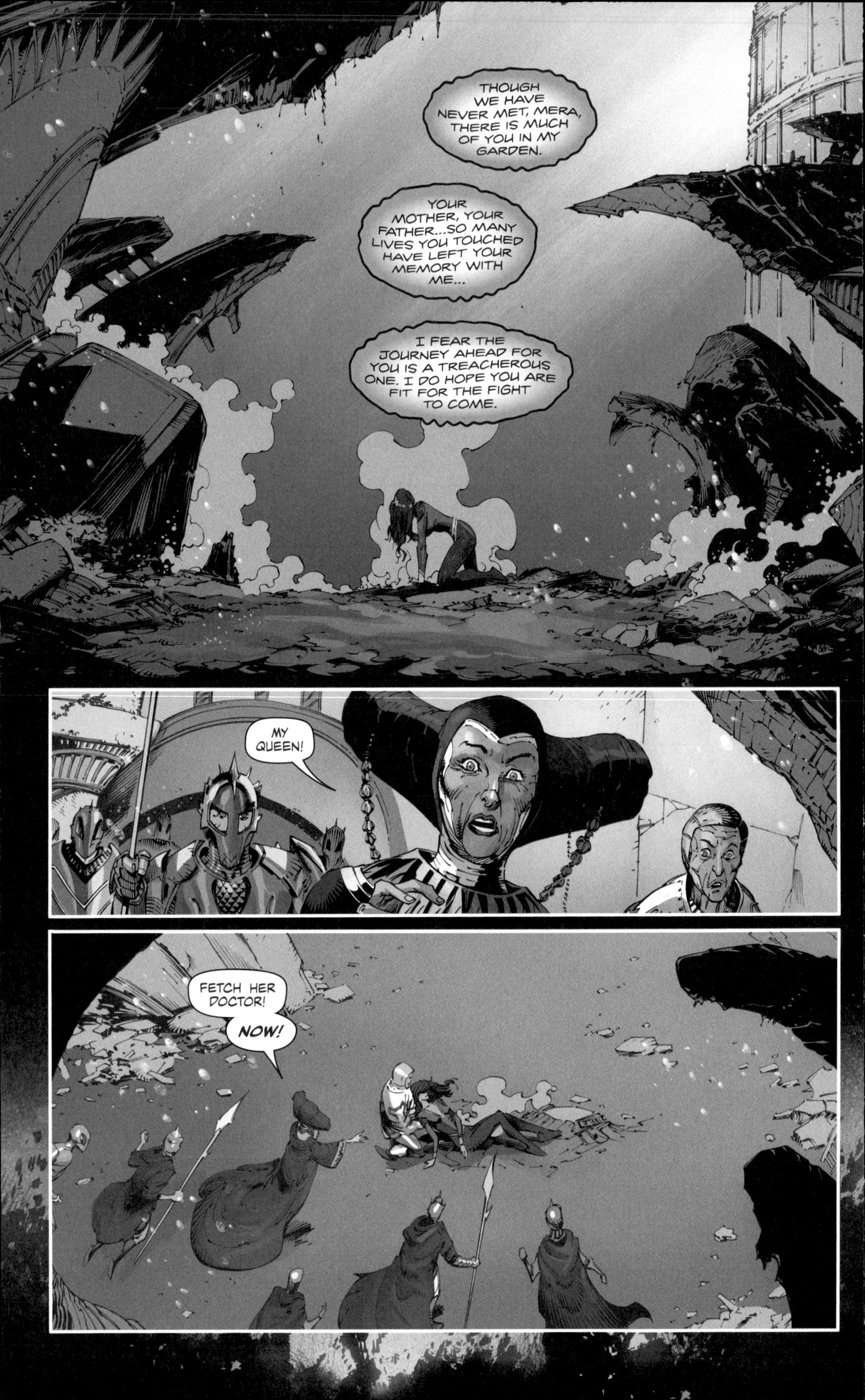
THOUGH WE HAVE NEVER MET, MERA, THERE IS MUCH OF YOU IN MY GARDEN.
YOUR MOTHER, YOUR FATHER...SO MANY LIVES YOU TOUCHED HAVE LEFT YOUR MEMORY WITH ME...
I FEAR THE JOURNEY AHEAD FOR YOU IS A TREACHEROUS ONE. I DO HOPE YOU ARE FIT FOR THE FIGHT TO COME.
MY QUEEN!
FETCH HER DOCTOR!
NOW!

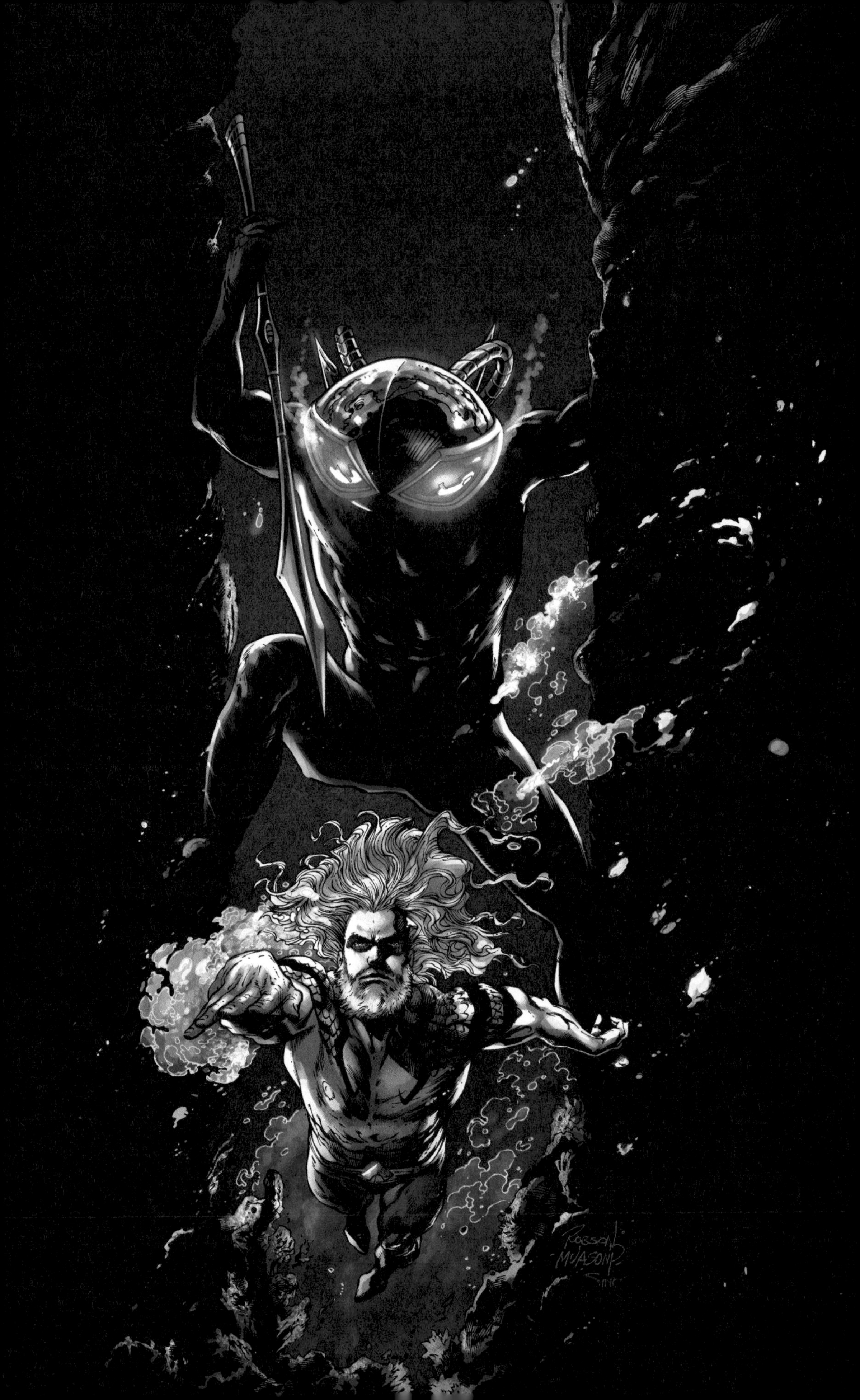

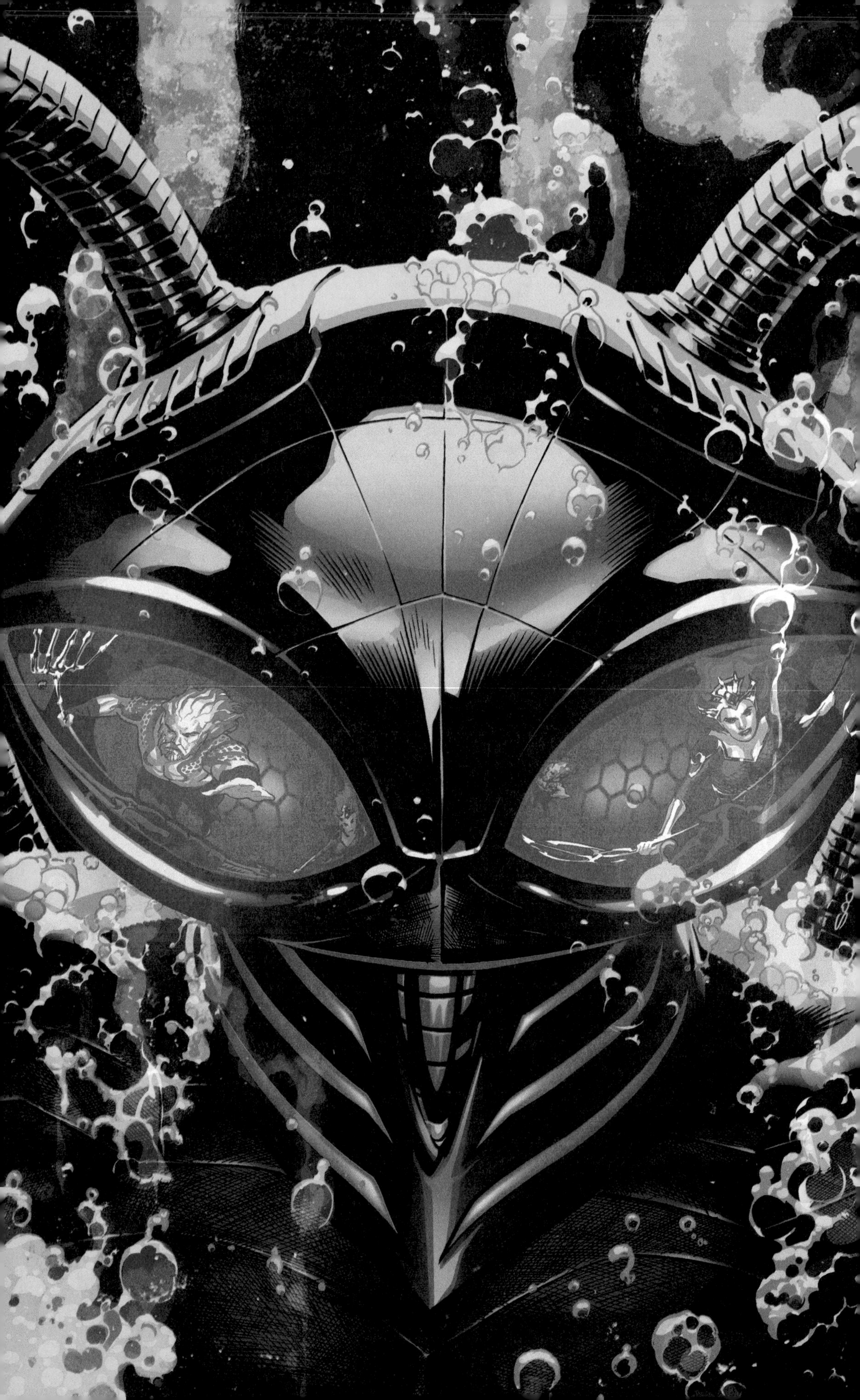

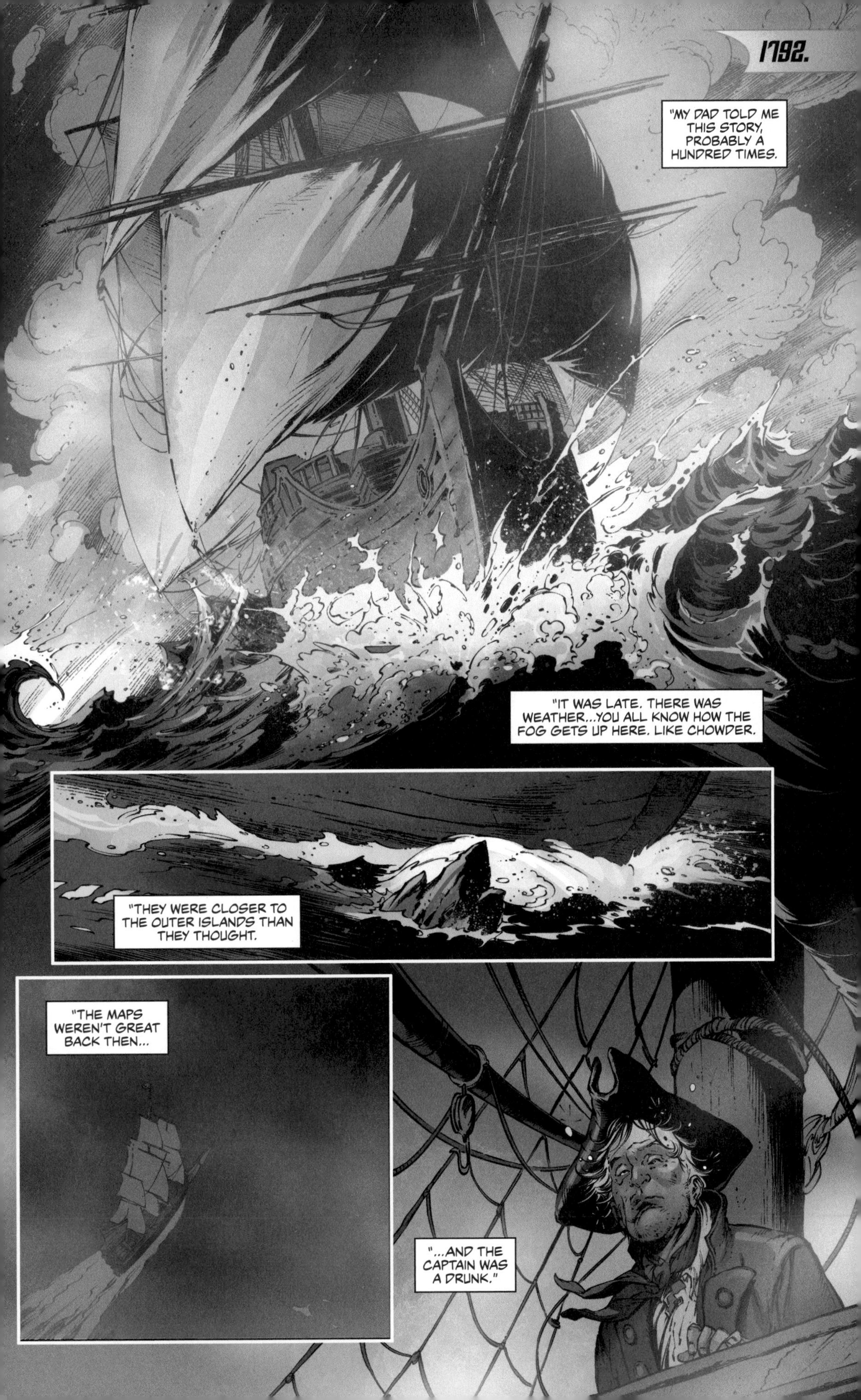
1792.
"MY DAD TOLD ME THIS STORY, PROBABLY A HUNDRED TIMES.
"IT WAS LATE. THERE WAS WEATHER...YOU ALL KNOW HOW THE FOG GETS UP HERE. LIKE CHOWDER.
"THEY WERE CLOSER TO THE OUTER ISLANDS THAN THEY THOUGHT.
"THE MAPS WEREN'T GREAT BACK THEN...
"...AND THE CAPTAIN WAS A DRUNK."

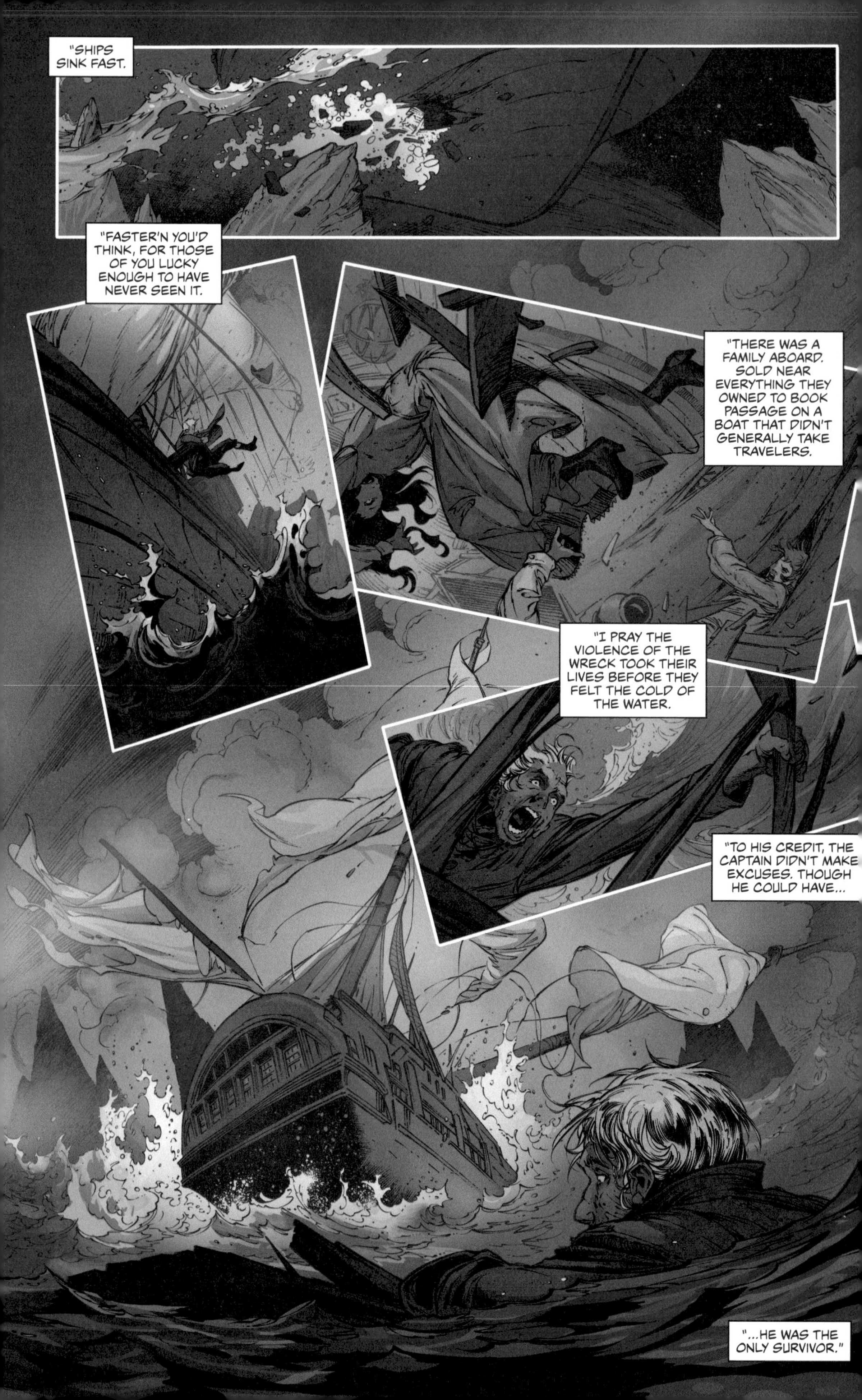
"SHIPS SINK FAST.
"FASTER'N YOU'D THINK, FOR THOSE OF YOU LUCKY ENOUGH TO HAVE NEVER SEEN IT.
"THERE WAS A FAMILY ABOARD. SOLD NEAR EVERYTHING THEY OWNED TO BOOK PASSAGE ON A BOAT THAT DIDN'T GENERALLY TAKE TRAVELERS.
"I PRAY THE VIOLENCE OF THE WRECK TOOK THEIR LIVES BEFORE THEY FELT THE COLD OF THE WATER.
"TO HIS CREDIT, THE CAPTAIN DIDN'T MAKE EXCUSES. THOUGH HE COULD HAVE...
"...HE WAS THE ONLY SURVIVOR."

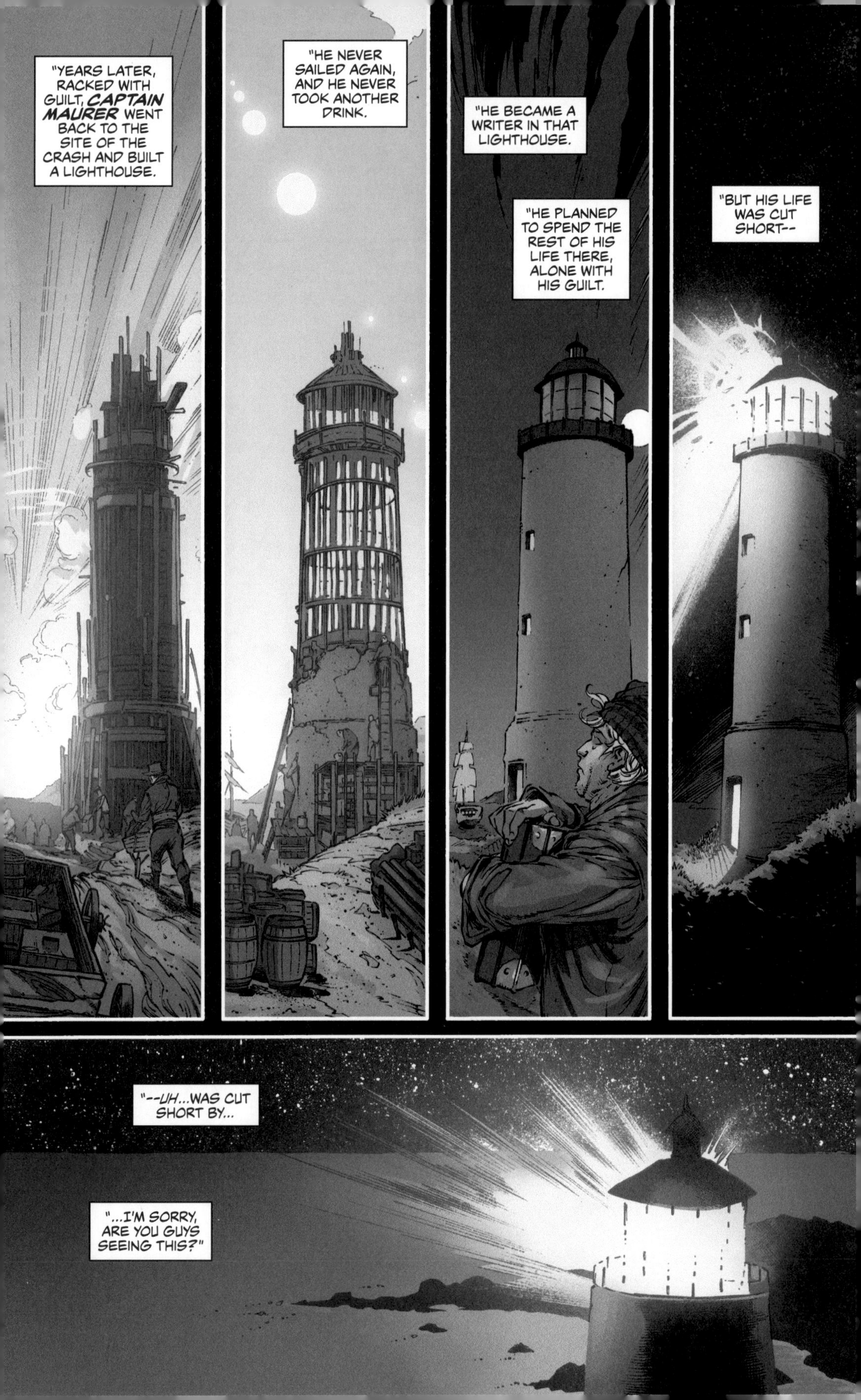
"YEARS LATER, RACKED WITH GUILT, CAPTAIN MAURER WENT BACK TO THE SITE OF THE CRASH AND BUILT A LIGHTHOUSE.
"HE NEVER SAILED AGAIN, AND HE NEVER TOOK ANOTHER DRINK.
"HE BECAME A WRITER IN THAT LIGHTHOUSE.
"HE PLANNED TO SPEND THE REST OF HIS LIFE THERE, ALONE WITH HIS GUILT.
"BUT HIS LIFE WAS CUT SHORT--
"--UH...WAS CUT SHORT BY...
"...I'M SORRY, ARE YOU GUYS SEEING THIS?"

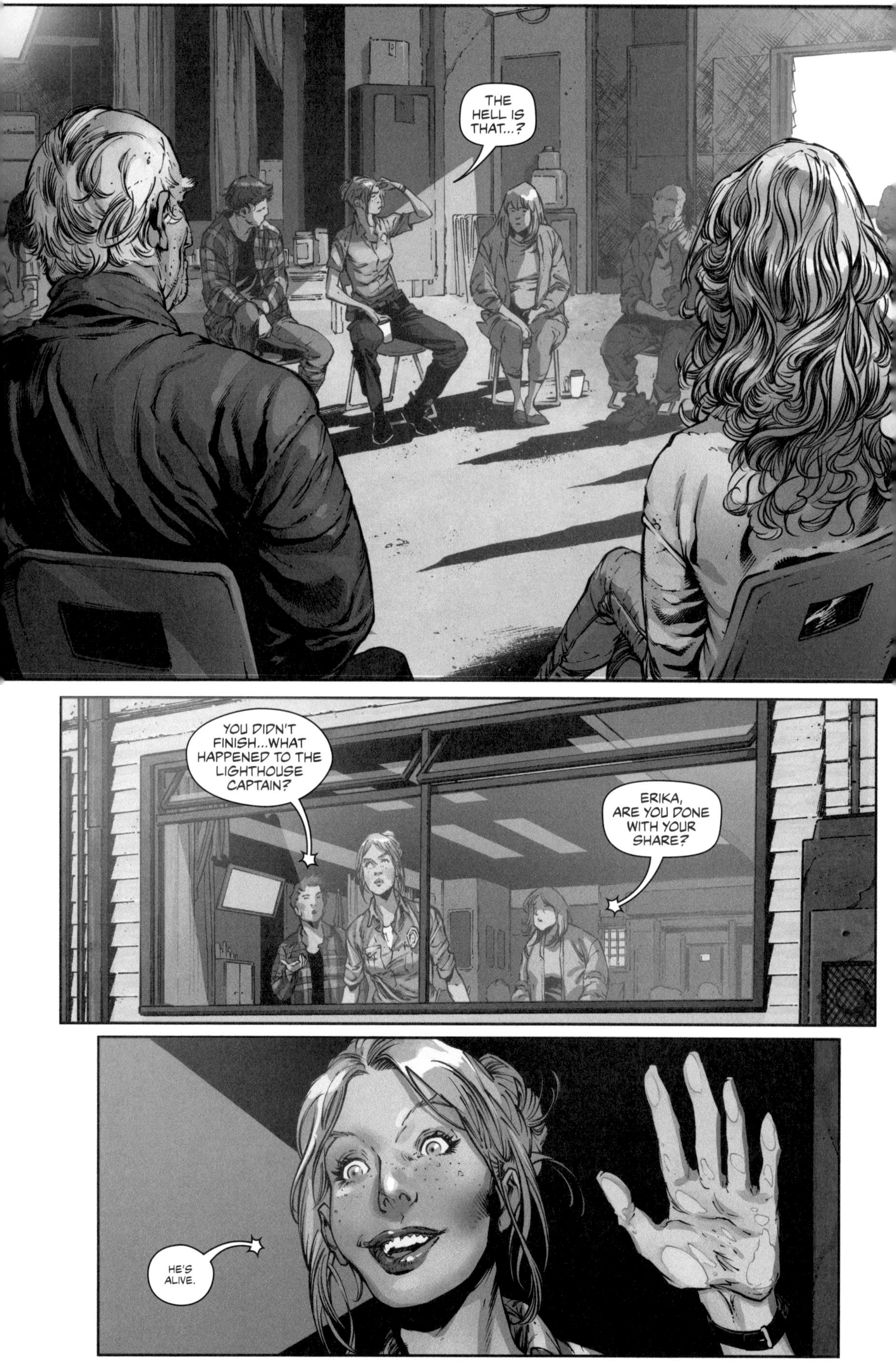
THE HELL IS THAT...?
YOU DIDN'T FINISH...WHAT HAPPENED TO THE LIGHTHOUSE CAPTAIN?
ERIKA, ARE YOU DONE WITH YOUR SHARE?
HE'S ALIVE.

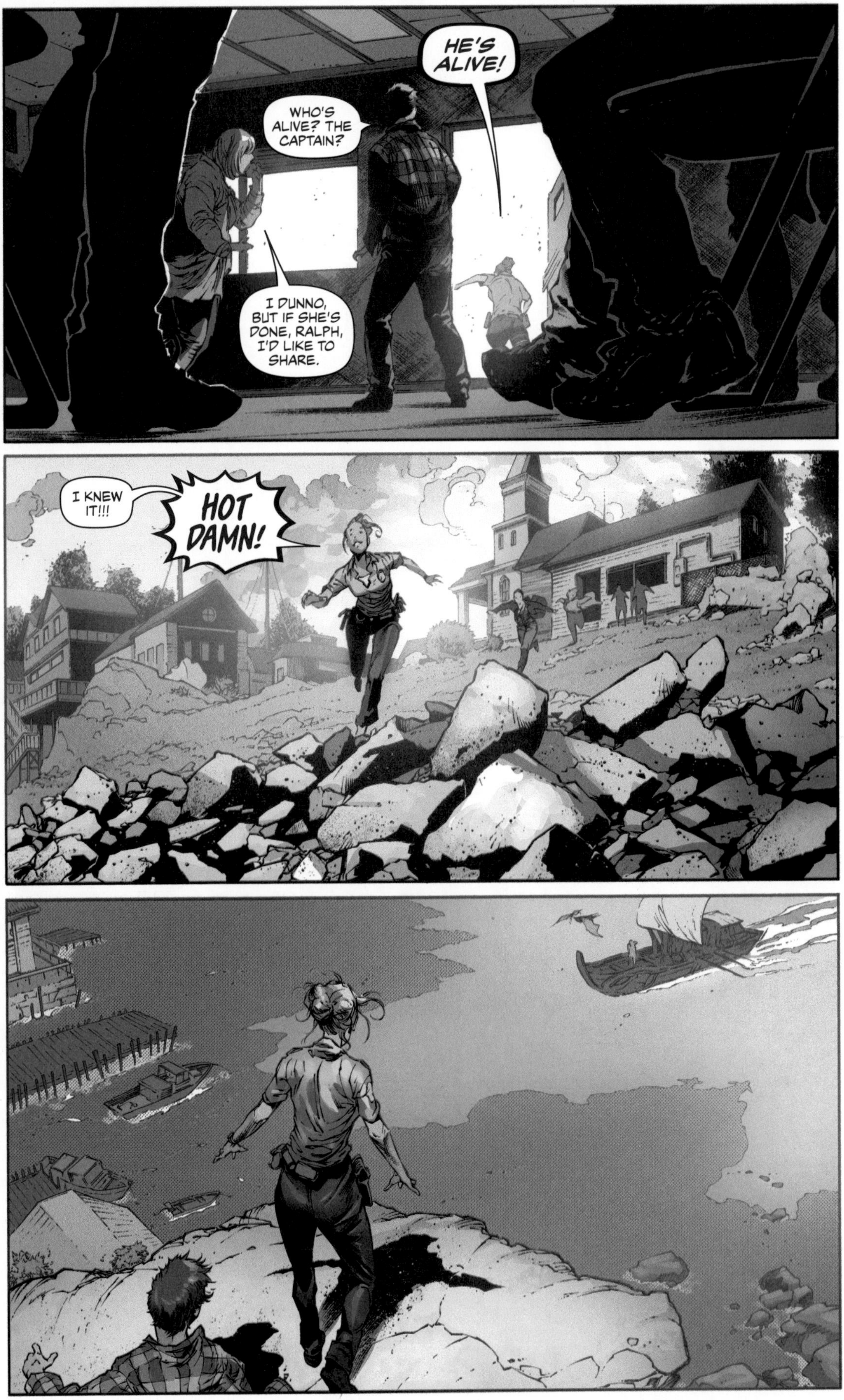
HE'S ALIVE!
WHO'S ALIVE? THE CAPTAIN?
I DUNNO, BUT IF SHE'S DONE, RALPH, I'D LIKE TO SHARE.
I KNEW IT!!!
HOT DAMN!

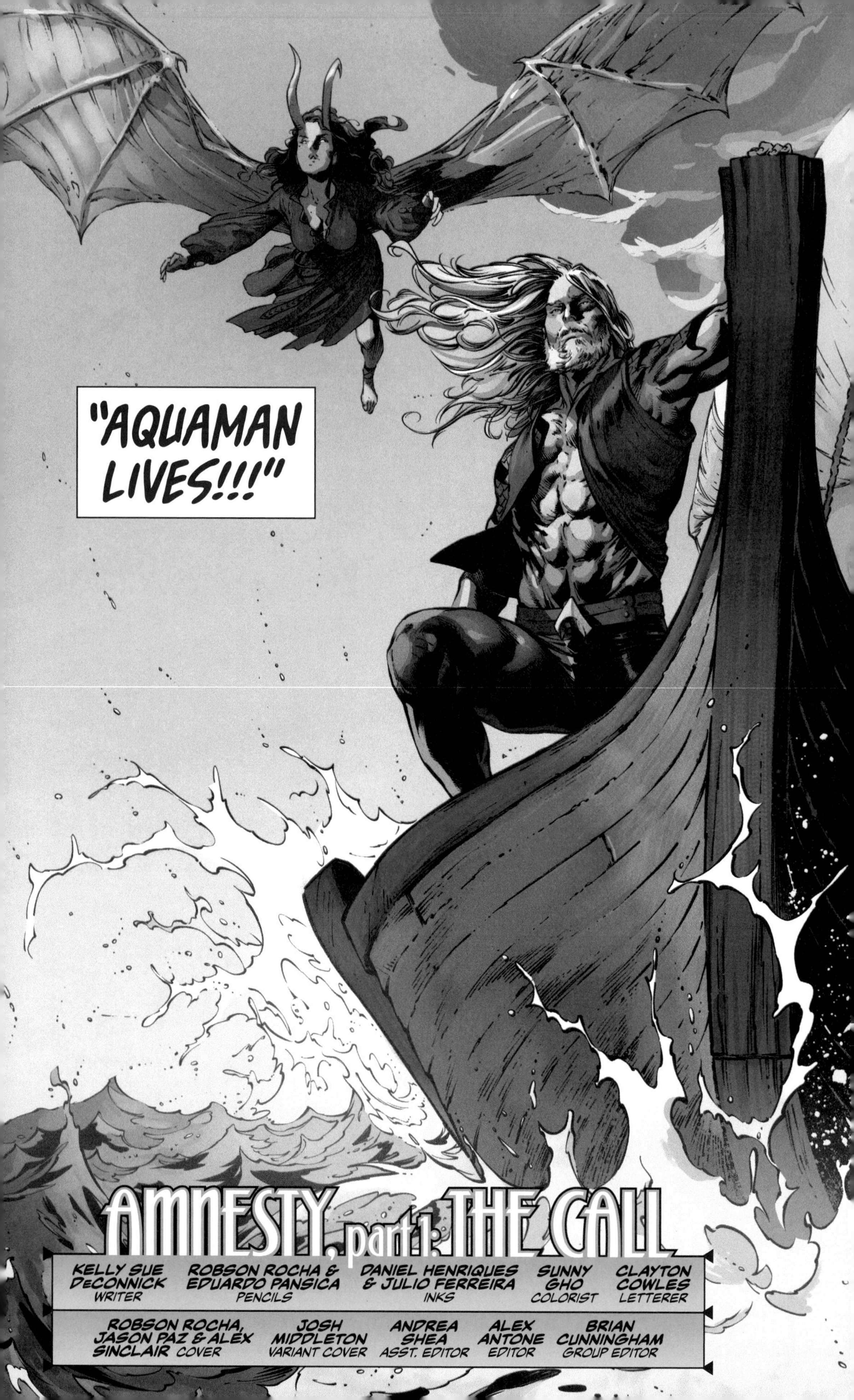
"AQUAMAN LIVES!!!"
AMNESTY, part 1: THE CALL
KELLY SUE DeCONNICK WRITER
ROBSON ROCHA & EDUARDO PANSICA PENCILS
DANIEL HENRIQUES & JULIO FERREIRA INKS
SUNNY GHO COLORIST
CLAYTON COWLES LETTERER
ROBSON ROCHA, JASON PAZ & ALEX SINCLAIR COVER
JOSH MIDDLETON VARIANT COVER
ANDREA SHEA ASST. EDITOR
ALEX ANTONE EDITOR
BRIAN CUNNINGHAM GROUP EDITOR

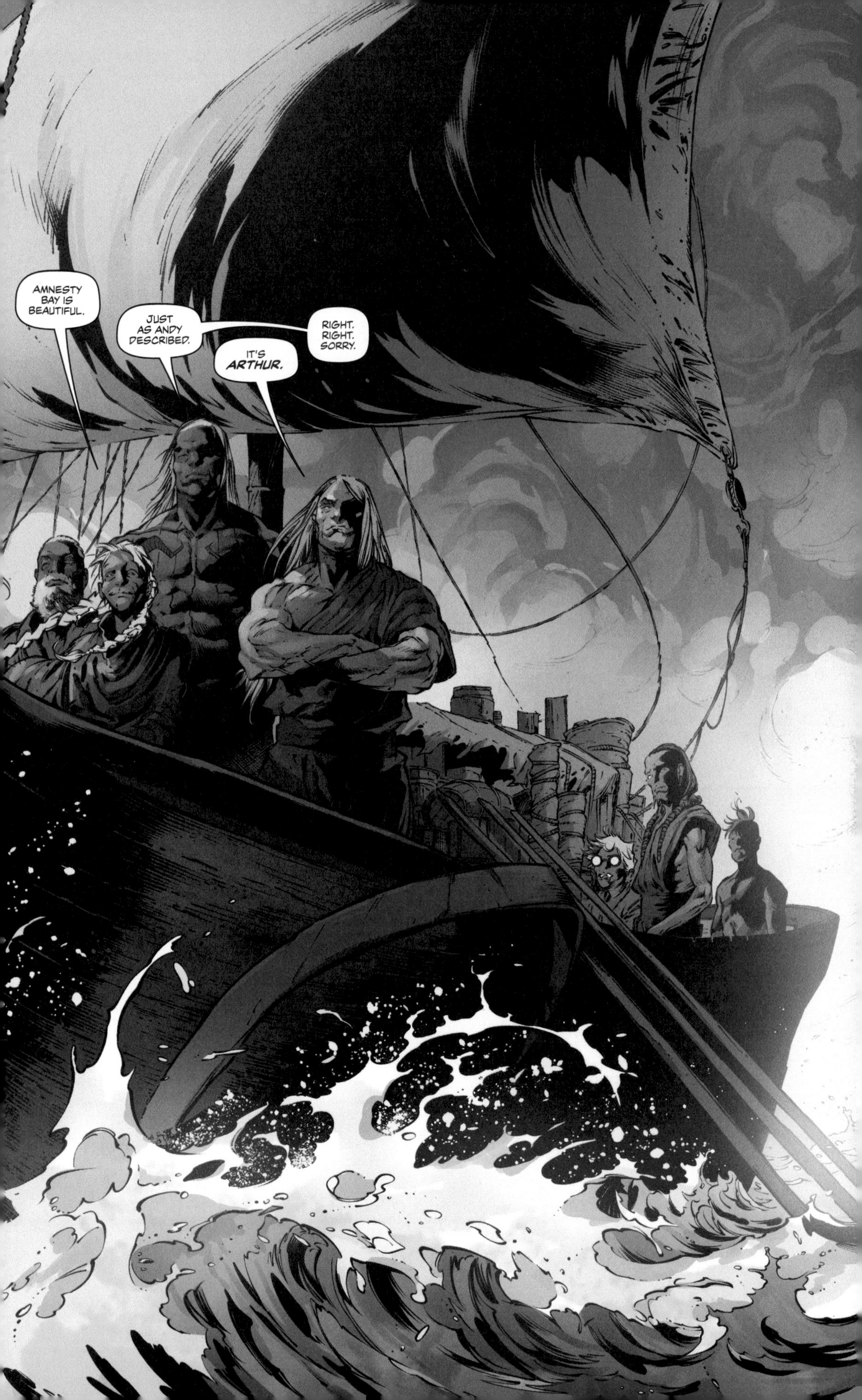
AMNESTY BAY IS BEAUTIFUL.
JUST AS ANDY DESCRIBED.
IT'S ARTHUR.
RIGHT. RIGHT. SORRY.

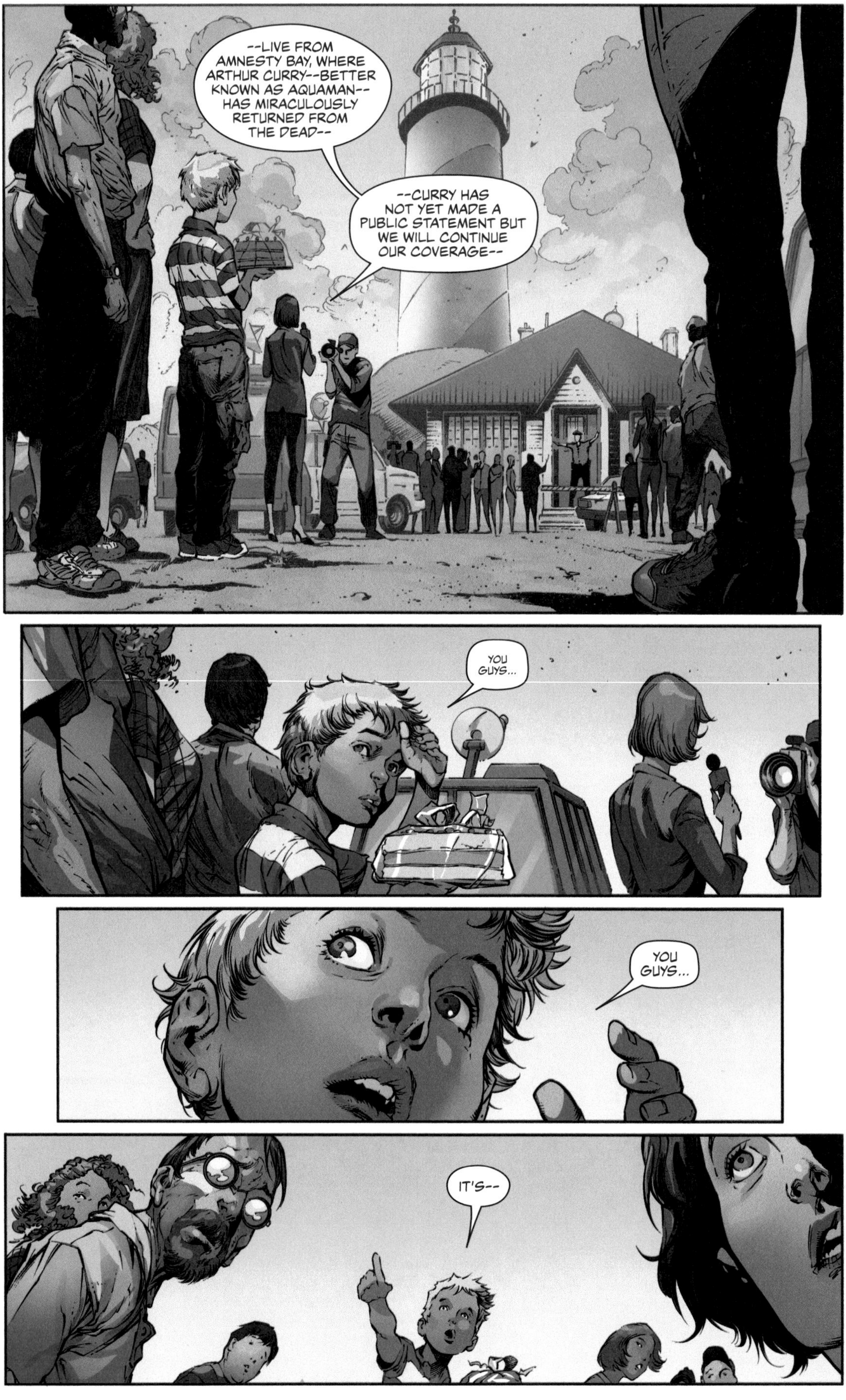
--LIVE FROM AMNESTY BAY, WHERE ARTHUR CURRY--BETTER KNOWN AS AQUAMAN--HAS MIRACULOUSLY RETURNED FROM THE DEAD--
--CURRY HAS NOT YET MADE A PUBLIC STATEMENT BUT WE WILL CONTINUE OUR COVERAGE--
YOU GUYS...
YOU GUYS...
IT'S--

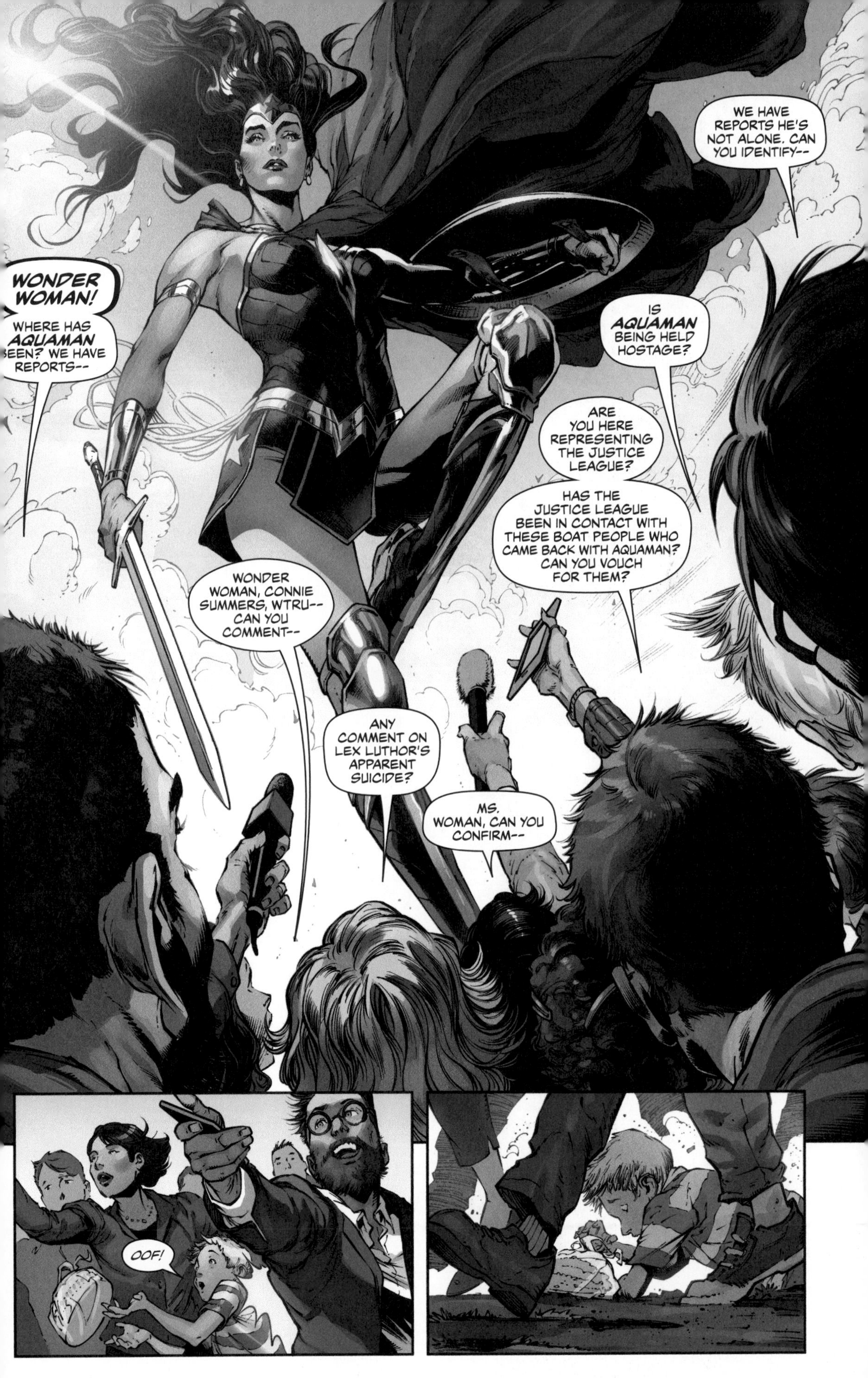

WONDER WOMAN! WHERE HAS AQUAMAN BEEN? WE HAVE REPORTS--
WE HAVE REPORTS HE'S NOT ALONE. CAN YOU IDENTIFY--
IS AQUAMAN BEING HELD HOSTAGE?
ARE YOU HERE REPRESENTING THE JUSTICE LEAGUE?
HAS THE JUSTICE LEAGUE BEEN IN CONTACT WITH THESE BOAT PEOPLE WHO CAME BACK WITH AQUAMAN? CAN YOU VOUCH FOR THEM?
WONDER WOMAN, CONNIE SUMMERS, WTRU-- CAN YOU COMMENT--
ANY COMMENT ON LEX LUTHOR'S APPARENT SUICIDE?
MS. WOMAN, CAN YOU CONFIRM--
OOF!

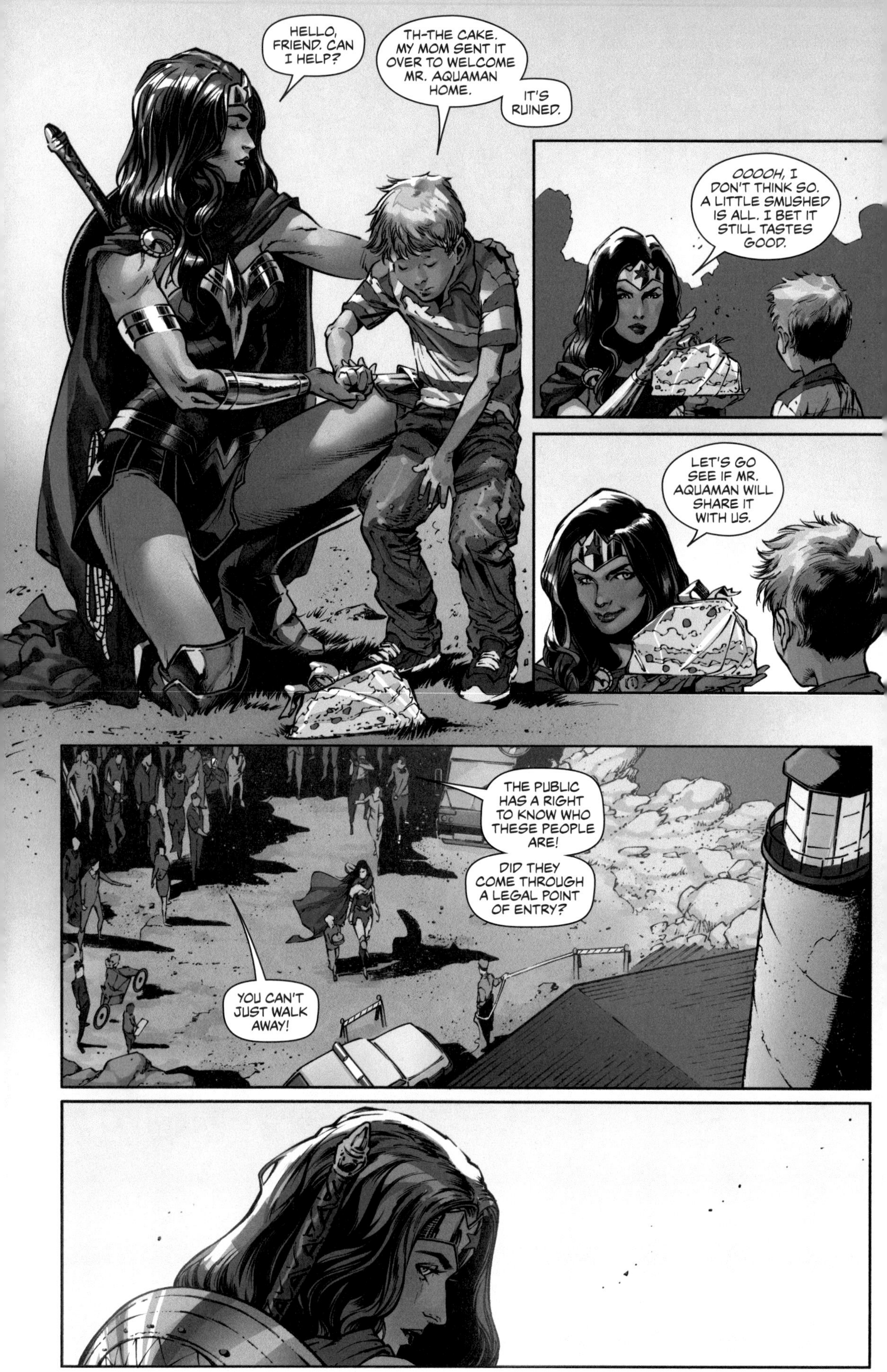
HELLO, FRIEND. CAN I HELP?
TH-THE CAKE. MY MOM SENT IT OVER TO WELCOME MR. AQUAMAN HOME.
IT'S RUINED.
OOOOH, I DON'T THINK SO. A LITTLE SMUSHED IS ALL. I BET IT STILL TASTES GOOD.
LET'S GO SEE IF MR. AQUAMAN WILL SHARE IT WITH US.
THE PUBLIC HAS A RIGHT TO KNOW WHO THESE PEOPLE ARE!
DID THEY COME THROUGH A LEGAL POINT OF ENTRY?
YOU CAN'T JUST WALK AWAY!

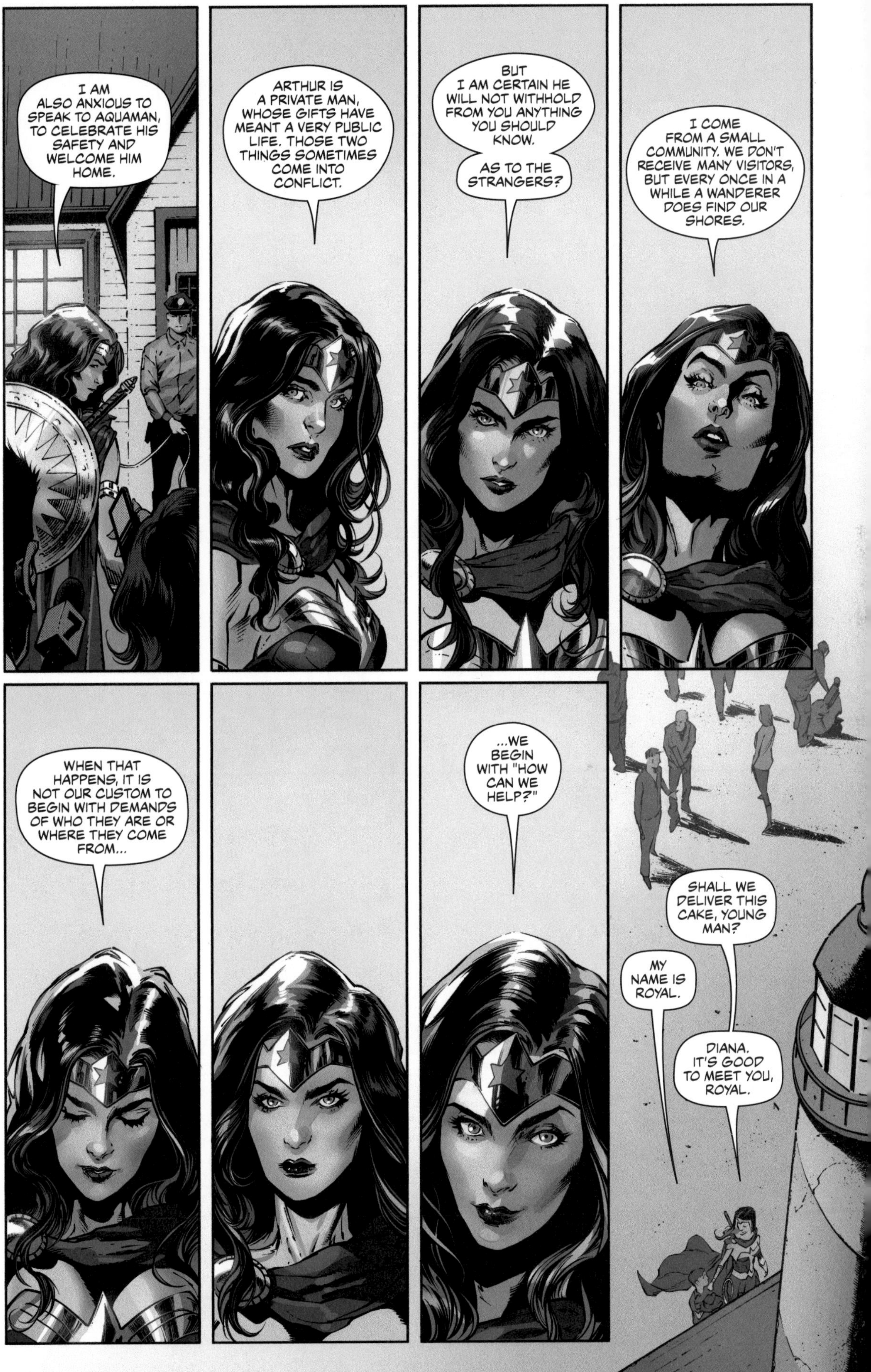
I AM ALSO ANXIOUS TO SPEAK TO AQUAMAN, TO CELEBRATE HIS SAFETY AND WELCOME HIM HOME.
ARTHUR IS A PRIVATE MAN, WHOSE GIFTS HAVE MEANT A VERY PUBLIC LIFE. THOSE TWO THINGS SOMETIMES COME INTO CONFLICT.
BUT I AM CERTAIN HE WILL NOT WITHHOLD FROM YOU ANYTHING YOU SHOULD KNOW.
AS TO THE STRANGERS?
I COME FROM A SMALL COMMUNITY. WE DON'T RECEIVE MANY VISITORS, BUT EVERY ONCE IN A WHILE A WANDERER DOES FIND OUR SHORES.
WHEN THAT HAPPENS, IT IS NOT OUR CUSTOM TO BEGIN WITH DEMANDS OF WHO THEY ARE OR WHERE THEY COME FROM...
...WE BEGIN WITH "HOW CAN WE HELP?"
SHALL WE DELIVER THIS CAKE, YOUNG MAN?
MY NAME IS ROYAL.
DIANA. IT'S GOOD TO MEET YOU, ROYAL.

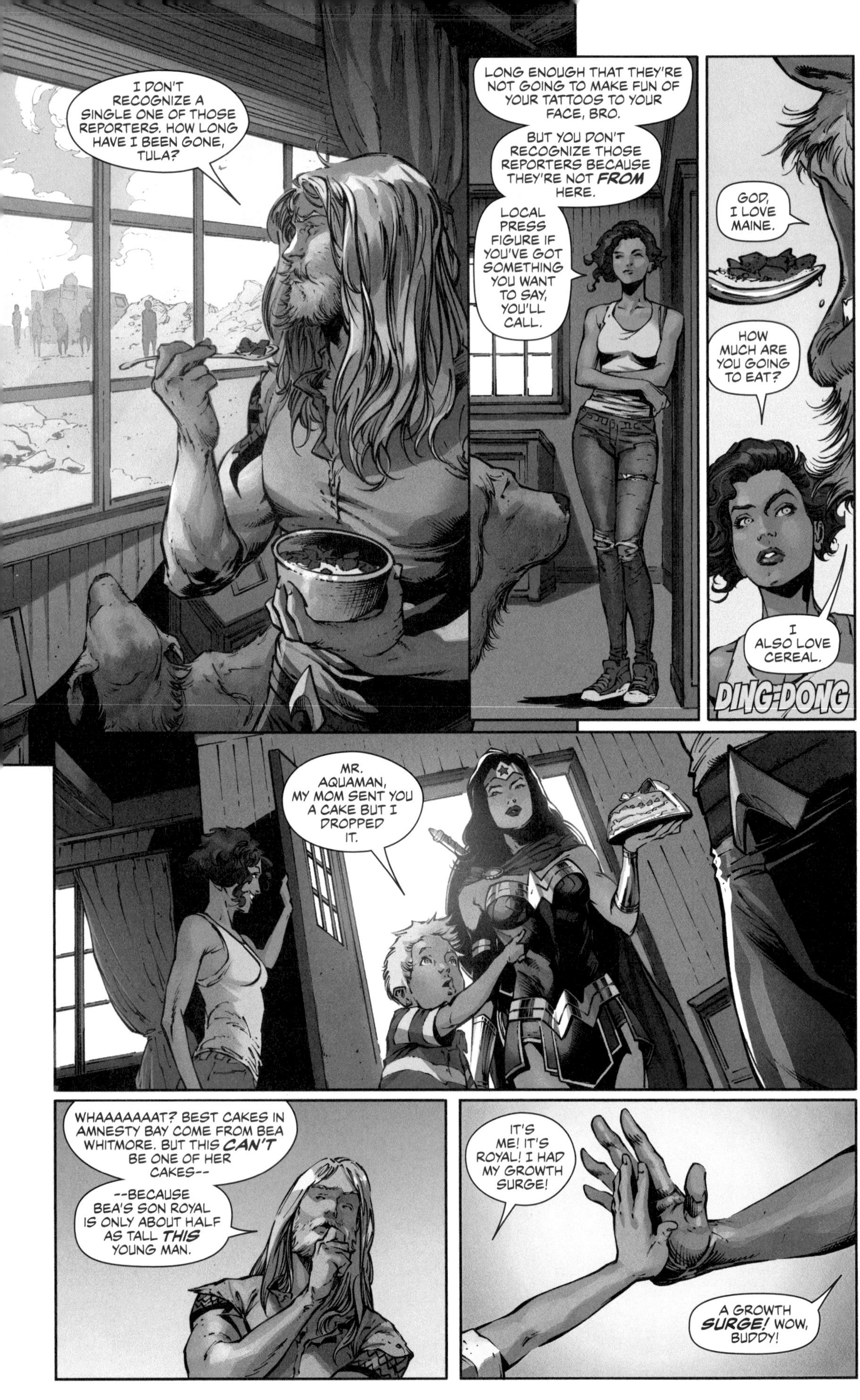
I DON'T RECOGNIZE A SINGLE ONE OF THOSE REPORTERS. HOW LONG HAVE I BEEN GONE, TULA?
LONG ENOUGH THAT THEY'RE NOT GOING TO MAKE FUN OF YOUR TATTOOS TO YOUR FACE, BRO.
BUT YOU DON'T RECOGNIZE THOSE REPORTERS BECAUSE THEY'RE NOT FROM HERE.
LOCAL PRESS FIGURE IF YOU'VE GOT SOMETHING YOU WANT TO SAY, YOU'LL CALL.
GOD, I LOVE MAINE.
HOW MUCH ARE YOU GOING TO EAT?
I ALSO LOVE CEREAL.
DING-DONG
MR. AQUAMAN, MY MOM SENT YOU A CAKE BUT I DROPPED IT.
WHAAAAAAAT? BEST CAKES IN AMNESTY BAY COME FROM BEA WHITMORE. BUT THIS CAN'T BE ONE OF HER CAKES--
--BECAUSE BEA'S SON ROYAL IS ONLY ABOUT HALF AS TALL THIS YOUNG MAN.
IT'S ME! IT'S ROYAL! I HAD MY GROWTH SURGE!
A GROWTH SURGE! WOW, BUDDY!

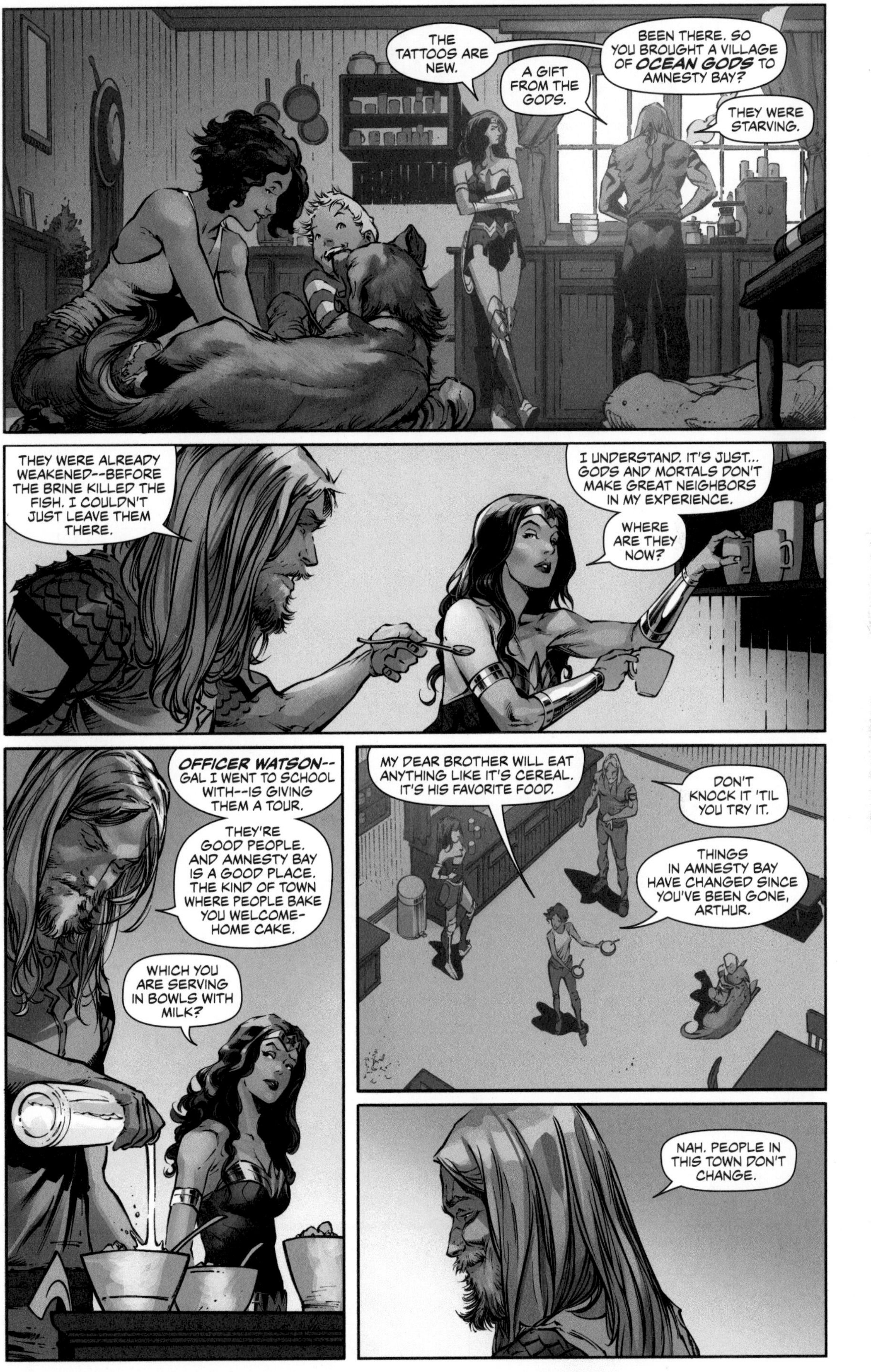

THE TATTOOS ARE NEW.
A GIFT FROM THE GODS.
BEEN THERE. SO YOU BROUGHT A VILLAGE OF OCEAN GODS TO AMNESTY BAY?
THEY WERE STARVING.
THEY WERE ALREADY WEAKENED--BEFORE THE BRINE KILLED THE FISH. I COULDN'T JUST LEAVE THEM THERE.
I UNDERSTAND. IT'S JUST... GODS AND MORTALS DON'T MAKE GREAT NEIGHBORS IN MY EXPERIENCE.
WHERE ARE THEY NOW?
OFFICER WATSON-- GAL I WENT TO SCHOOL WITH--IS GIVING THEM A TOUR.
THEY'RE GOOD PEOPLE. AND AMNESTY BAY IS A GOOD PLACE. THE KIND OF TOWN WHERE PEOPLE BAKE YOU WELCOME-HOME CAKE.
WHICH YOU ARE SERVING IN BOWLS WITH MILK?
MY DEAR BROTHER WILL EAT ANYTHING LIKE IT'S CEREAL. IT'S HIS FAVORITE FOOD.
DON'T KNOCK IT 'TIL YOU TRY IT.
THINGS IN AMNESTY BAY HAVE CHANGED SINCE YOU'VE BEEN GONE, ARTHUR.
NAH. PEOPLE IN THIS TOWN DON'T CHANGE.

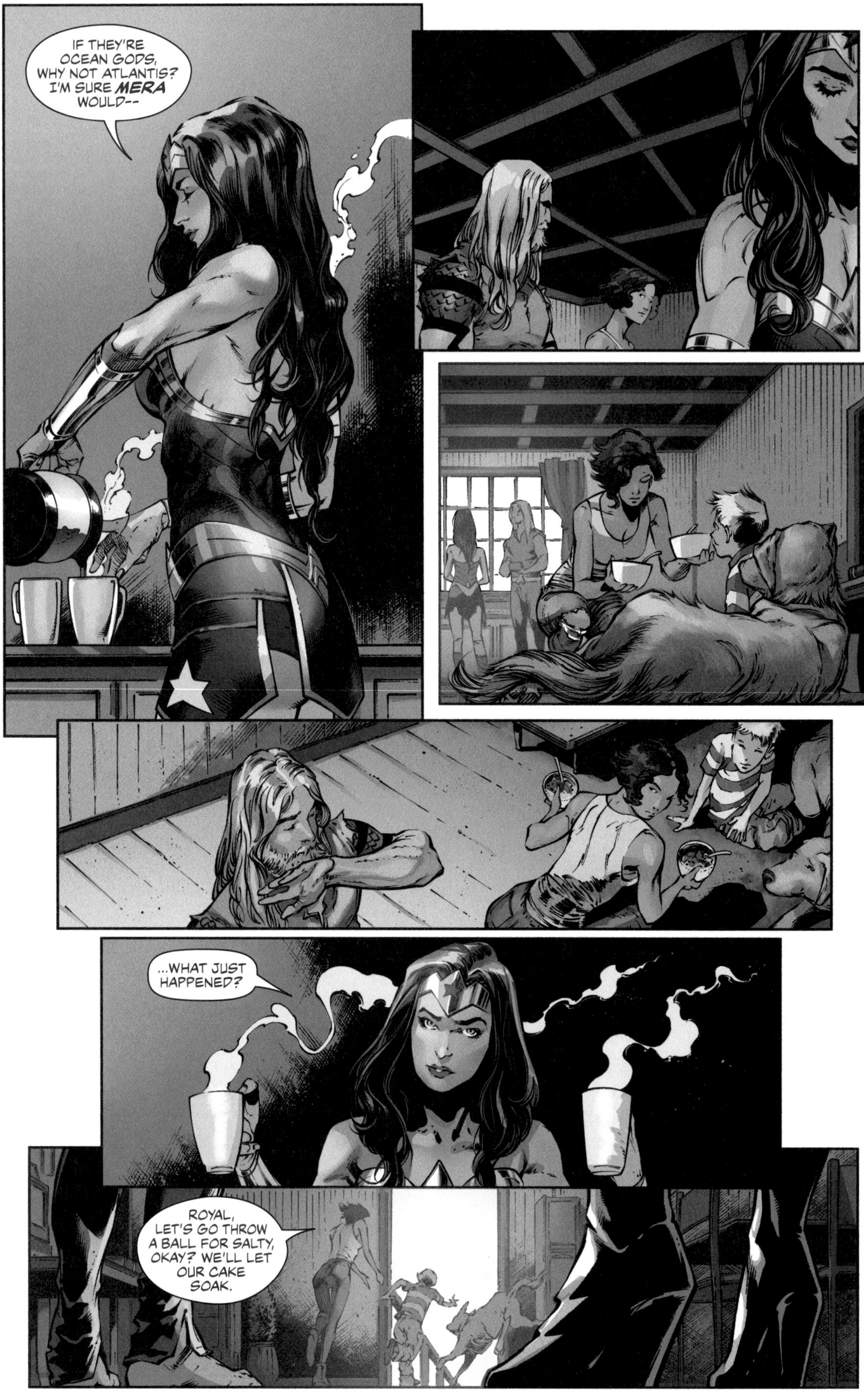
IF THEY'RE OCEAN GODS, WHY NOT ATLANTIS? I'M SURE MERA WOULD--
...WHAT JUST HAPPENED?
ROYAL, LET'S GO THROW A BALL FOR SALTY, OKAY? WE'LL LET OUR CAKE SOAK.

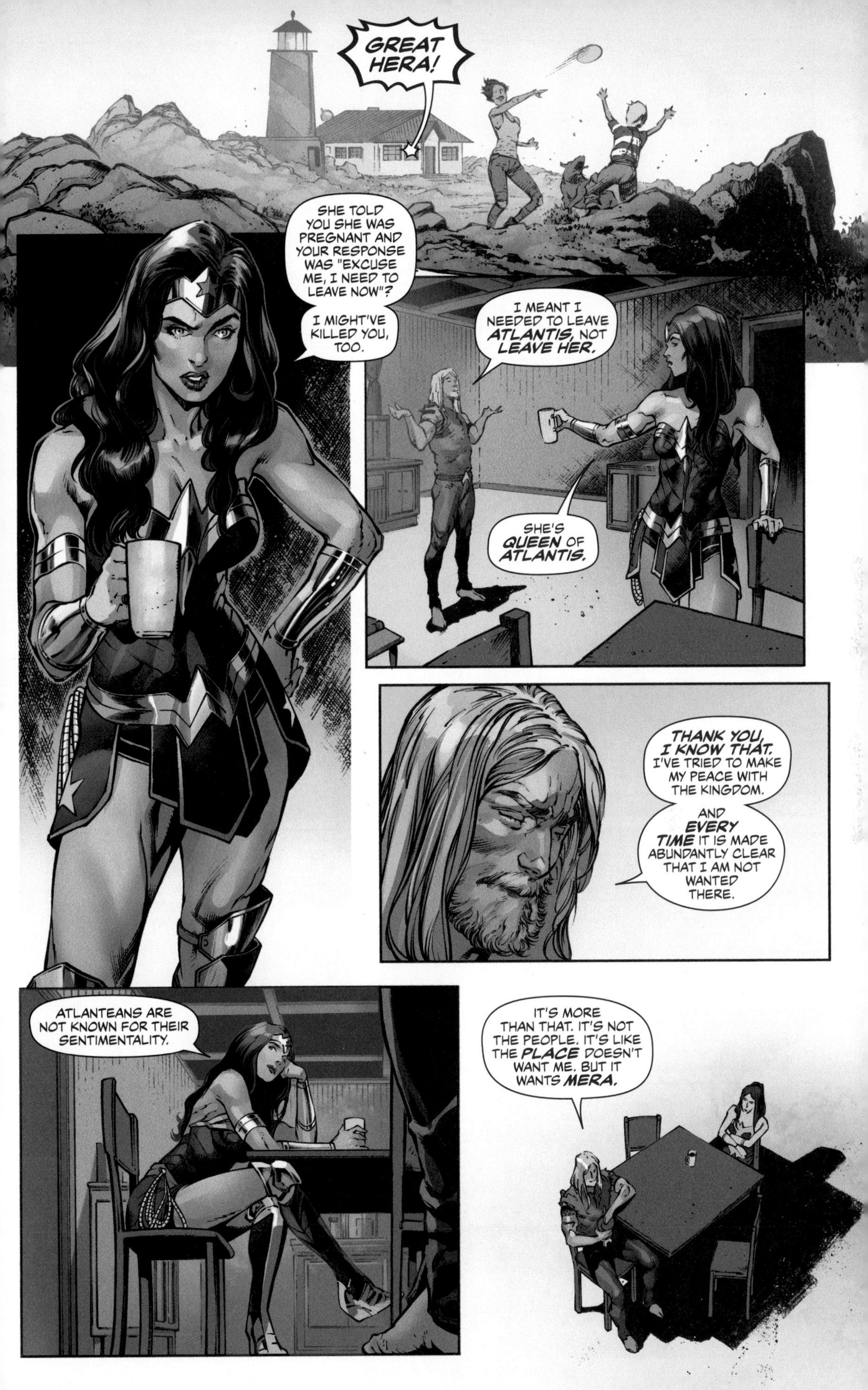
GREAT HERA!
SHE TOLD YOU SHE WAS PREGNANT AND YOUR RESPONSE WAS "EXCUSE ME, I NEED TO LEAVE NOW"?
I MIGHT'VE KILLED YOU, TOO.
I MEANT I NEEDED TO LEAVE ATLANTIS, NOT LEAVE HER.
SHE'S QUEEN OF ATLANTIS.
THANK YOU, I KNOW THAT. I'VE TRIED TO MAKE MY PEACE WITH THE KINGDOM.
AND EVERY TIME IT IS MADE ABUNDANTLY CLEAR THAT I AM NOT WANTED THERE.
ATLANTEANS ARE NOT KNOWN FOR THEIR SENTIMENTALITY.
IT'S MORE THAN THAT. IT'S NOT THE PEOPLE. IT'S LIKE THE PLACE DOESN'T WANT ME. BUT IT WANTS MERA.

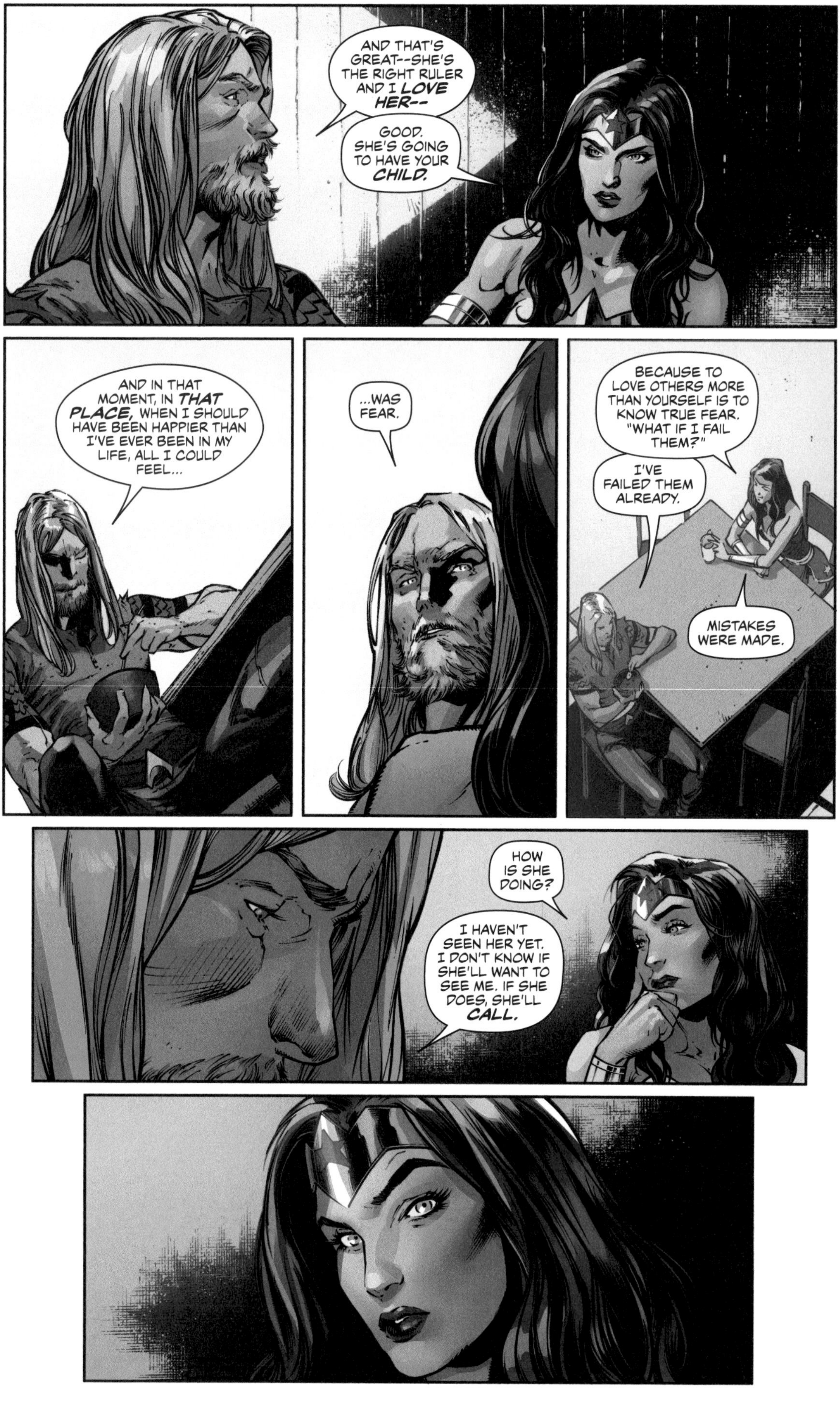
AND THAT'S GREAT--SHE'S THE RIGHT RULER AND I LOVE HER--
GOOD. SHE'S GOING TO HAVE YOUR CHILD.
AND IN THAT MOMENT, IN THAT PLACE, WHEN I SHOULD HAVE BEEN HAPPIER THAN I'VE EVER BEEN IN MY LIFE, ALL I COULD FEEL...
...WAS FEAR.
BECAUSE TO LOVE OTHERS MORE THAN YOURSELF IS TO KNOW TRUE FEAR. "WHAT IF I FAIL THEM?"
I'VE FAILED THEM ALREADY.
MISTAKES WERE MADE.
HOW IS SHE DOING?
I HAVEN'T SEEN HER YET. I DON'T KNOW IF SHE'LL WANT TO SEE ME. IF SHE DOES, SHE'LL CALL.

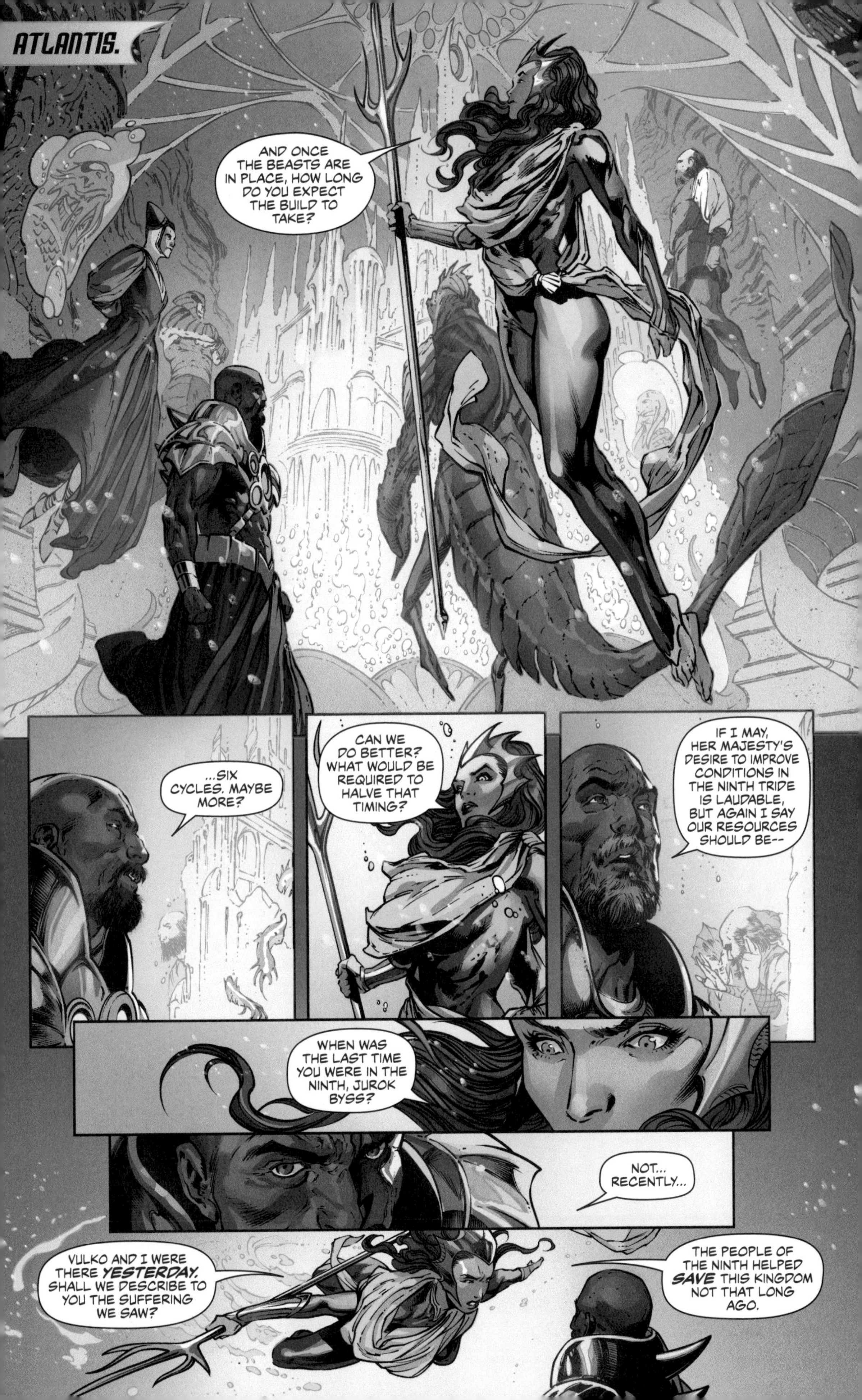
ATLANTIS.
AND ONCE THE BEASTS ARE IN PLACE, HOW LONG DO YOU EXPECT THE BUILD TO TAKE?
...SIX CYCLES. MAYBE MORE?
CAN WE DO BETTER? WHAT WOULD BE REQUIRED TO HALVE THAT TIMING?
IF I MAY, HER MAJESTY'S DESIRE TO IMPROVE CONDITIONS IN THE NINTH TRIDE IS LAUDABLE, BUT AGAIN I SAY OUR RESOURCES SHOULD BE--
WHEN WAS THE LAST TIME YOU WERE IN THE NINTH, JUROK BYSS?
NOT... RECENTLY...
VULKO AND I WERE THERE YESTERDAY. SHALL WE DESCRIBE TO YOU THE SUFFERING WE SAW?
THE PEOPLE OF THE NINTH HELPED SAVE THIS KINGDOM NOT THAT LONG AGO.

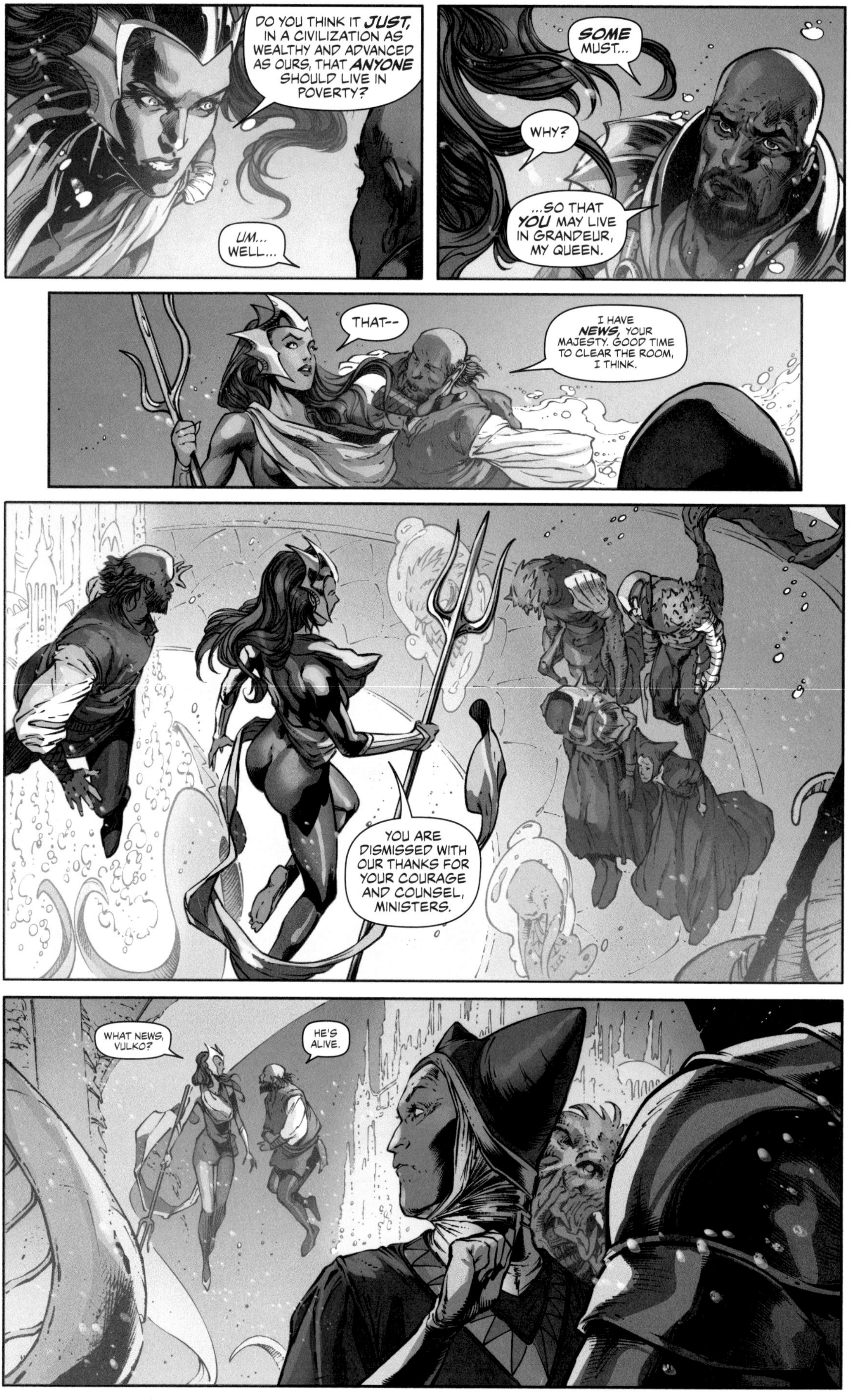

DO YOU THINK IT JUST, IN A CIVILIZATION AS WEALTHY AND ADVANCED AS OURS, THAT ANYONE SHOULD LIVE IN POVERTY?
UM... WELL...
SOME MUST...
WHY?
...SO THAT YOU MAY LIVE IN GRANDEUR, MY QUEEN.
THAT--
I HAVE NEWS, YOUR MAJESTY. GOOD TIME TO CLEAR THE ROOM, I THINK.
YOU ARE DISMISSED WITH OUR THANKS FOR YOUR COURAGE AND COUNSEL, MINISTERS.
WHAT NEWS, VULKO?
HE'S ALIVE.

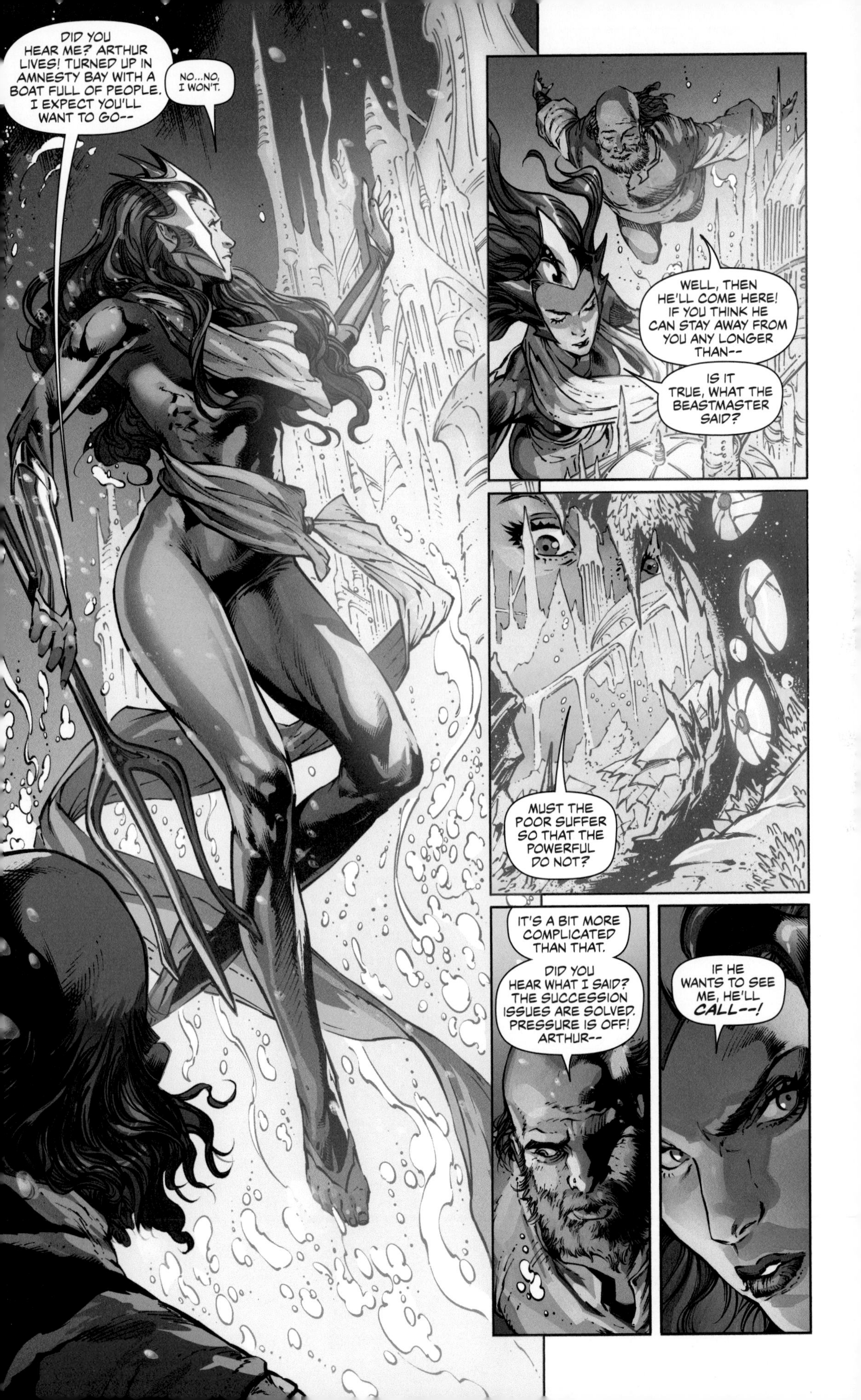
DID YOU HEAR ME? ARTHUR LIVES! TURNED UP IN AMNESTY BAY WITH A BOAT FULL OF PEOPLE. I EXPECT YOU'LL WANT TO GO--
NO...NO, I WON'T.
WELL, THEN HE'LL COME HERE! IF YOU THINK HE CAN STAY AWAY FROM YOU ANY LONGER THAN--
IS IT TRUE, WHAT THE BEASTMASTER SAID?
MUST THE POOR SUFFER SO THAT THE POWERFUL DO NOT?
IT'S A BIT MORE COMPLICATED THAN THAT.
DID YOU HEAR WHAT I SAID? THE SUCCESSION ISSUES ARE SOLVED. PRESSURE IS OFF! ARTHUR--
IF HE WANTS TO SEE ME, HE'LL CALL--!

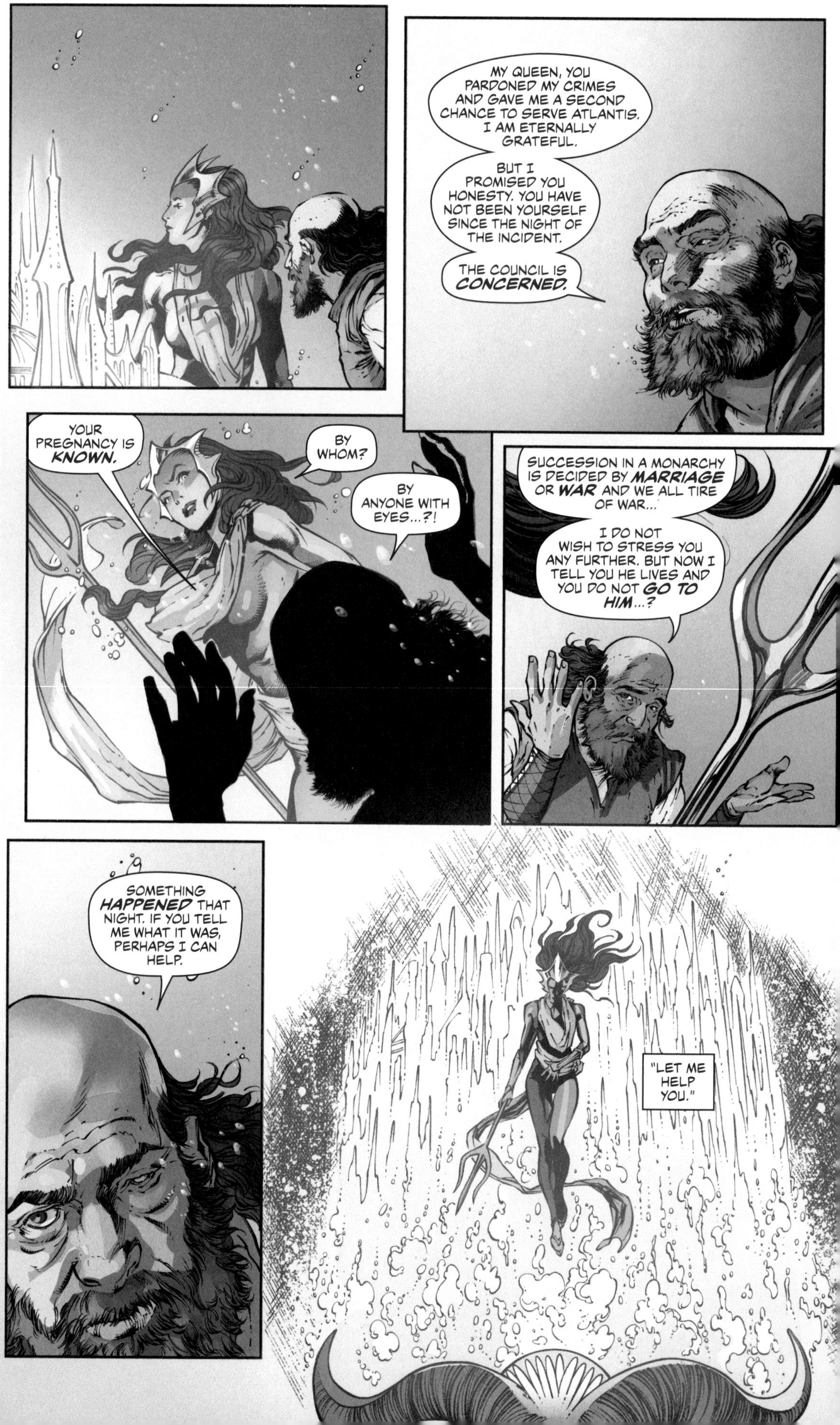
MY QUEEN, YOU PARDONED MY CRIMES AND GAVE ME A SECOND CHANCE TO SERVE ATLANTIS. I AM ETERNALLY GRATEFUL.
BUT I PROMISED YOU HONESTY. YOU HAVE NOT BEEN YOURSELF SINCE THE NIGHT OF THE INCIDENT.
THE COUNCIL IS *CONCERNED.*
YOUR PREGNANCY IS *KNOWN.*
BY WHOM?
BY ANYONE WITH EYES...?!
SUCCESSION IN A MONARCHY IS DECIDED BY *MARRIAGE* OR *WAR* AND WE ALL TIRE OF WAR...
I DO NOT WISH TO STRESS YOU ANY FURTHER. BUT NOW I TELL YOU HE LIVES AND YOU DO NOT *GO TO HIM*...?
SOMETHING *HAPPENED* THAT NIGHT. IF YOU TELL ME WHAT IT WAS, PERHAPS I CAN HELP.
"LET ME HELP YOU."

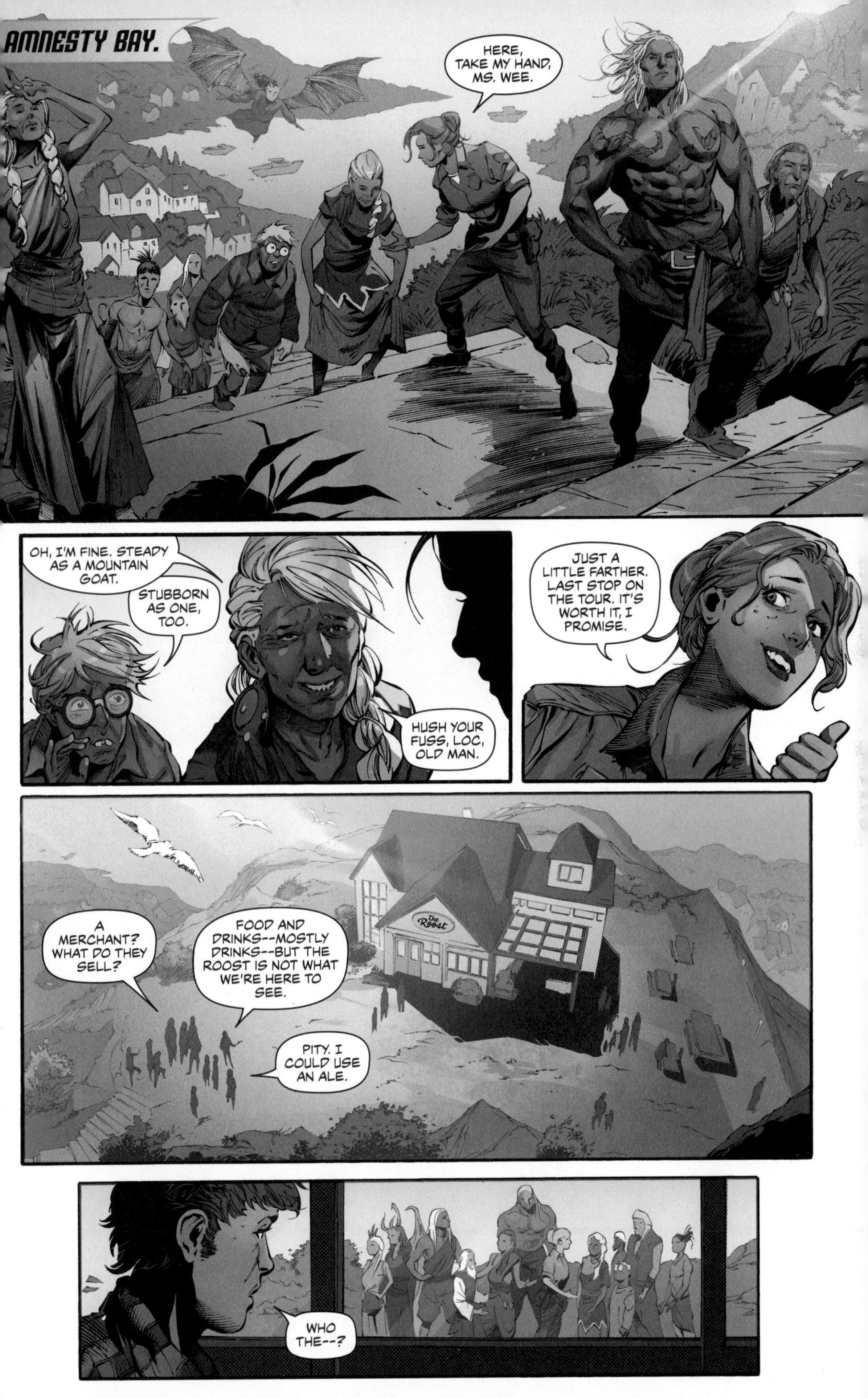
AMNESTY BAY.
HERE, TAKE MY HAND, MS. WEE.
OH, I'M FINE. STEADY AS A MOUNTAIN GOAT.
STUBBORN AS ONE, TOO.
HUSH YOUR FUSS, LOC, OLD MAN.
JUST A LITTLE FARTHER. LAST STOP ON THE TOUR. IT'S WORTH IT, I PROMISE.
The Roost
A MERCHANT? WHAT DO THEY SELL?
FOOD AND DRINKS--MOSTLY DRINKS--BUT THE ROOST IS NOT WHAT WE'RE HERE TO SEE.
PITY. I COULD USE AN ALE.
WHO THE--?

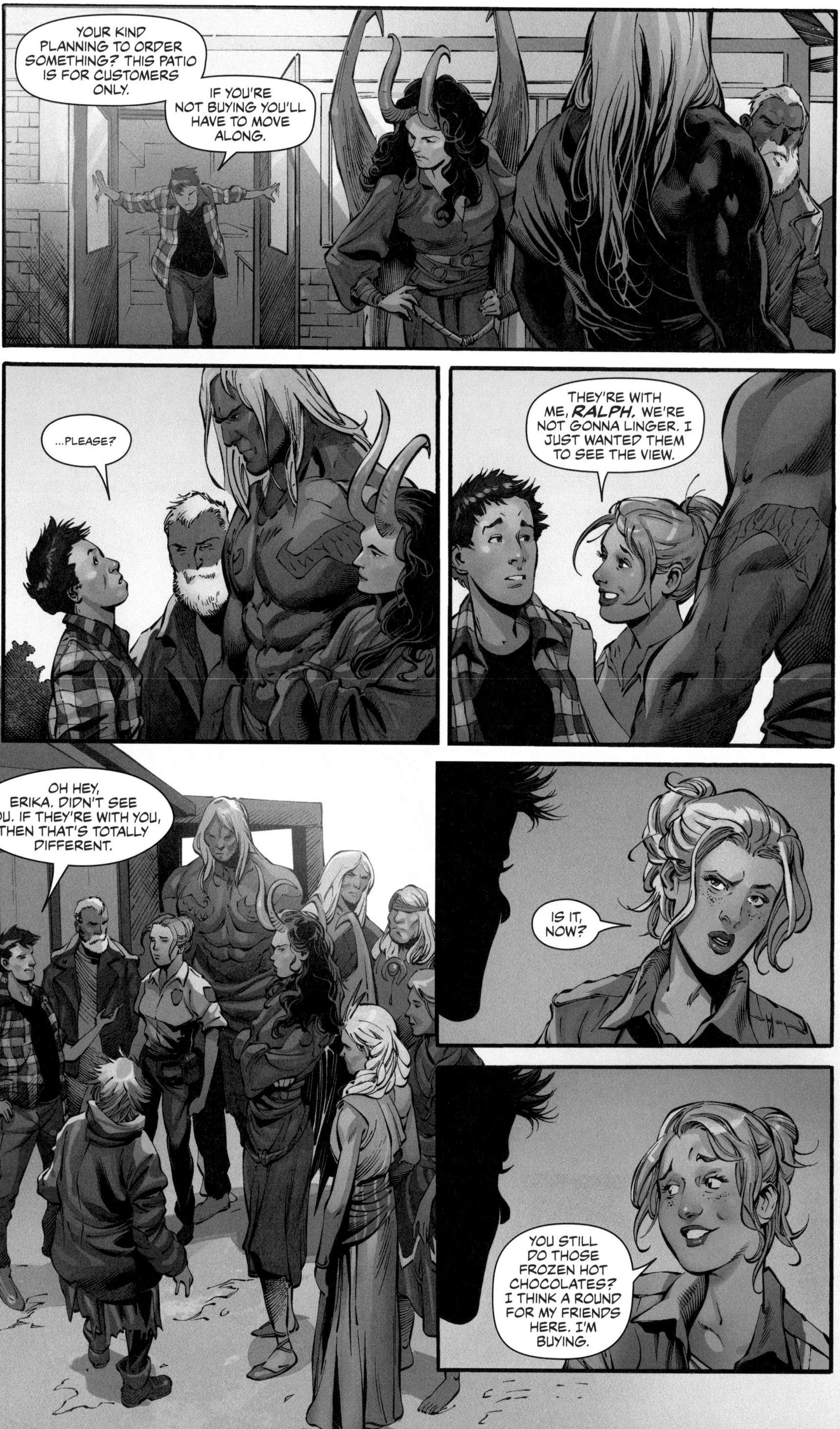
YOUR KIND PLANNING TO ORDER SOMETHING? THIS PATIO IS FOR CUSTOMERS ONLY.
IF YOU'RE NOT BUYING YOU'LL HAVE TO MOVE ALONG.
...PLEASE?
THEY'RE WITH ME, RALPH. WE'RE NOT GONNA LINGER. I JUST WANTED THEM TO SEE THE VIEW.
OH HEY, ERIKA. DIDN'T SEE YOU. IF THEY'RE WITH YOU, THEN THAT'S TOTALLY DIFFERENT.
IS IT, NOW?
YOU STILL DO THOSE FROZEN HOT CHOCOLATES? I THINK A ROUND FOR MY FRIENDS HERE. I'M BUYING.

COULDN'T ASK FOR A BETTER TOUR GUIDE. ERIKA HERE KNOWS *EVERYTHING* THERE IS TO KNOW ABOUT THIS OLD TOWN.

SHE WAS JUST TELLING ME A STORY ABOUT THE OLD LIGHTHOUSE AND A SHIPWRECK--

--IN A *PRIVATE* MEETING. THE SECOND *A* IS FOR *ANONYMOUS*, RALPH.

SORRY.

"OUR KIND" HAVE A PARTICULAR FONDNESS FOR STORIES, YOU KNOW.

WELL, IT'S NOT THAT GREAT OF A STORY, I'M AFRAID. DOESN'T HAVE MUCH OF AN ENDING.

SHIP CAPTAIN IN THE 1700s WAS A DRUNK, WRECKED HIS SHIP AND EVERYONE ON BOARD DIED EXCEPT HIM.

THE GUILT ATE HIM UP. HE CAME BACK AND BUILT A LIGHTHOUSE. THEN HE DISAPPEARED. THAT'S KIND OF IT.

YOU'RE RIGHT. YOU'RE NOT VERY GOOD AT STORIES.

WAS IT ARTHUR'S LIGHTHOUSE HE BUILT?

NO--OH NO--THE *OLD* LIGHTHOUSE. I'LL SHOW YOU.

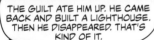

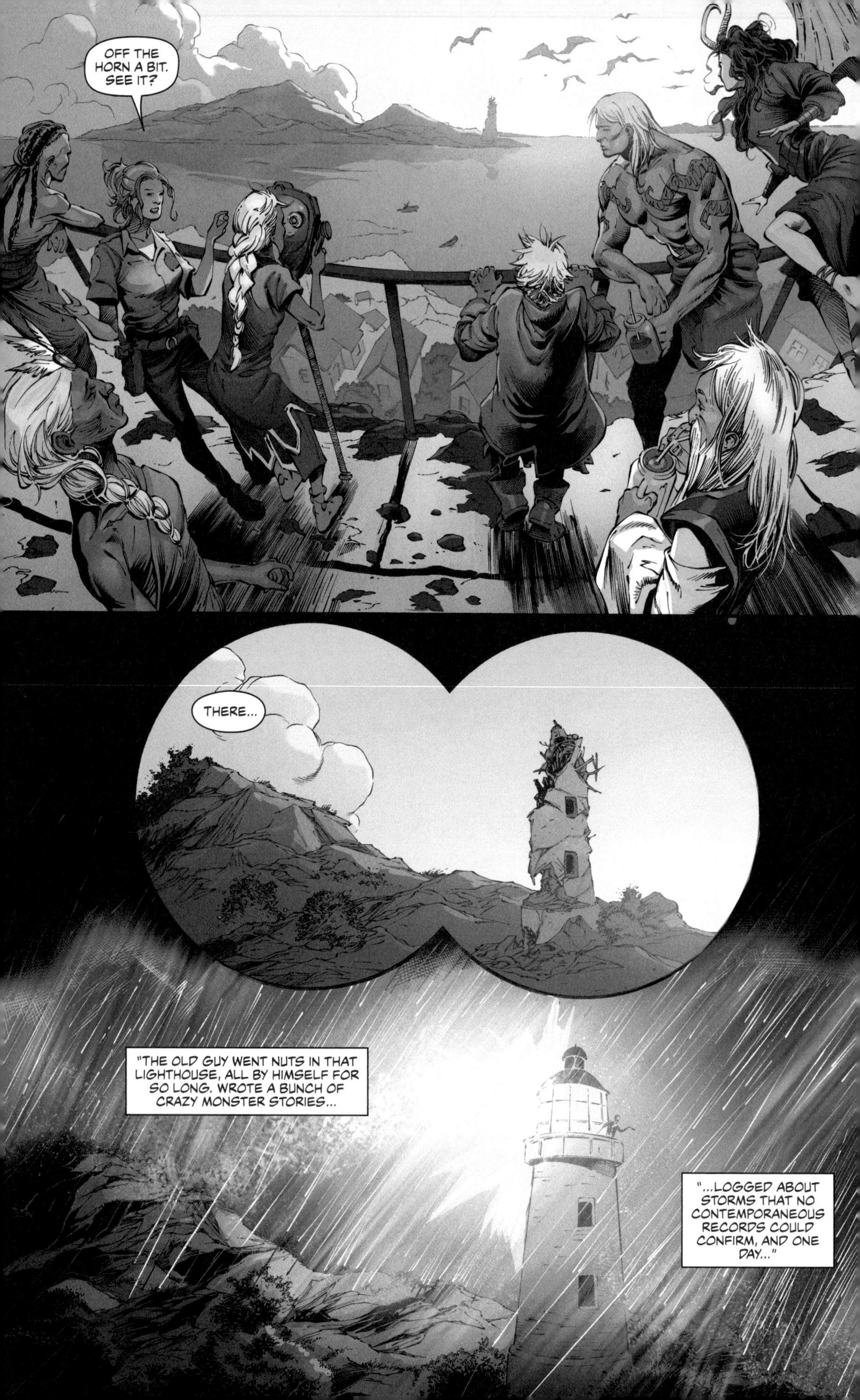
OFF THE HORN A BIT. SEE IT?
THERE...
"THE OLD GUY WENT NUTS IN THAT LIGHTHOUSE, ALL BY HIMSELF FOR SO LONG. WROTE A BUNCH OF CRAZY MONSTER STORIES...
"...LOGGED ABOUT STORMS THAT NO CONTEMPORANEOUS RECORDS COULD CONFIRM, AND ONE DAY..."

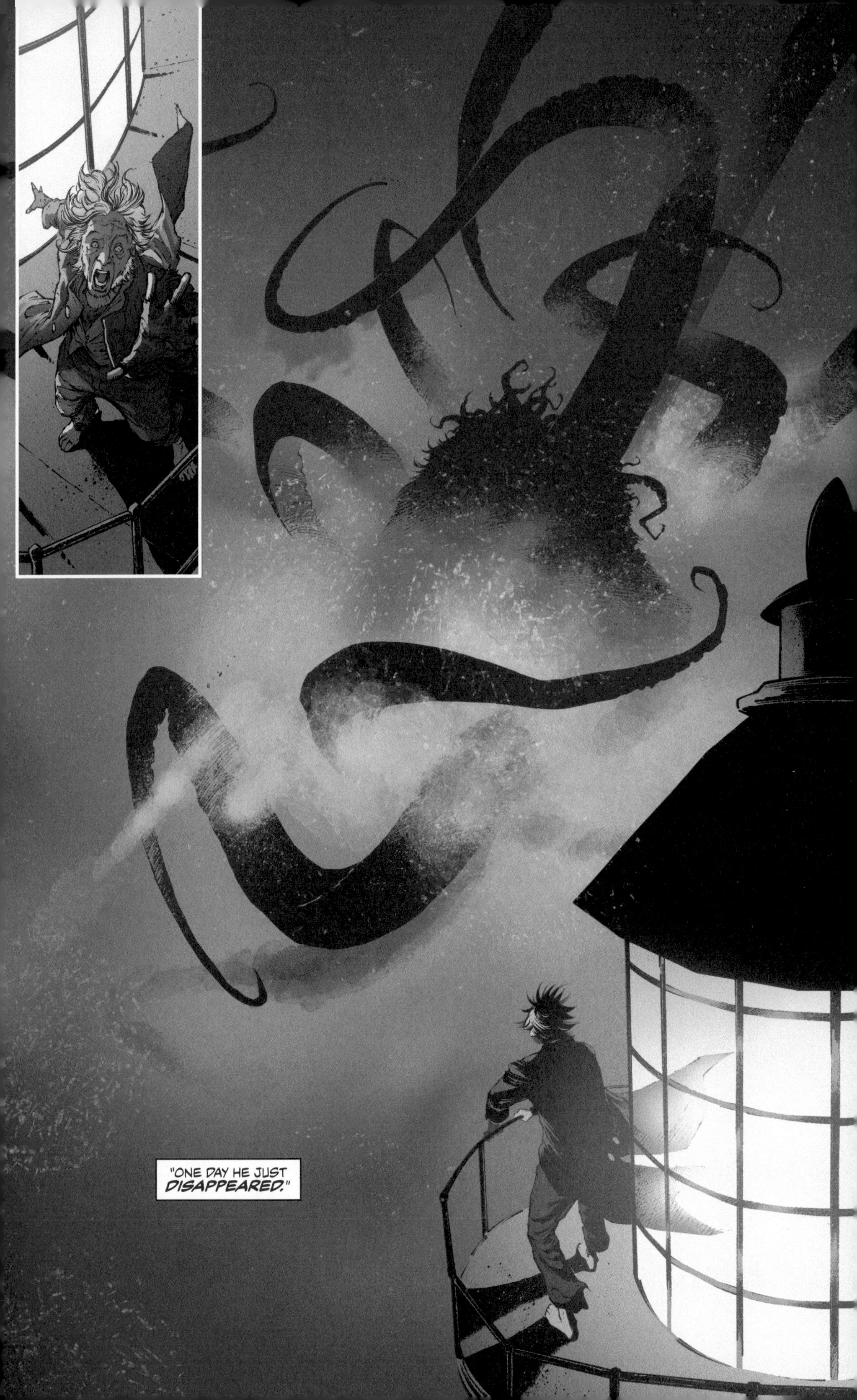
"ONE DAY HE JUST DISAPPEARED."

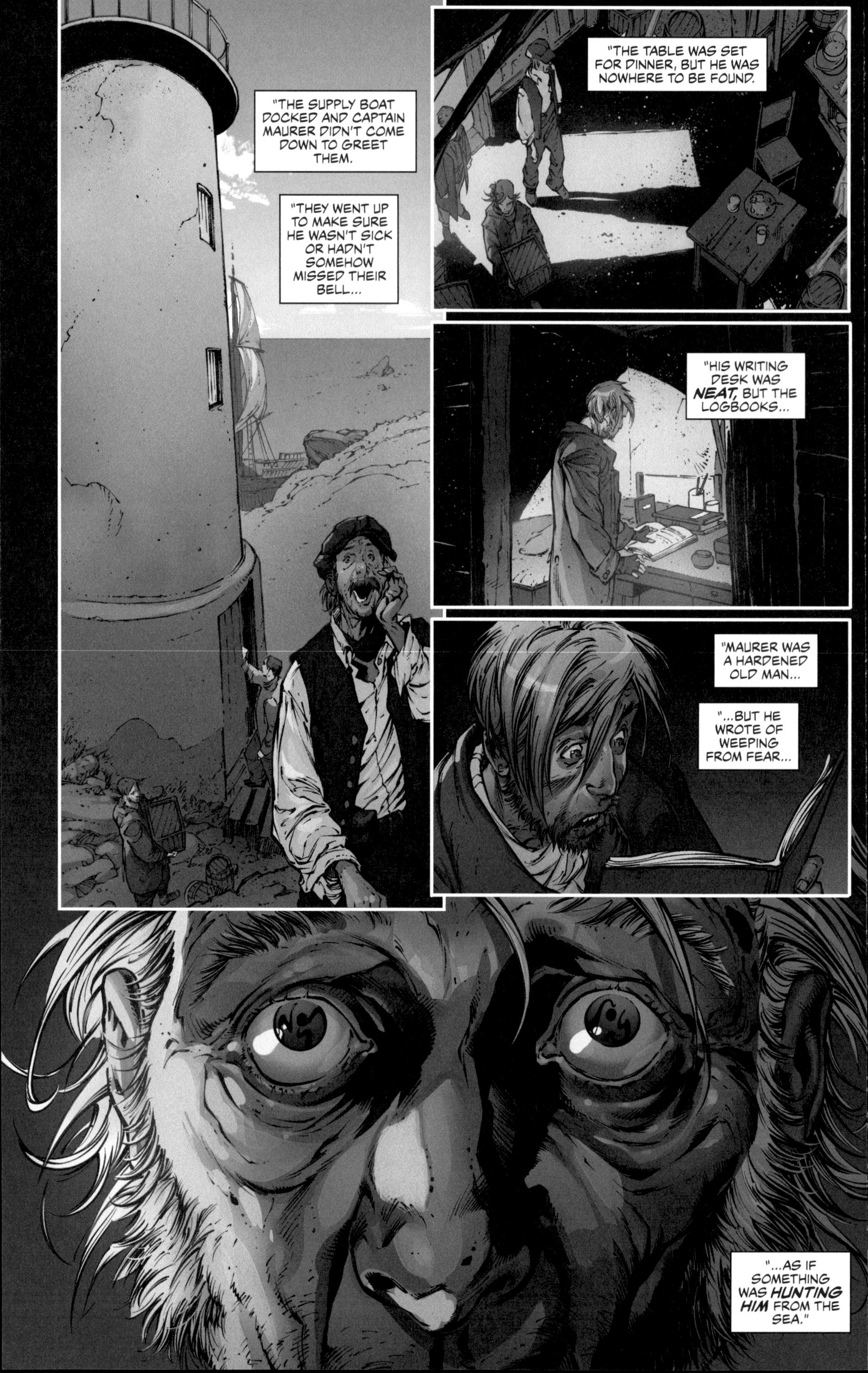
"THE SUPPLY BOAT DOCKED AND CAPTAIN MAURER DIDN'T COME DOWN TO GREET THEM.
"THEY WENT UP TO MAKE SURE HE WASN'T SICK OR HADN'T SOMEHOW MISSED THEIR BELL...
"THE TABLE WAS SET FOR DINNER, BUT HE WAS NOWHERE TO BE FOUND.
"HIS WRITING DESK WAS ***NEAT,*** BUT THE LOGBOOKS...
"MAURER WAS A HARDENED OLD MAN...
"...BUT HE WROTE OF WEEPING FROM FEAR...
"...AS IF SOMETHING WAS ***HUNTING HIM*** FROM THE SEA."

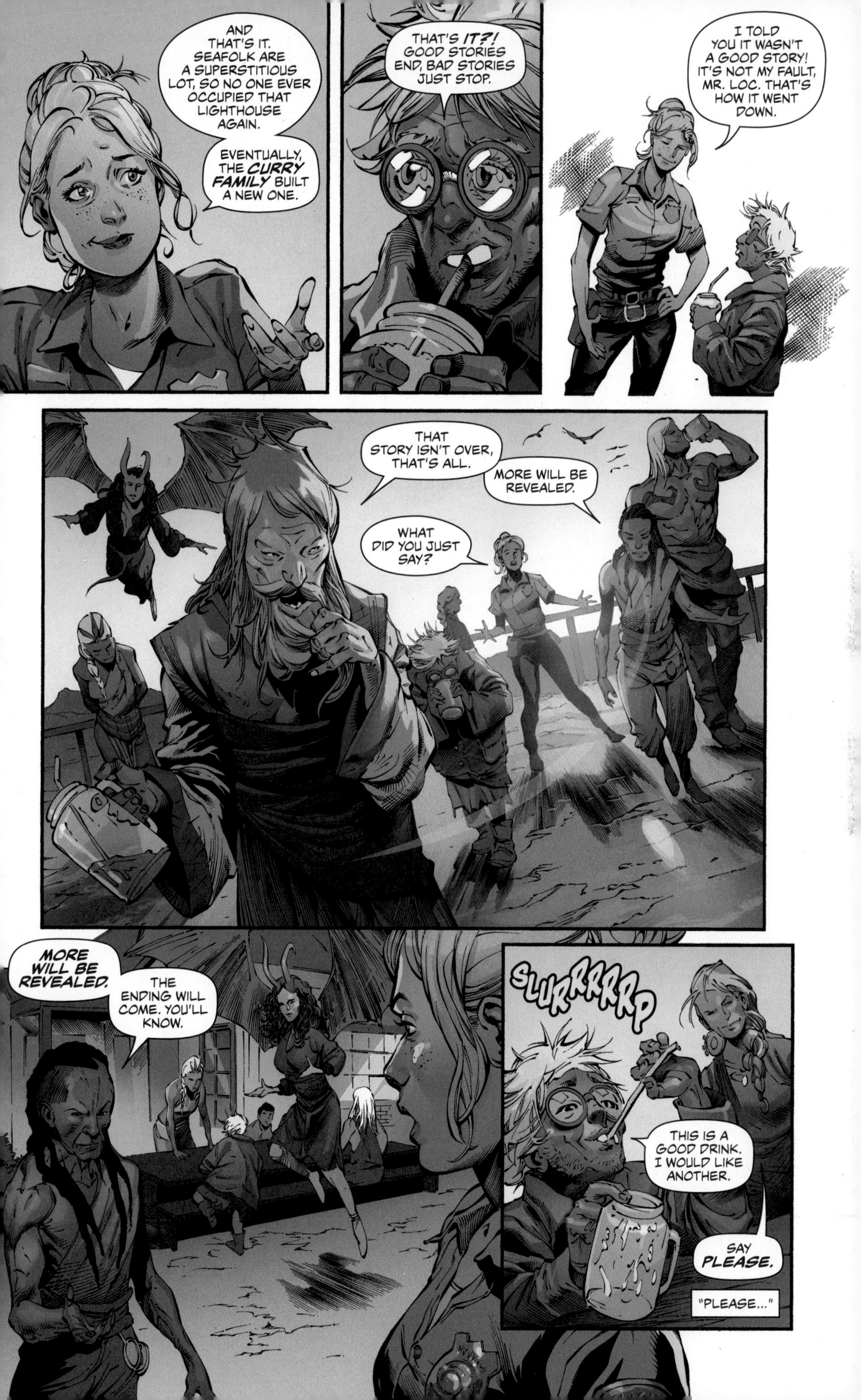
AND THAT'S IT. SEAFOLK ARE A SUPERSTITIOUS LOT, SO NO ONE EVER OCCUPIED THAT LIGHTHOUSE AGAIN.
EVENTUALLY, THE CURRY FAMILY BUILT A NEW ONE.
THAT'S IT?! GOOD STORIES END, BAD STORIES JUST STOP.
I TOLD YOU IT WASN'T A GOOD STORY! IT'S NOT MY FAULT, MR. LOC. THAT'S HOW IT WENT DOWN.
THAT STORY ISN'T OVER, THAT'S ALL.
MORE WILL BE REVEALED.
WHAT DID YOU JUST SAY?
MORE WILL BE REVEALED.
THE ENDING WILL COME. YOU'LL KNOW.
SLURRRRRP
THIS IS A GOOD DRINK. I WOULD LIKE ANOTHER.
SAY PLEASE.
"PLEASE..."

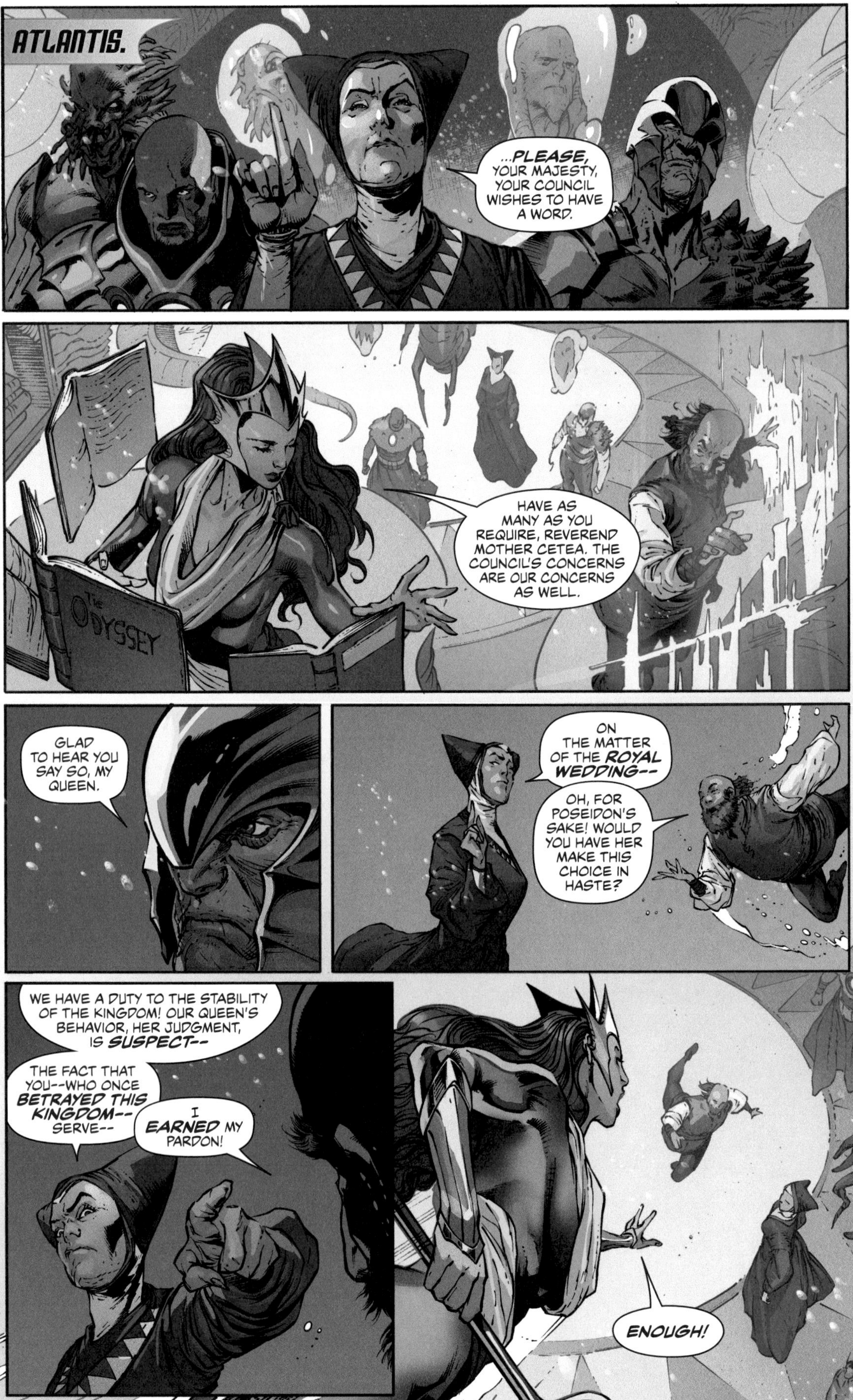
ATLANTIS.
...PLEASE, YOUR MAJESTY, YOUR COUNCIL WISHES TO HAVE A WORD.
THE ODYSSEY
HAVE AS MANY AS YOU REQUIRE, REVEREND MOTHER CETEA. THE COUNCIL'S CONCERNS ARE OUR CONCERNS AS WELL.
GLAD TO HEAR YOU SAY SO, MY QUEEN.
ON THE MATTER OF THE ROYAL WEDDING--
OH, FOR POSEIDON'S SAKE! WOULD YOU HAVE HER MAKE THIS CHOICE IN HASTE?
WE HAVE A DUTY TO THE STABILITY OF THE KINGDOM! OUR QUEEN'S BEHAVIOR, HER JUDGMENT, IS SUSPECT--
THE FACT THAT YOU--WHO ONCE BETRAYED THIS KINGDOM--SERVE--
I EARNED MY PARDON!
ENOUGH!

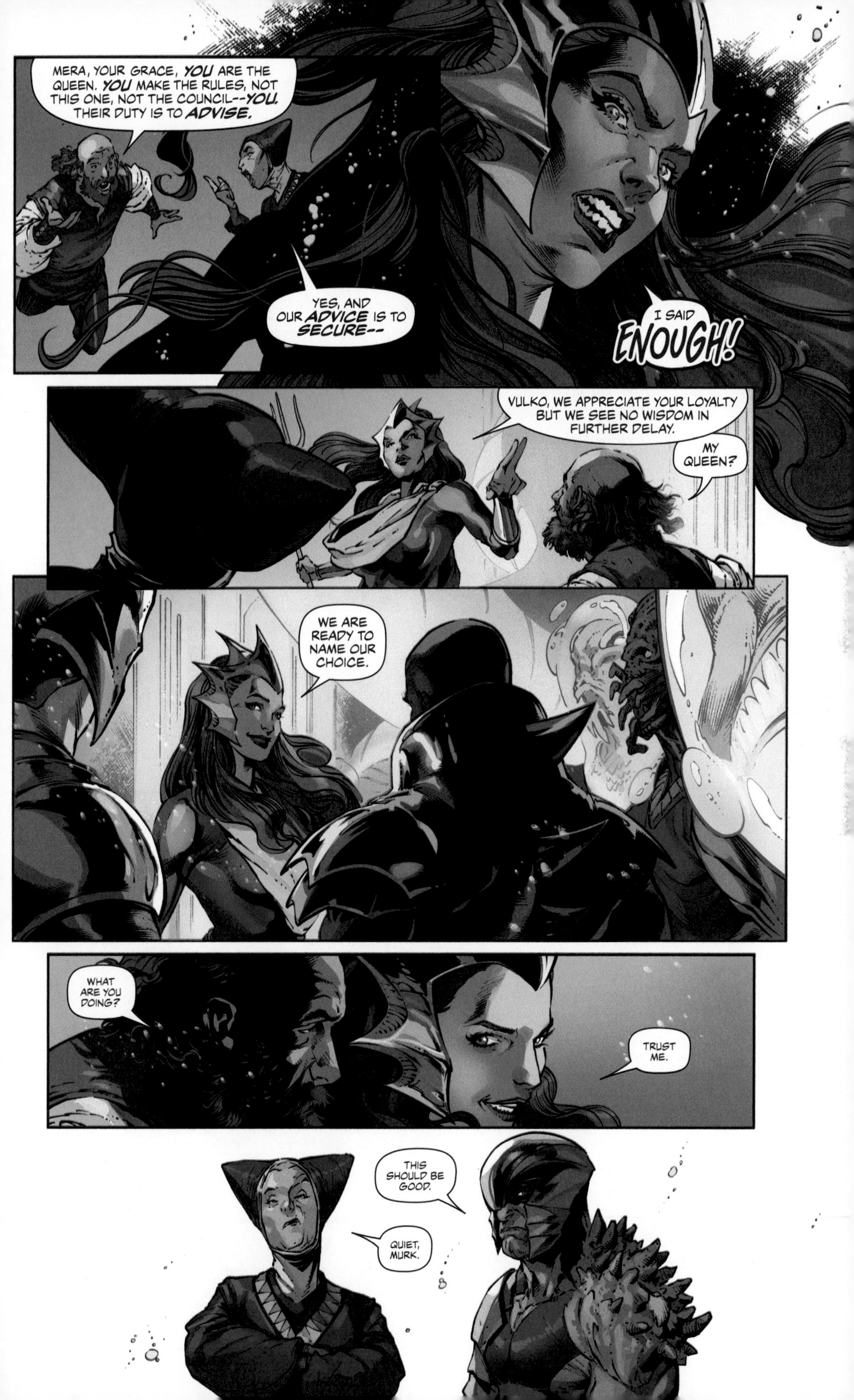
MERA, YOUR GRACE, YOU ARE THE QUEEN. YOU MAKE THE RULES, NOT THIS ONE, NOT THE COUNCIL--YOU. THEIR DUTY IS TO ADVISE.
YES, AND OUR ADVICE IS TO SECURE--
I SAID ENOUGH!
VULKO, WE APPRECIATE YOUR LOYALTY BUT WE SEE NO WISDOM IN FURTHER DELAY.
MY QUEEN?
WE ARE READY TO NAME OUR CHOICE.
WHAT ARE YOU DOING?
TRUST ME.
THIS SHOULD BE GOOD.
QUIET, MURK.

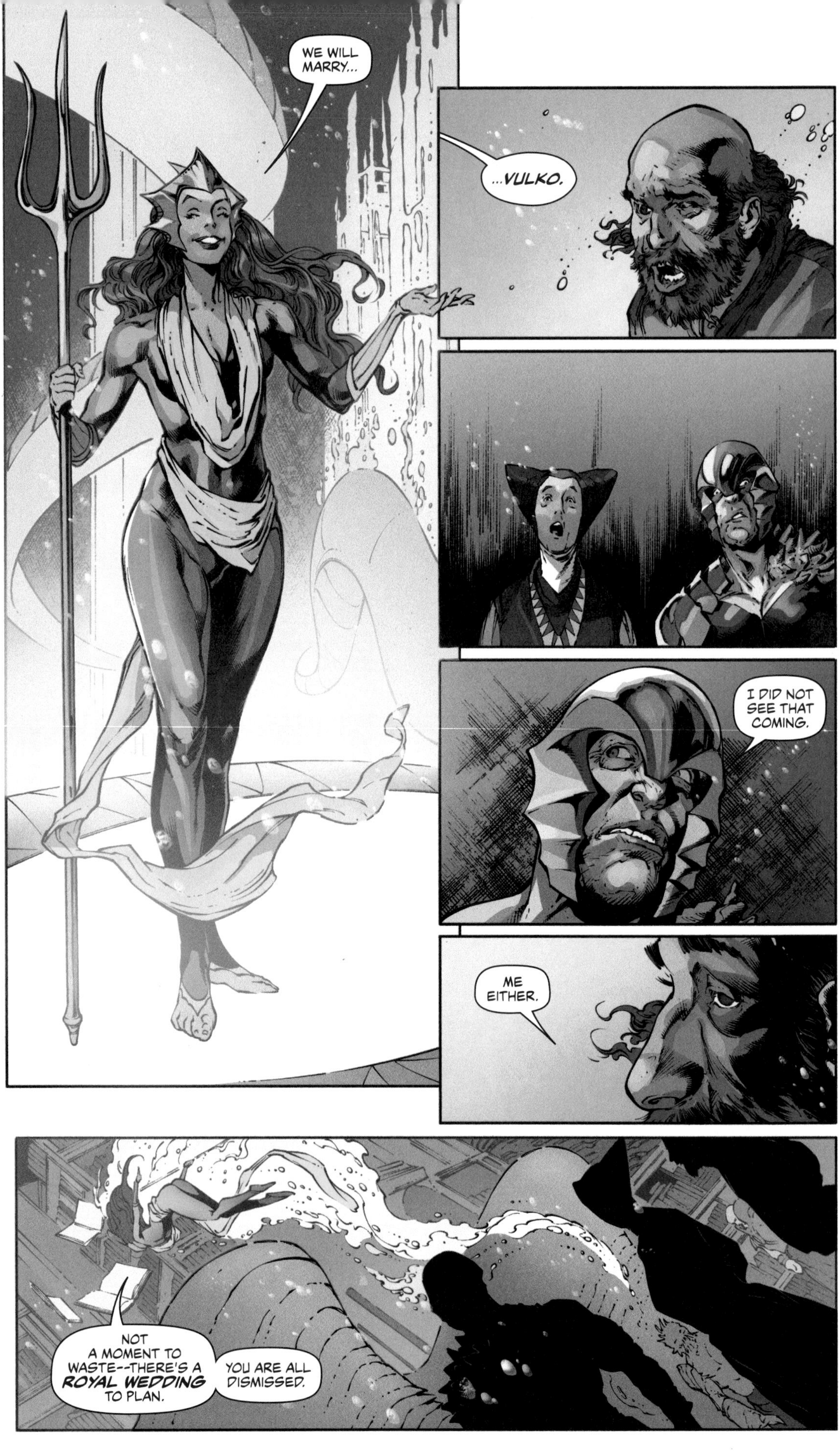
WE WILL MARRY...
...VULKO.
I DID NOT SEE THAT COMING.
ME EITHER.
NOT A MOMENT TO WASTE--THERE'S A ROYAL WEDDING TO PLAN.
YOU ARE ALL DISMISSED.

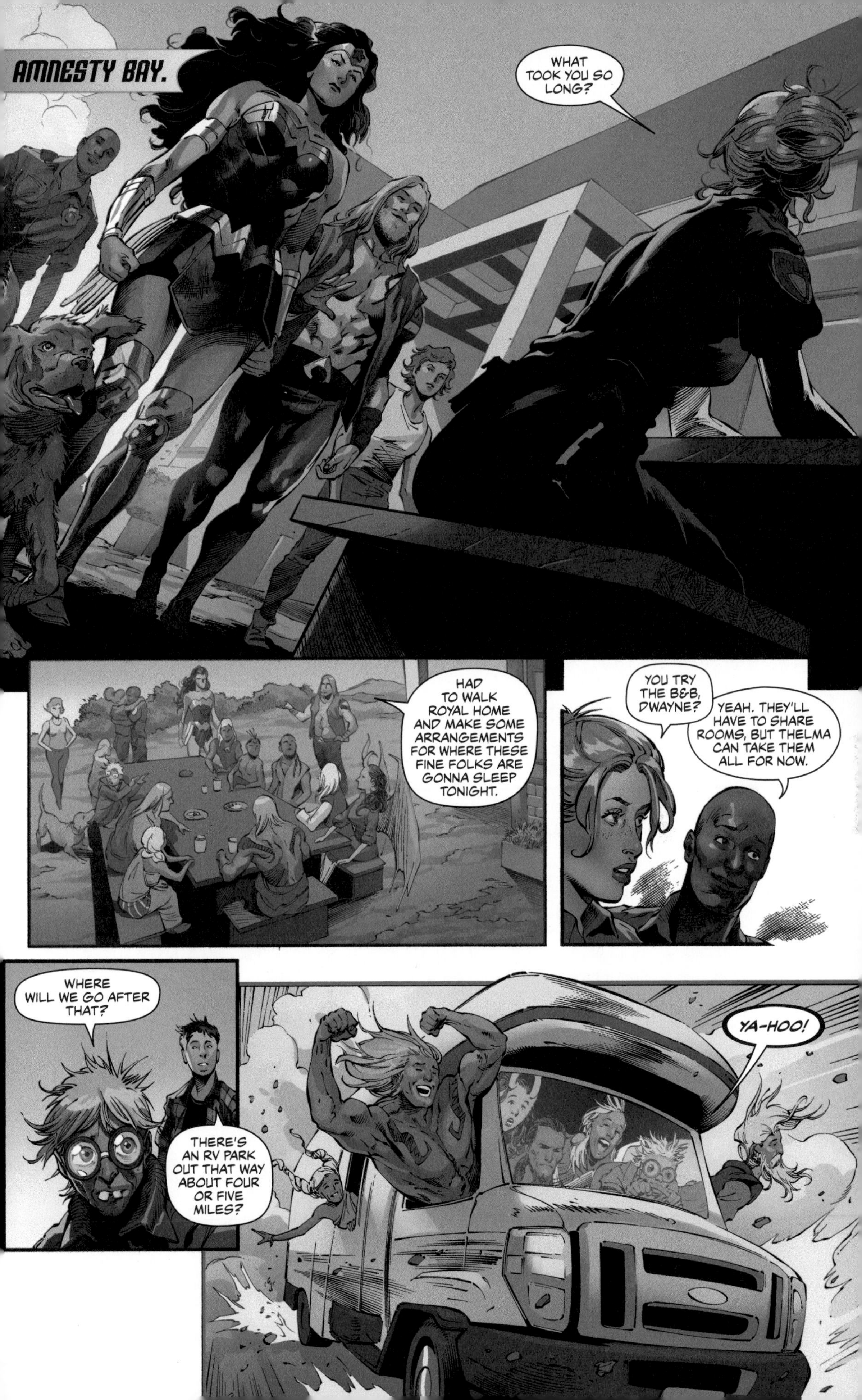
AMNESTY BAY.
WHAT TOOK YOU SO LONG?
HAD TO WALK ROYAL HOME AND MAKE SOME ARRANGEMENTS FOR WHERE THESE FINE FOLKS ARE GONNA SLEEP TONIGHT.
YOU TRY THE B&B, DWAYNE?
YEAH. THEY'LL HAVE TO SHARE ROOMS, BUT THELMA CAN TAKE THEM ALL FOR NOW.
WHERE WILL WE GO AFTER THAT?
THERE'S AN RV PARK OUT THAT WAY ABOUT FOUR OR FIVE MILES?
YA-HOO!

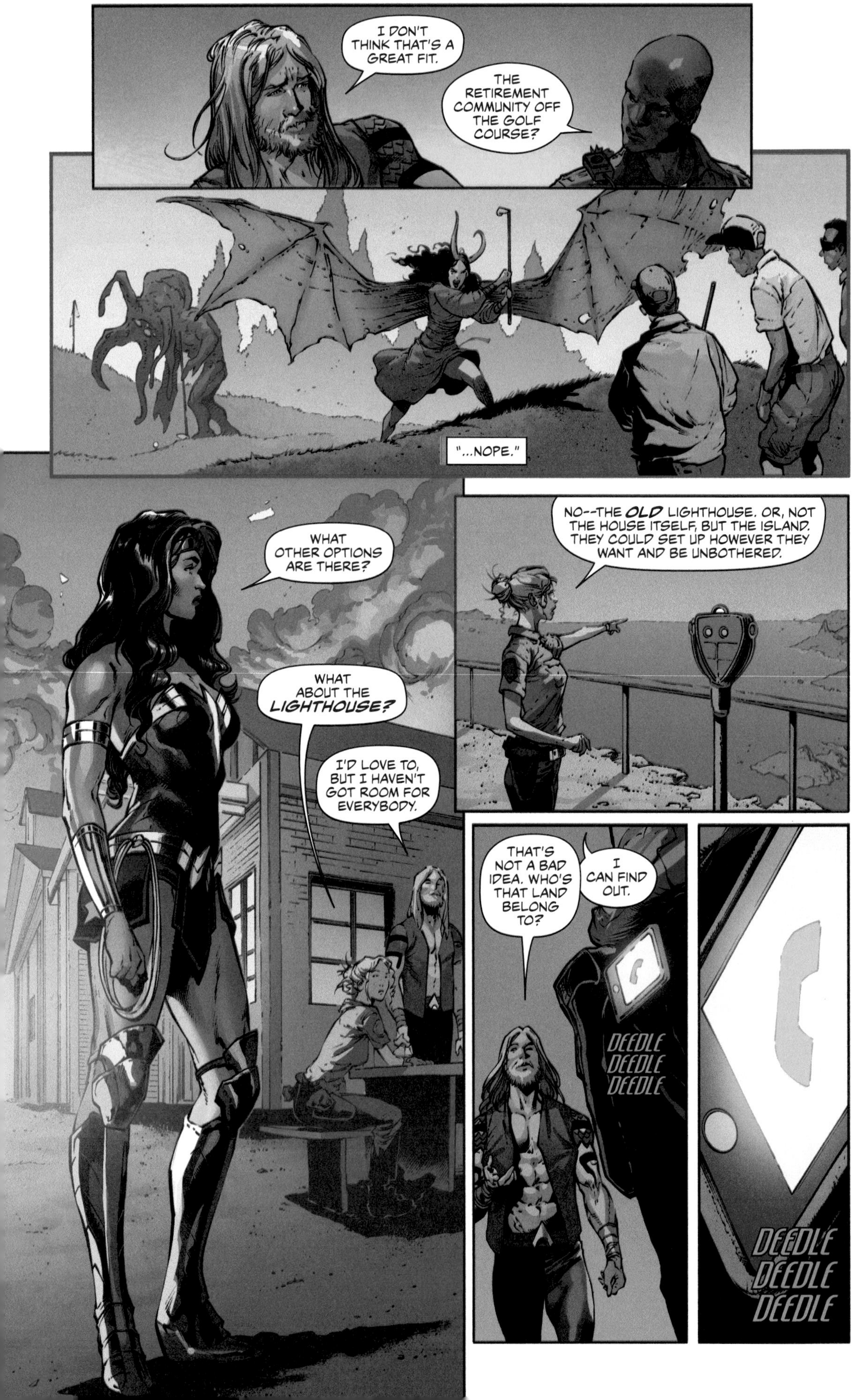
I DON'T THINK THAT'S A GREAT FIT.
THE RETIREMENT COMMUNITY OFF THE GOLF COURSE?
"...NOPE."
WHAT OTHER OPTIONS ARE THERE?
WHAT ABOUT THE LIGHTHOUSE?
I'D LOVE TO, BUT I HAVEN'T GOT ROOM FOR EVERYBODY.
NO--THE OLD LIGHTHOUSE. OR, NOT THE HOUSE ITSELF, BUT THE ISLAND. THEY COULD SET UP HOWEVER THEY WANT AND BE UNBOTHERED.
THAT'S NOT A BAD IDEA. WHO'S THAT LAND BELONG TO?
I CAN FIND OUT.
DEEDLE DEEDLE DEEDLE
DEEDLE DEEDLE DEEDLE

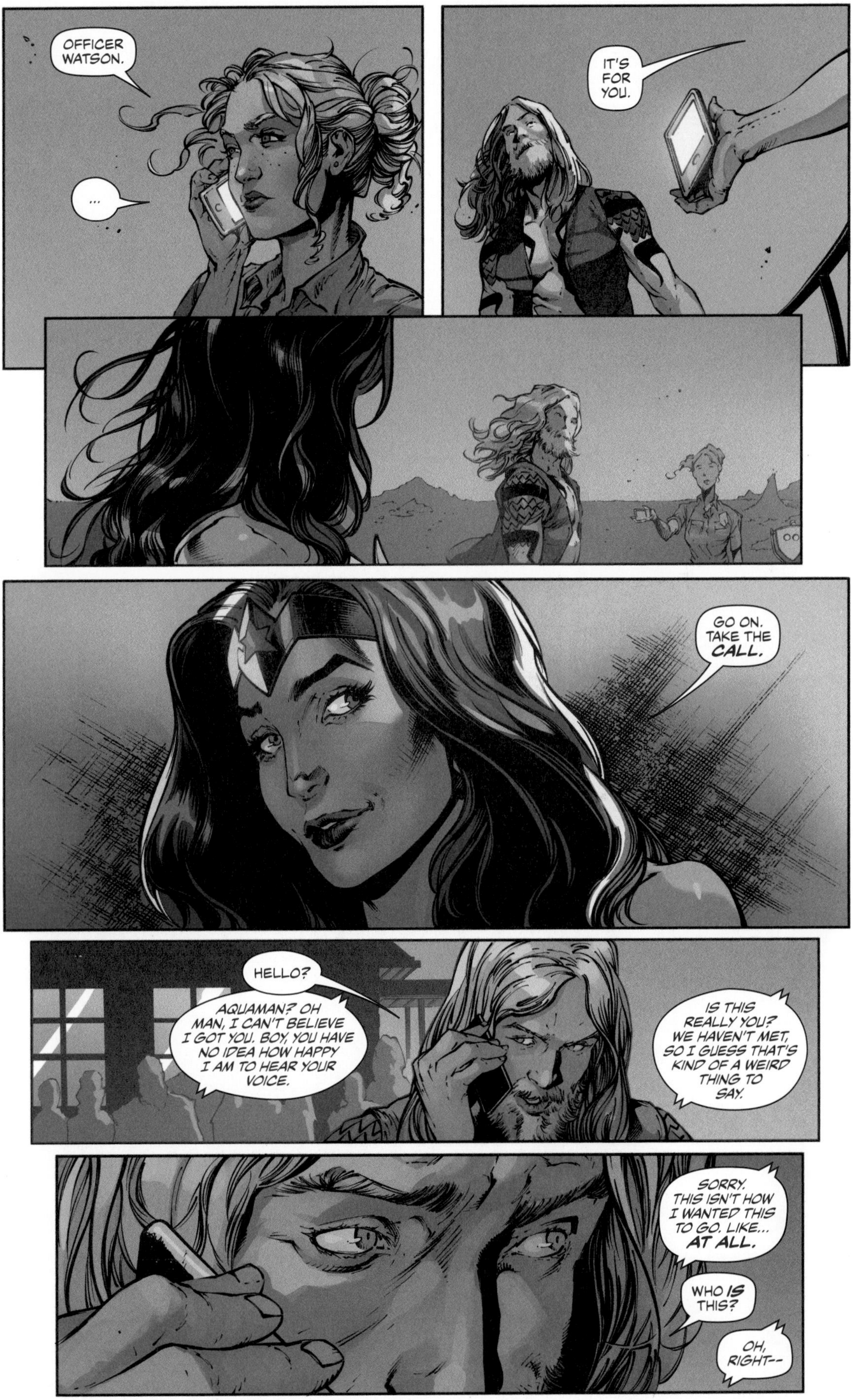

OFFICER WATSON.
...
IT'S FOR YOU.
GO ON. TAKE THE CALL.
HELLO?
AQUAMAN? OH MAN, I CAN'T BELIEVE I GOT YOU. BOY, YOU HAVE NO IDEA HOW HAPPY I AM TO HEAR YOUR VOICE.
IS THIS REALLY YOU? WE HAVEN'T MET, SO I GUESS THAT'S KIND OF A WEIRD THING TO SAY.
SORRY. THIS ISN'T HOW I WANTED THIS TO GO. LIKE... AT ALL.
WHO IS THIS?
OH, RIGHT--

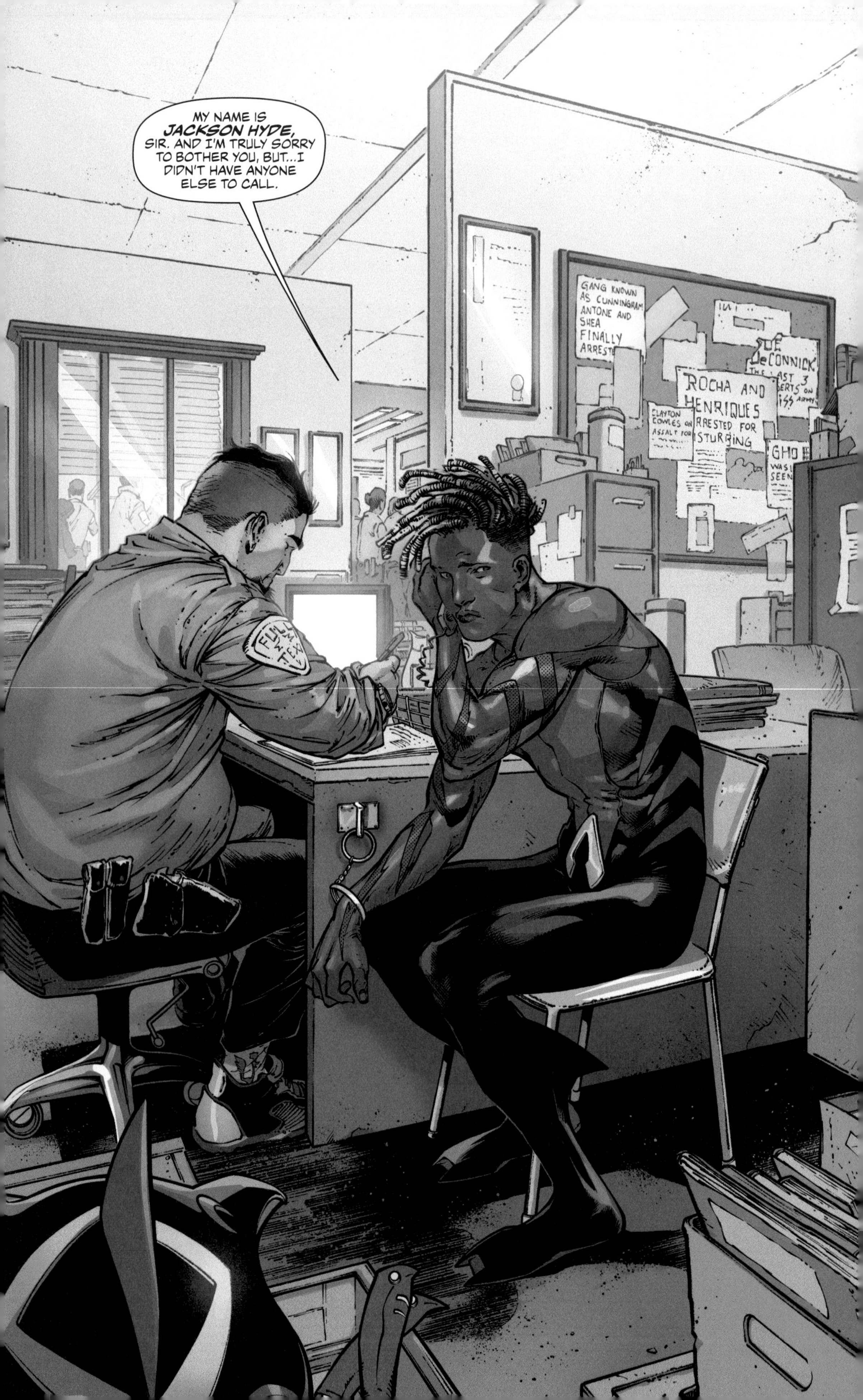
MY NAME IS JACKSON HYDE, SIR. AND I'M TRULY SORRY TO BOTHER YOU, BUT...I DIDN'T HAVE ANYONE ELSE TO CALL.

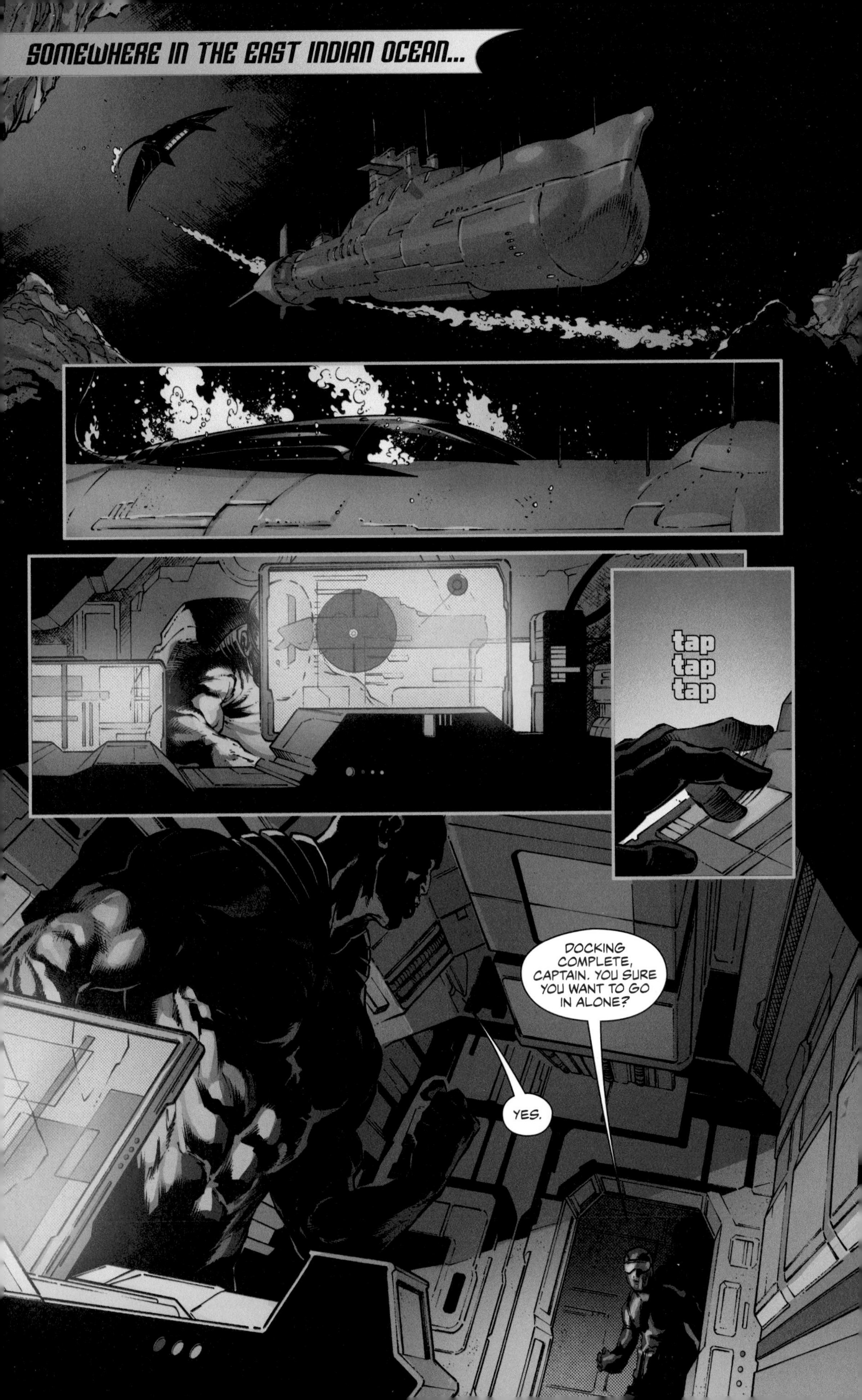
SOMEWHERE IN THE EAST INDIAN OCEAN...
tap
tap
tap
DOCKING COMPLETE, CAPTAIN. YOU SURE YOU WANT TO GO IN ALONE?
YES.

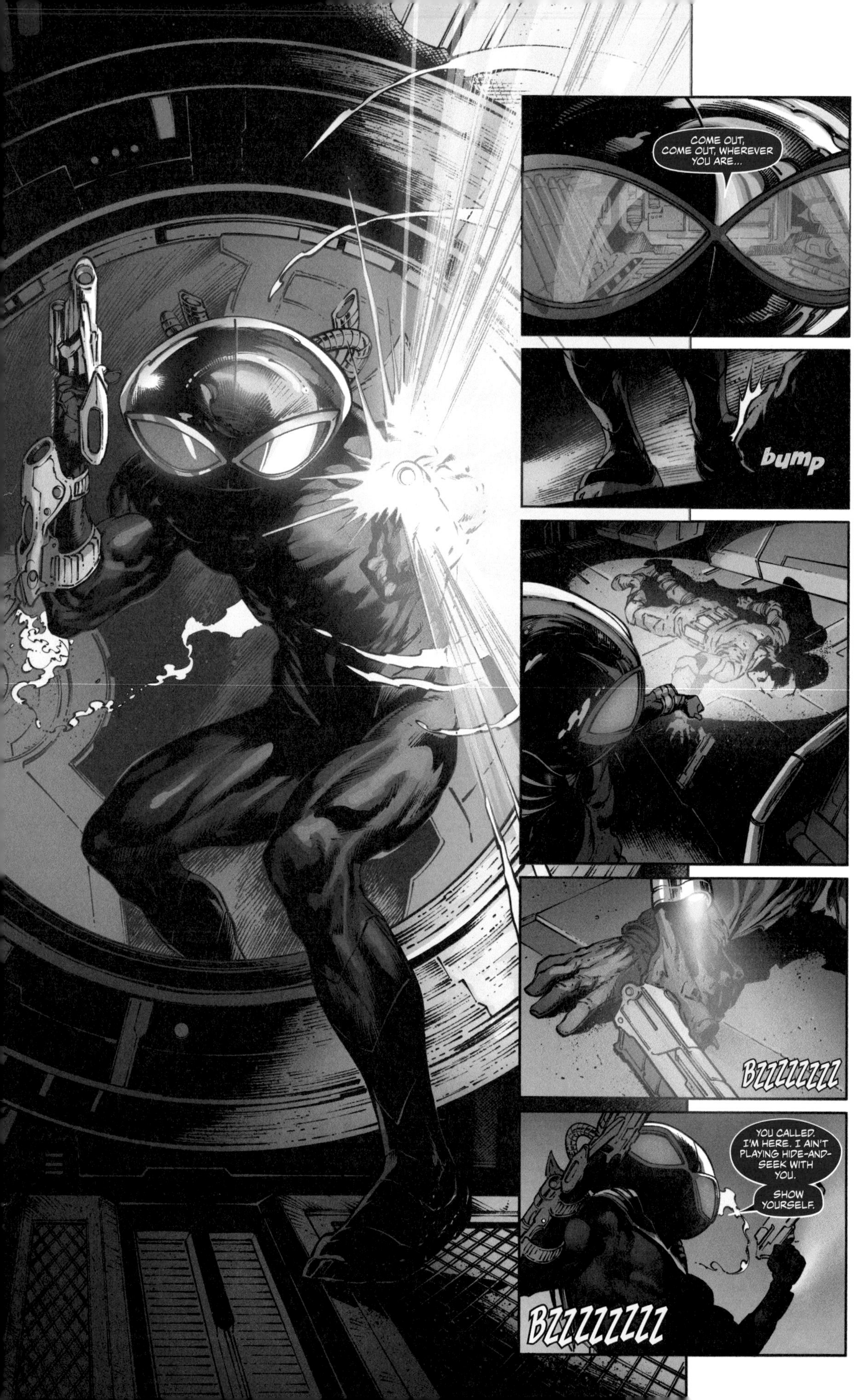
COME OUT, COME OUT, WHEREVER YOU ARE...
bump
BZZZZZZZZ
YOU CALLED. I'M HERE. I AIN'T PLAYING HIDE-AND-SEEK WITH YOU.
SHOW YOURSELF.
BZZZZZZZZ

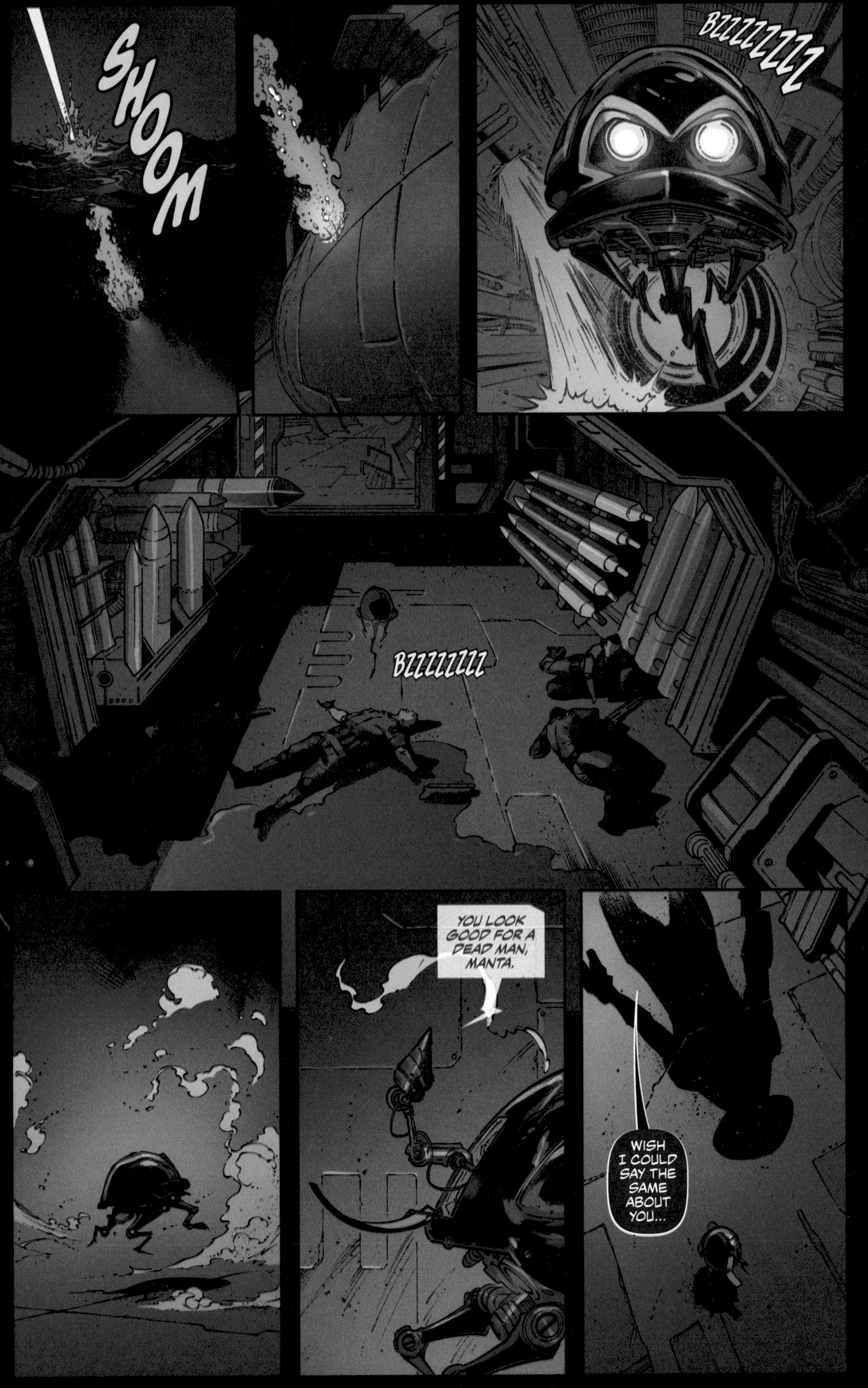
SHOOM
BZZZZZZZZ
BZZZZZZZZ
YOU LOOK GOOD FOR A DEAD MAN, MANTA.
WISH I COULD SAY THE SAME ABOUT YOU...

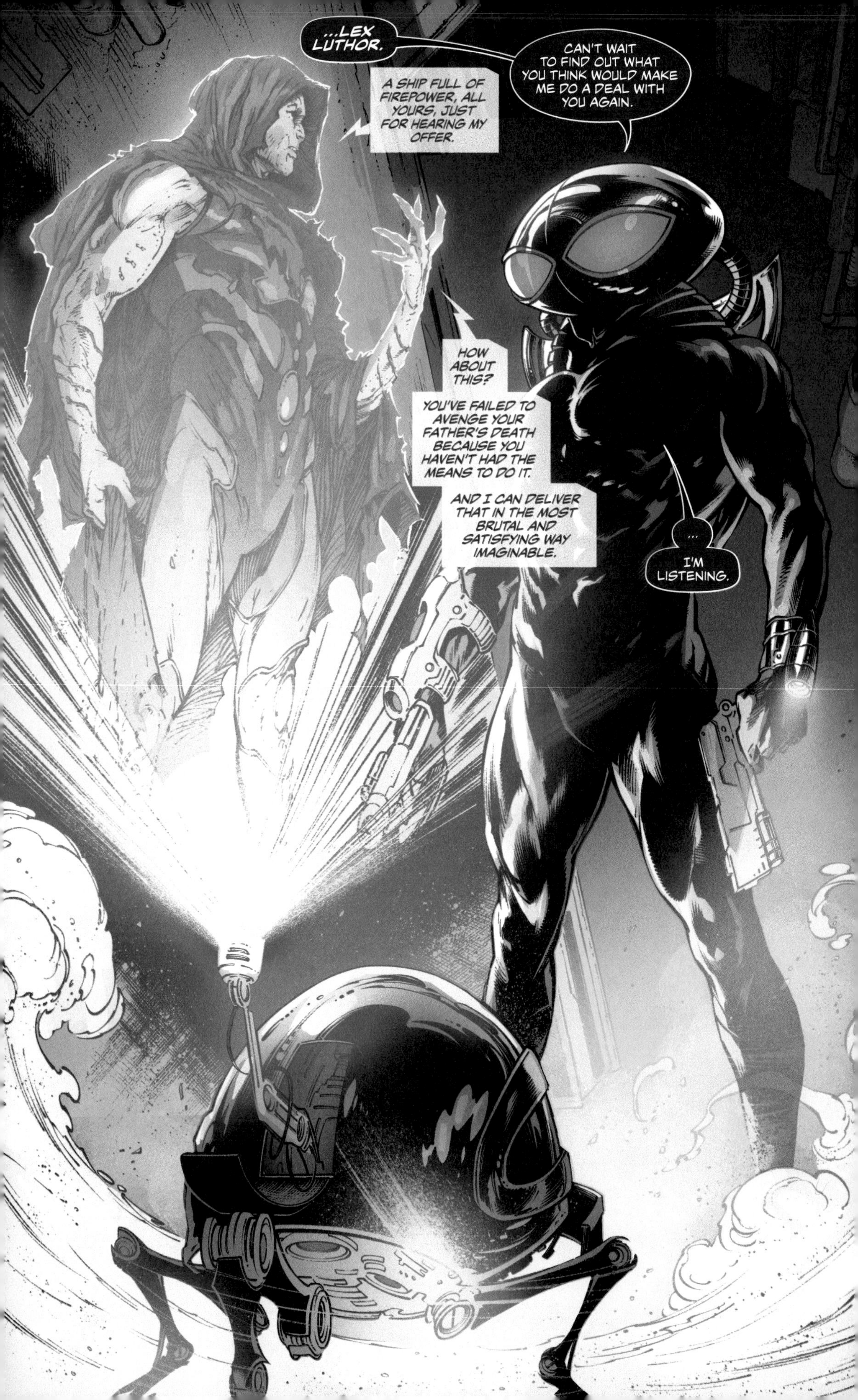
...LEX LUTHOR.
CAN'T WAIT TO FIND OUT WHAT YOU THINK WOULD MAKE ME DO A DEAL WITH YOU AGAIN.
A SHIP FULL OF FIREPOWER, ALL YOURS, JUST FOR HEARING MY OFFER.
HOW ABOUT THIS?
YOU'VE FAILED TO AVENGE YOUR FATHER'S DEATH BECAUSE YOU HAVEN'T HAD THE MEANS TO DO IT.
AND I CAN DELIVER THAT IN THE MOST BRUTAL AND SATISFYING WAY IMAGINABLE.
...
I'M LISTENING.

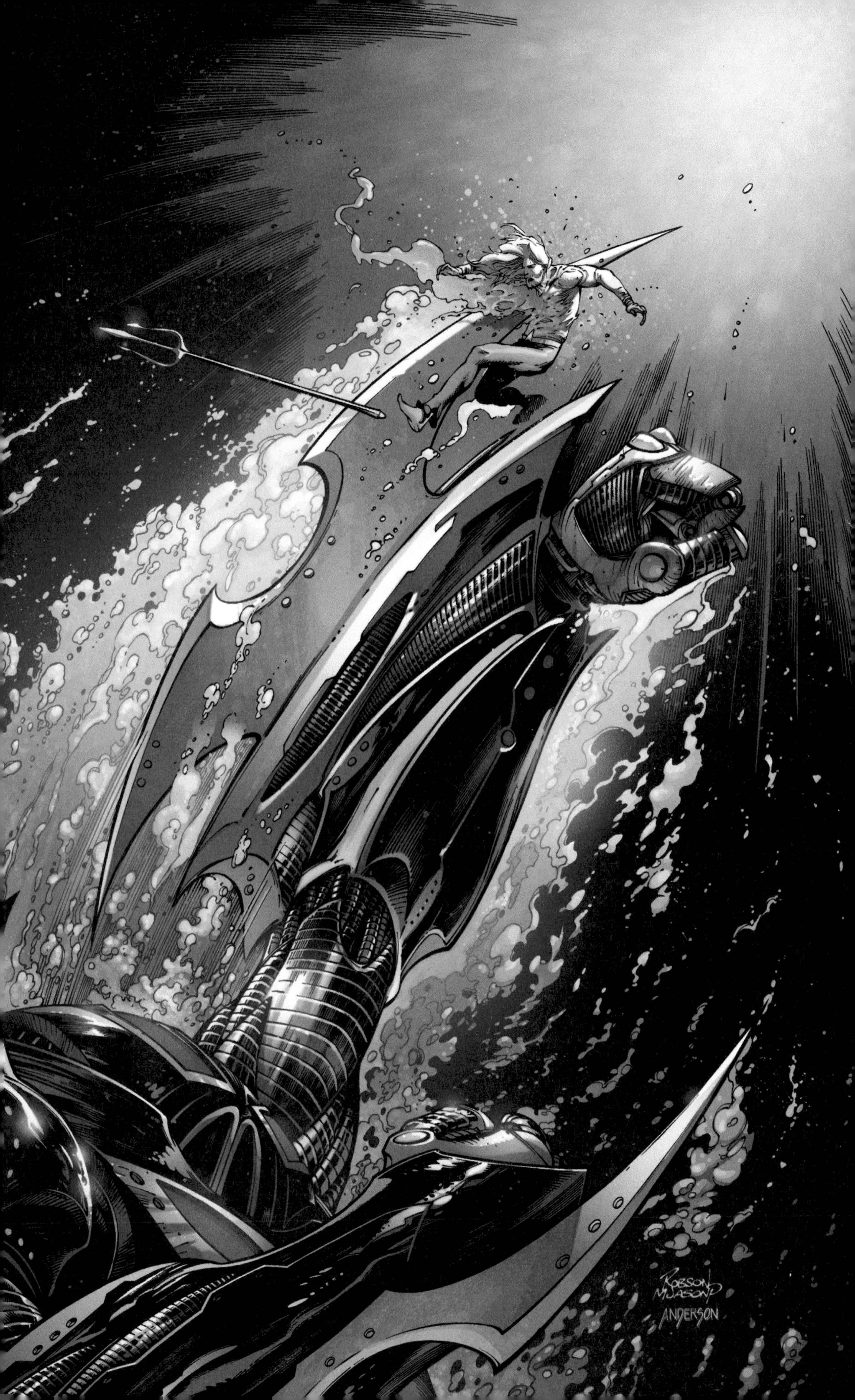
ROBSON
MJASON
ANDERSON

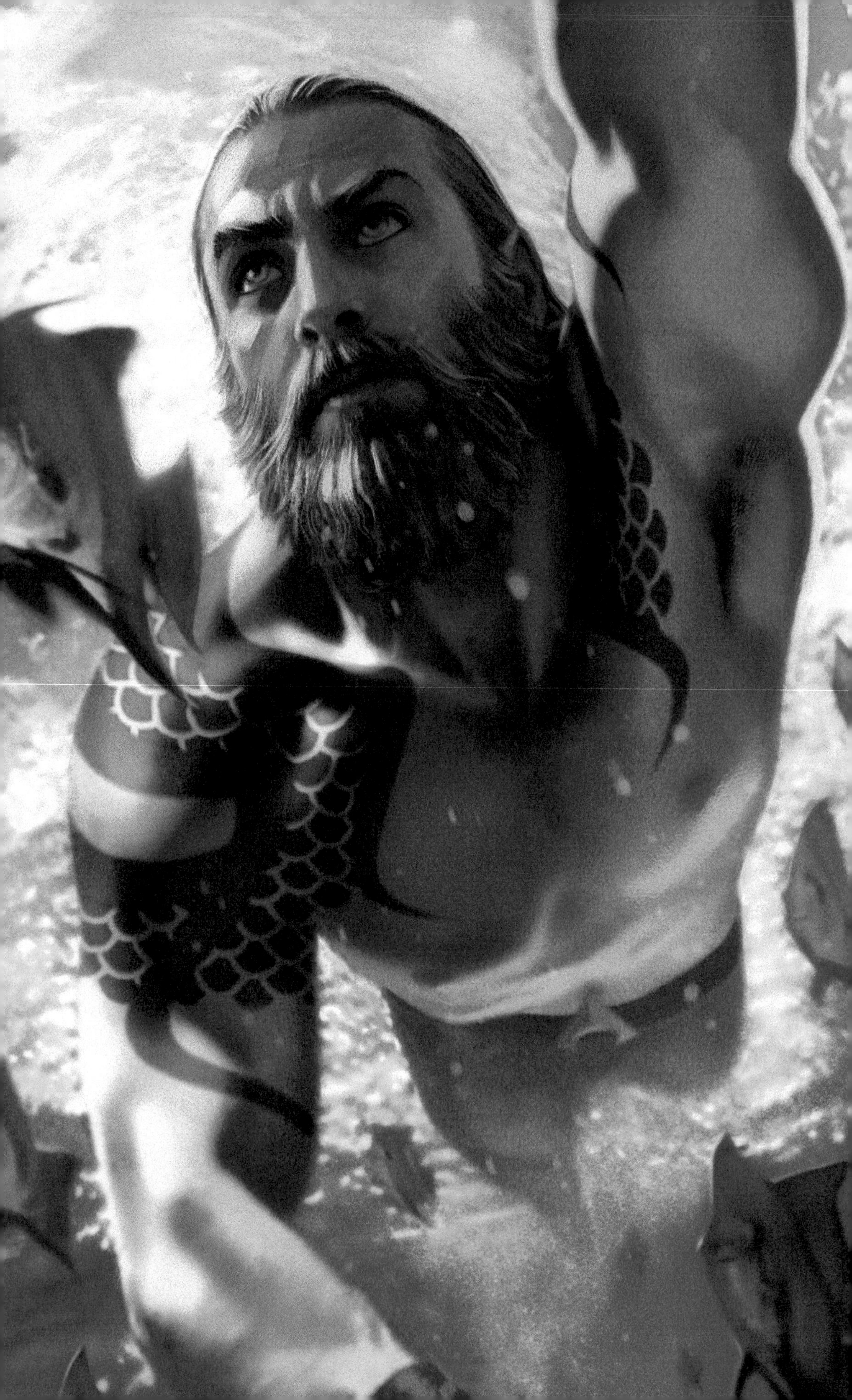

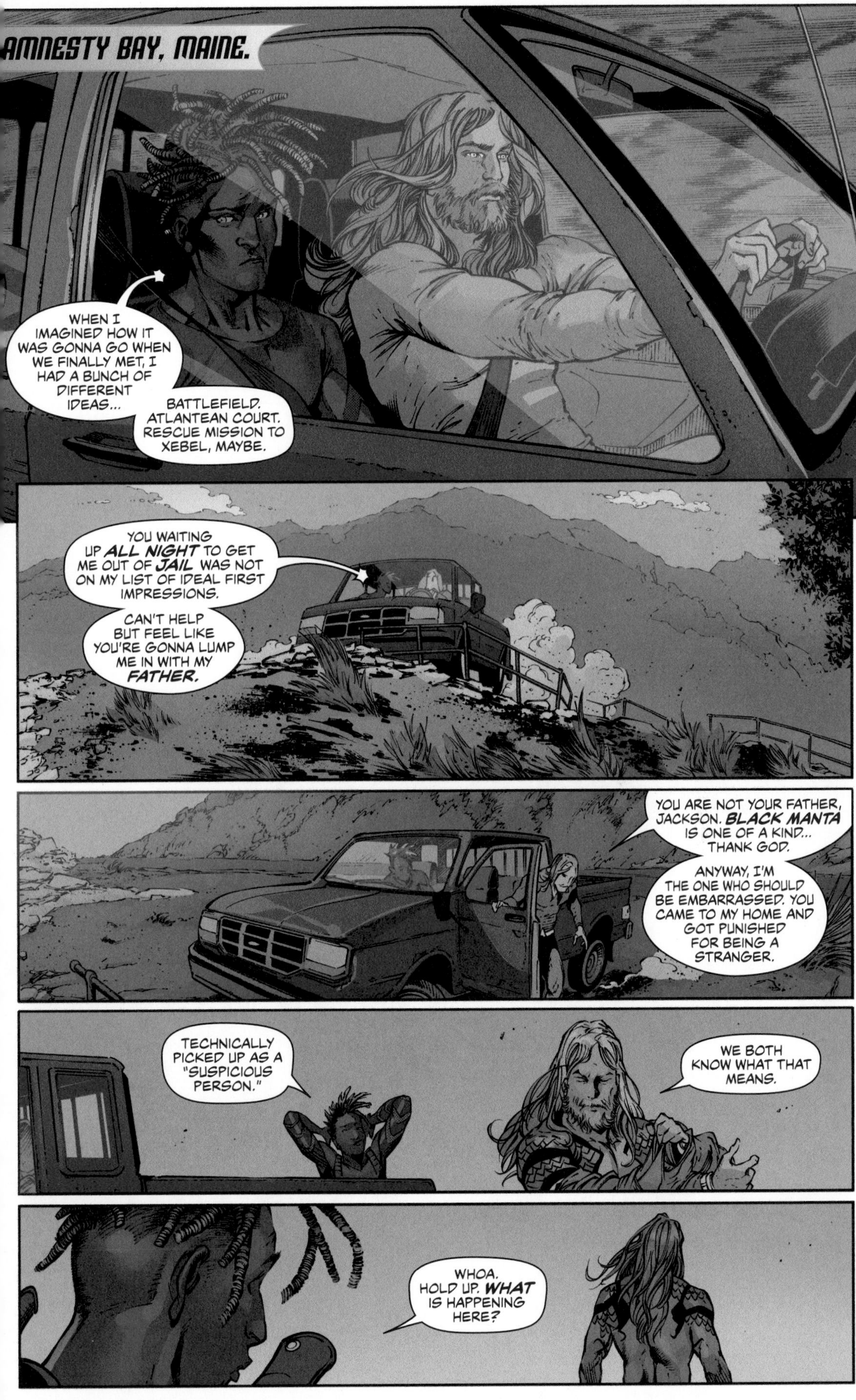
AMNESTY BAY, MAINE.
WHEN I IMAGINED HOW IT WAS GONNA GO WHEN WE FINALLY MET, I HAD A BUNCH OF DIFFERENT IDEAS...
BATTLEFIELD. ATLANTEAN COURT. RESCUE MISSION TO XEBEL, MAYBE.
YOU WAITING UP ALL NIGHT TO GET ME OUT OF JAIL WAS NOT ON MY LIST OF IDEAL FIRST IMPRESSIONS.
CAN'T HELP BUT FEEL LIKE YOU'RE GONNA LUMP ME IN WITH MY FATHER.
YOU ARE NOT YOUR FATHER, JACKSON. BLACK MANTA IS ONE OF A KIND... THANK GOD.
ANYWAY, I'M THE ONE WHO SHOULD BE EMBARRASSED. YOU CAME TO MY HOME AND GOT PUNISHED FOR BEING A STRANGER.
TECHNICALLY PICKED UP AS A "SUSPICIOUS PERSON."
WE BOTH KNOW WHAT THAT MEANS.
WHOA, HOLD UP. WHAT IS HAPPENING HERE?

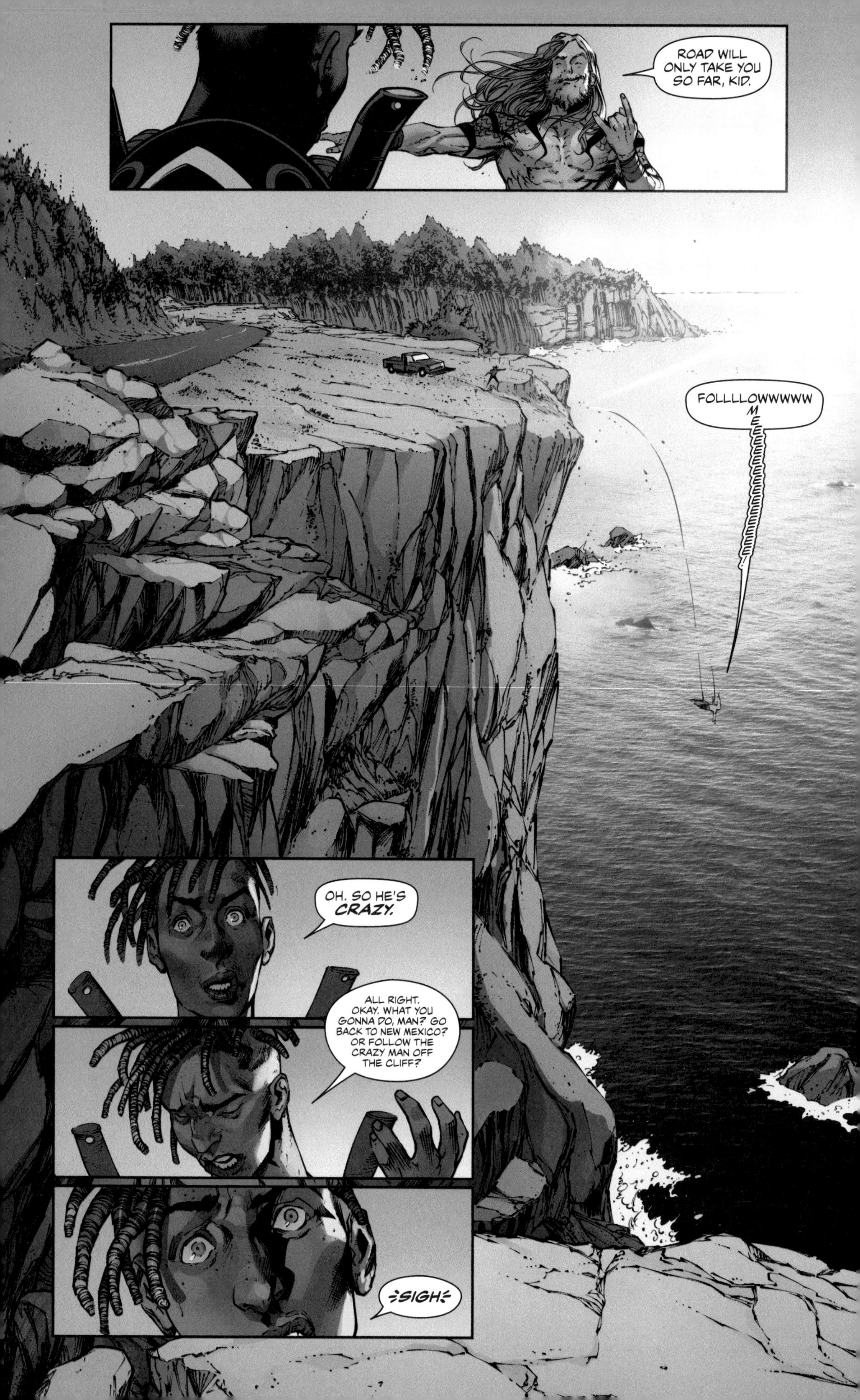
ROAD WILL ONLY TAKE YOU SO FAR, KID.
FOLLLLOWWWWW MEEEEEEEEEEEEEEEE!
OH. SO HE'S CRAZY.
ALL RIGHT. OKAY. WHAT YOU GONNA DO, MAN? GO BACK TO NEW MEXICO? OR FOLLOW THE CRAZY MAN OFF THE CLIFF?
SIGH

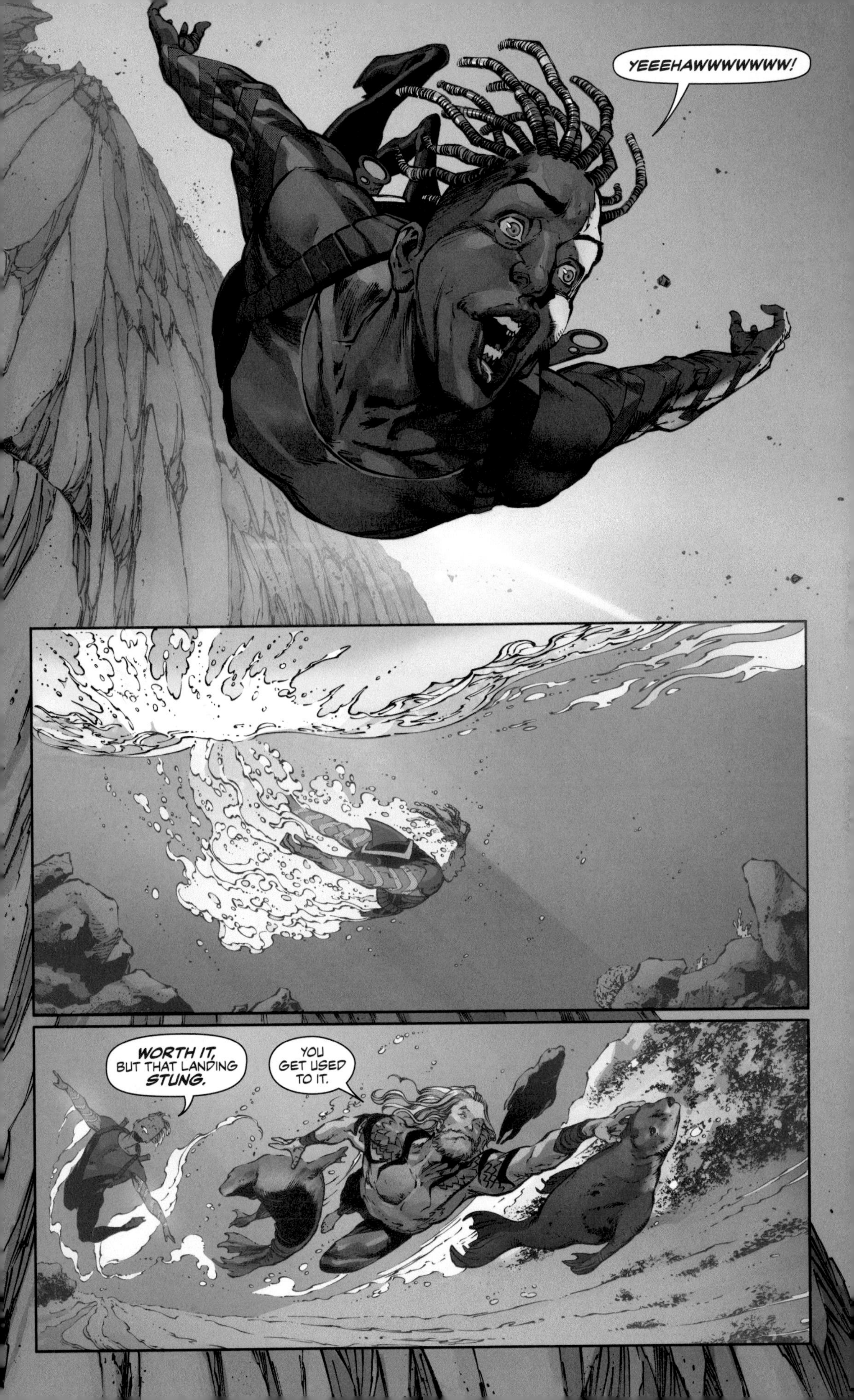
YEEEHAWWWWWWW!
WORTH IT, BUT THAT LANDING STUNG.
YOU GET USED TO IT.

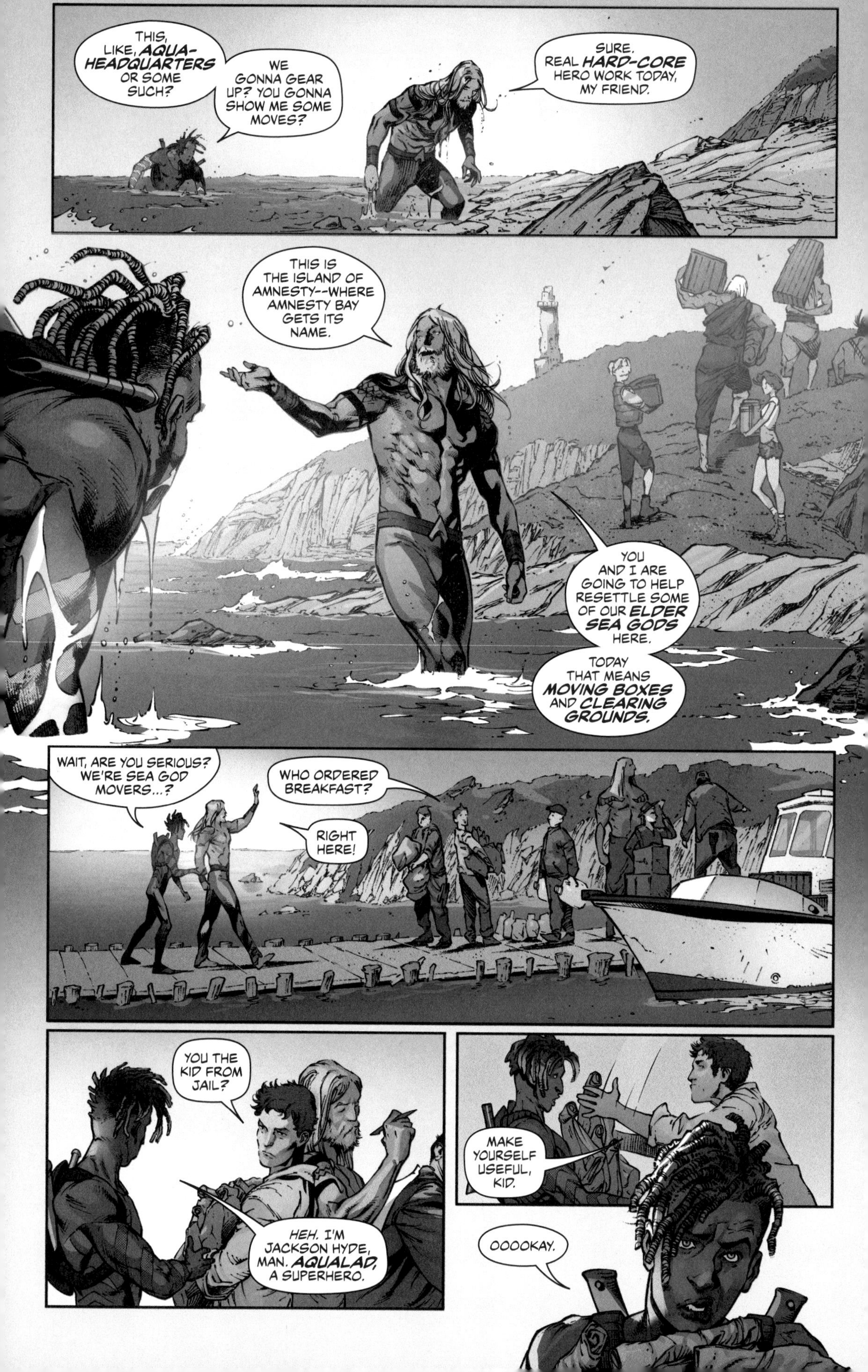

THIS, LIKE, AQUA-HEADQUARTERS OR SOME SUCH?
WE GONNA GEAR UP? YOU GONNA SHOW ME SOME MOVES?
SURE. REAL HARD-CORE HERO WORK TODAY, MY FRIEND.
THIS IS THE ISLAND OF AMNESTY--WHERE AMNESTY BAY GETS ITS NAME.
YOU AND I ARE GOING TO HELP RESETTLE SOME OF OUR ELDER SEA GODS HERE.
TODAY THAT MEANS MOVING BOXES AND CLEARING GROUNDS.
WAIT, ARE YOU SERIOUS? WE'RE SEA GOD MOVERS...?
WHO ORDERED BREAKFAST?
RIGHT HERE!
YOU THE KID FROM JAIL?
HEH. I'M JACKSON HYDE, MAN. AQUALAD, A SUPERHERO.
MAKE YOURSELF USEFUL, KID.
OOOOKAY.

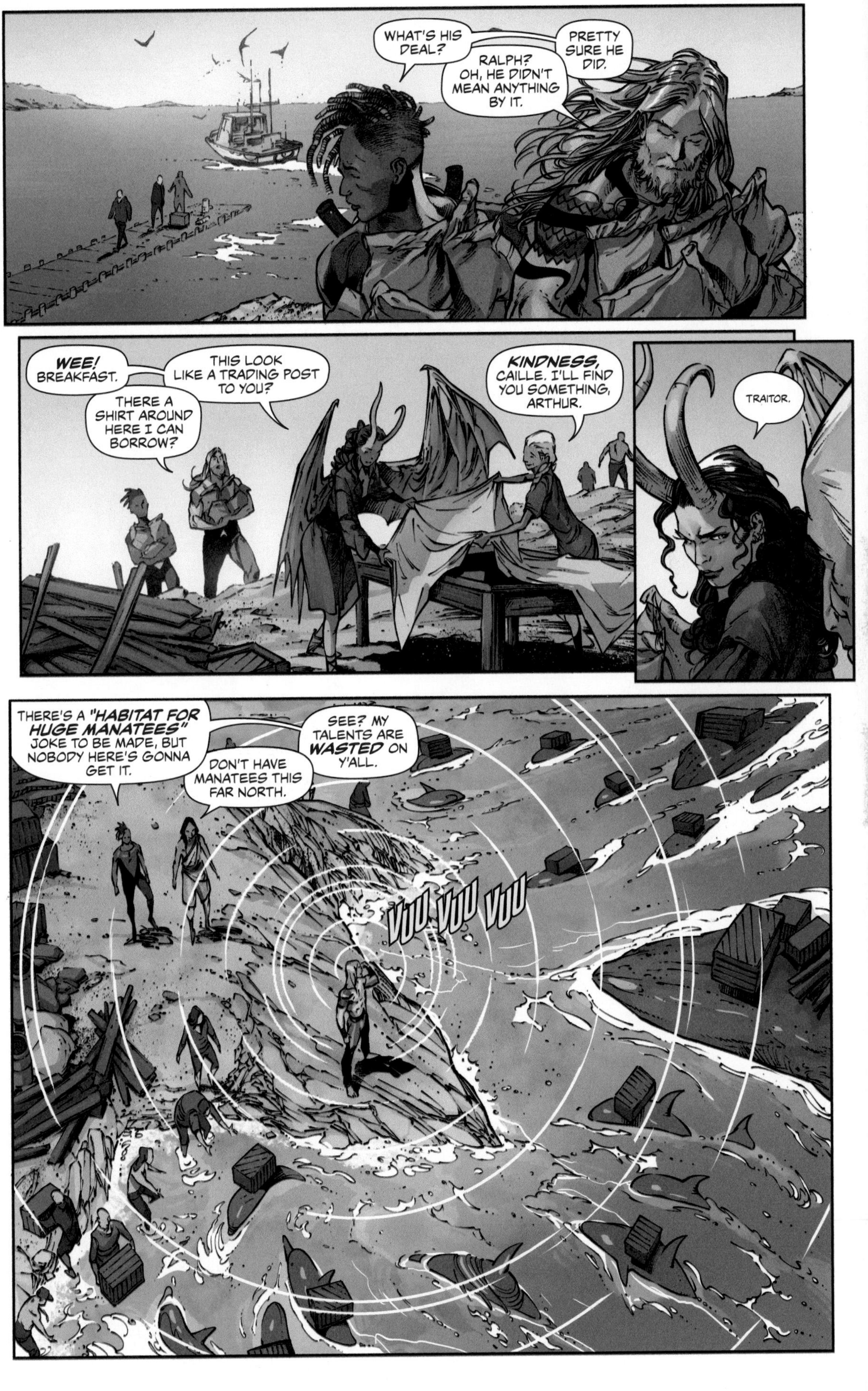
WHAT'S HIS DEAL?
RALPH? OH, HE DIDN'T MEAN ANYTHING BY IT.
PRETTY SURE HE DID.
WEE! BREAKFAST.
THERE A SHIRT AROUND HERE I CAN BORROW?
THIS LOOK LIKE A TRADING POST TO YOU?
KINDNESS, CAILLE. I'LL FIND YOU SOMETHING, ARTHUR.
TRAITOR.
THERE'S A **"HABITAT FOR HUGE MANATEES"** JOKE TO BE MADE, BUT NOBODY HERE'S GONNA GET IT.
DON'T HAVE MANATEES THIS FAR NORTH.
SEE? MY TALENTS ARE **WASTED** ON Y'ALL.
VUU VUU VUU

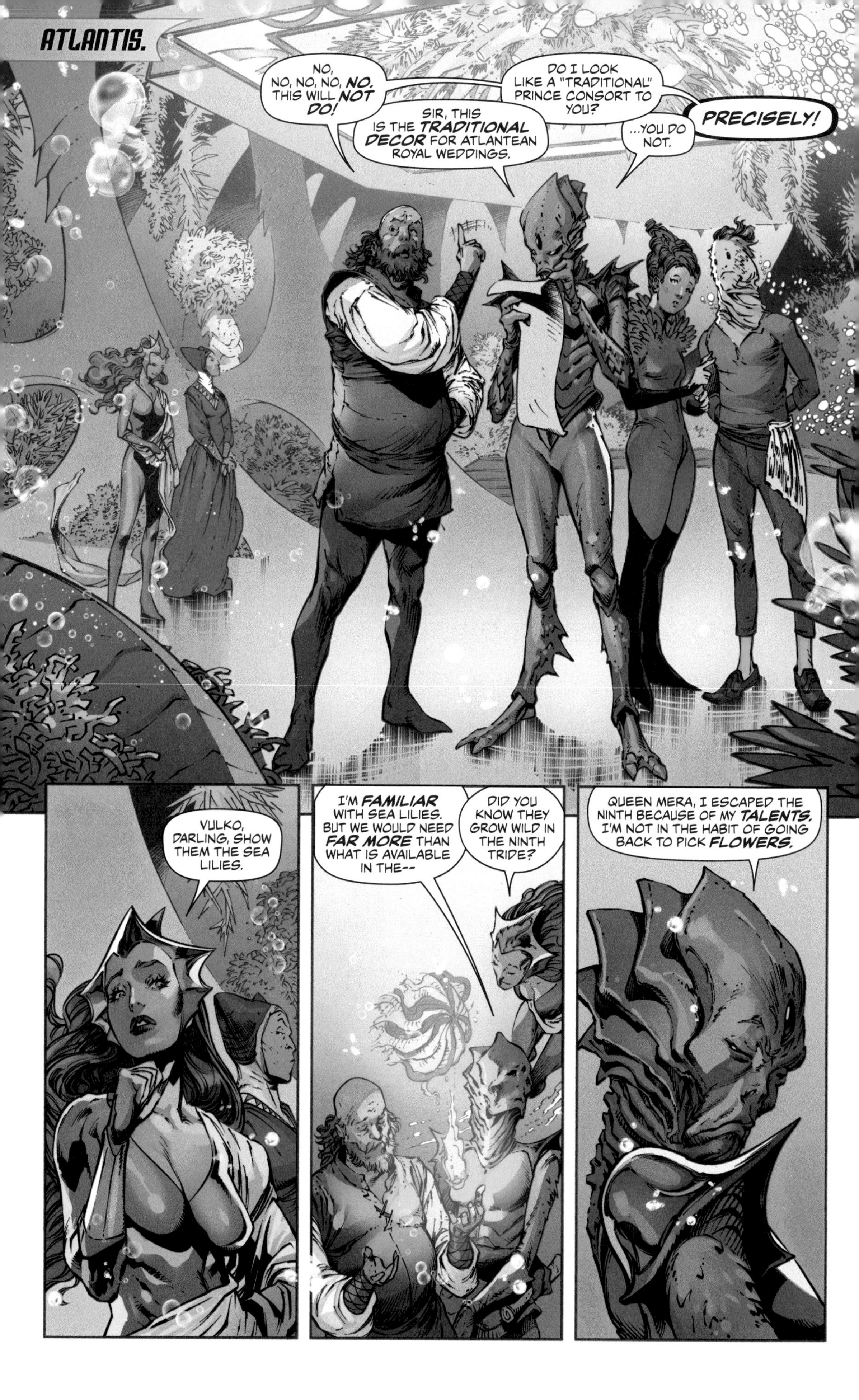
ATLANTIS.
NO, NO, NO, NO, NO. THIS WILL NOT DO!
SIR, THIS IS THE TRADITIONAL DECOR FOR ATLANTEAN ROYAL WEDDINGS.
DO I LOOK LIKE A "TRADITIONAL" PRINCE CONSORT TO YOU?
...YOU DO NOT.
PRECISELY!
VULKO, DARLING, SHOW THEM THE SEA LILIES.
I'M FAMILIAR WITH SEA LILIES. BUT WE WOULD NEED FAR MORE THAN WHAT IS AVAILABLE IN THE--
DID YOU KNOW THEY GROW WILD IN THE NINTH TRIDE?
QUEEN MERA, I ESCAPED THE NINTH BECAUSE OF MY TALENTS. I'M NOT IN THE HABIT OF GOING BACK TO PICK FLOWERS.

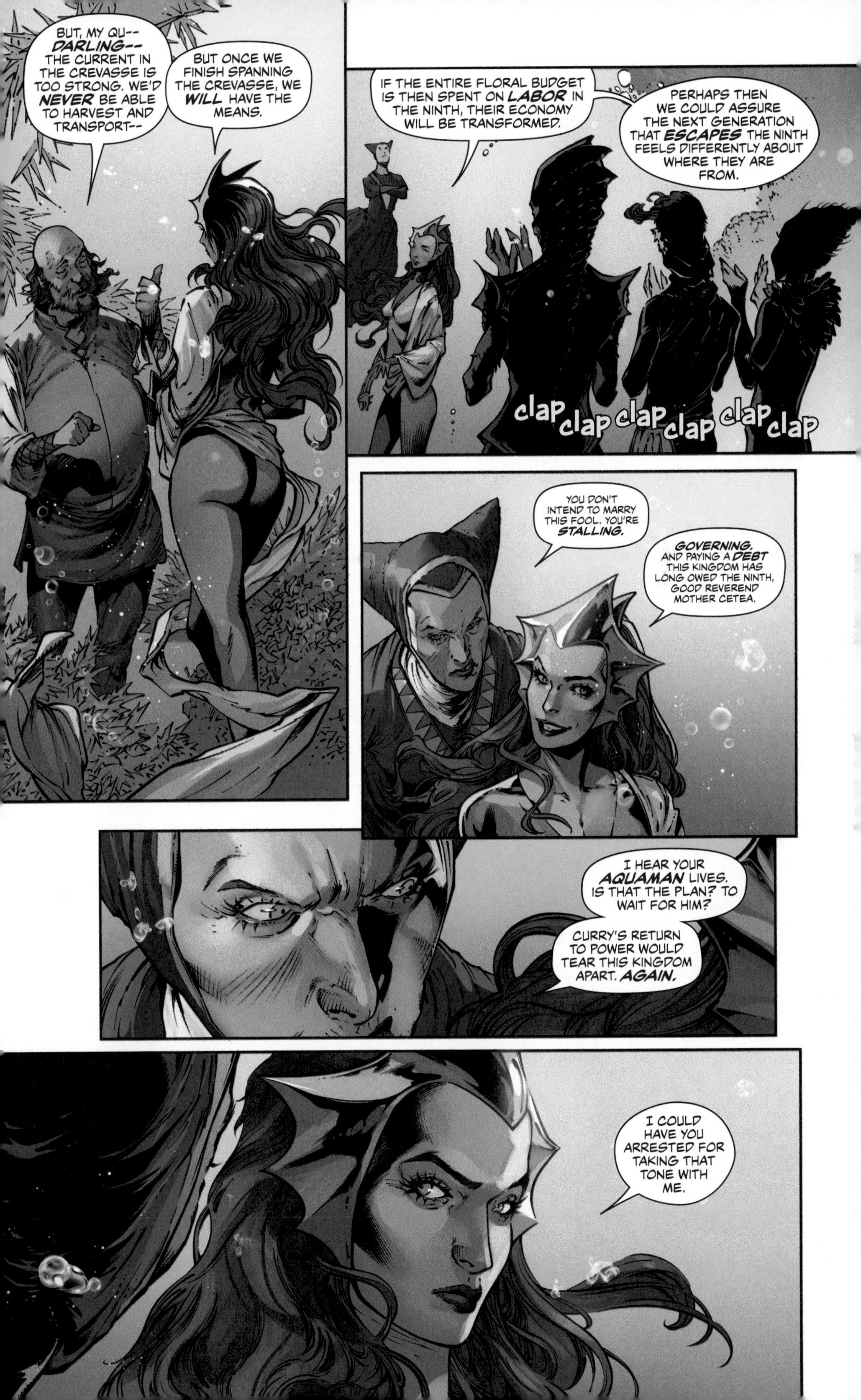
BUT, MY QU-- DARLING-- THE CURRENT IN THE CREVASSE IS TOO STRONG. WE'D NEVER BE ABLE TO HARVEST AND TRANSPORT--
BUT ONCE WE FINISH SPANNING THE CREVASSE, WE WILL HAVE THE MEANS.
IF THE ENTIRE FLORAL BUDGET IS THEN SPENT ON LABOR IN THE NINTH, THEIR ECONOMY WILL BE TRANSFORMED.
PERHAPS THEN WE COULD ASSURE THE NEXT GENERATION THAT ESCAPES THE NINTH FEELS DIFFERENTLY ABOUT WHERE THEY ARE FROM.
clap clap clap clap clap clap
YOU DON'T INTEND TO MARRY THIS FOOL. YOU'RE STALLING.
GOVERNING. AND PAYING A DEBT THIS KINGDOM HAS LONG OWED THE NINTH, GOOD REVEREND MOTHER CETEA.
I HEAR YOUR AQUAMAN LIVES. IS THAT THE PLAN? TO WAIT FOR HIM?
CURRY'S RETURN TO POWER WOULD TEAR THIS KINGDOM APART. AGAIN.
I COULD HAVE YOU ARRESTED FOR TAKING THAT TONE WITH ME.

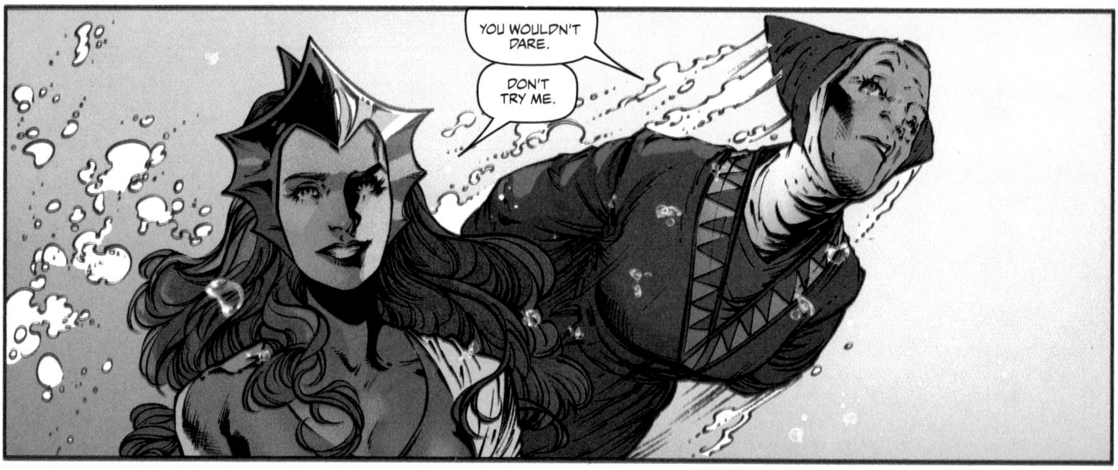
YOU WOULDN'T DARE.
DON'T TRY ME.

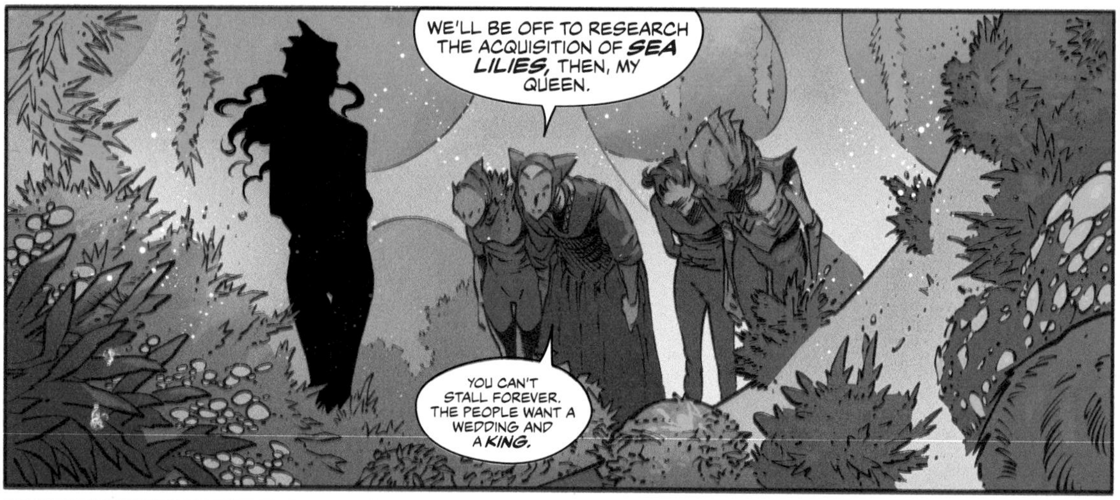
WE'LL BE OFF TO RESEARCH THE ACQUISITION OF SEA LILIES, THEN, MY QUEEN.
YOU CAN'T STALL FOREVER. THE PEOPLE WANT A WEDDING AND A KING.

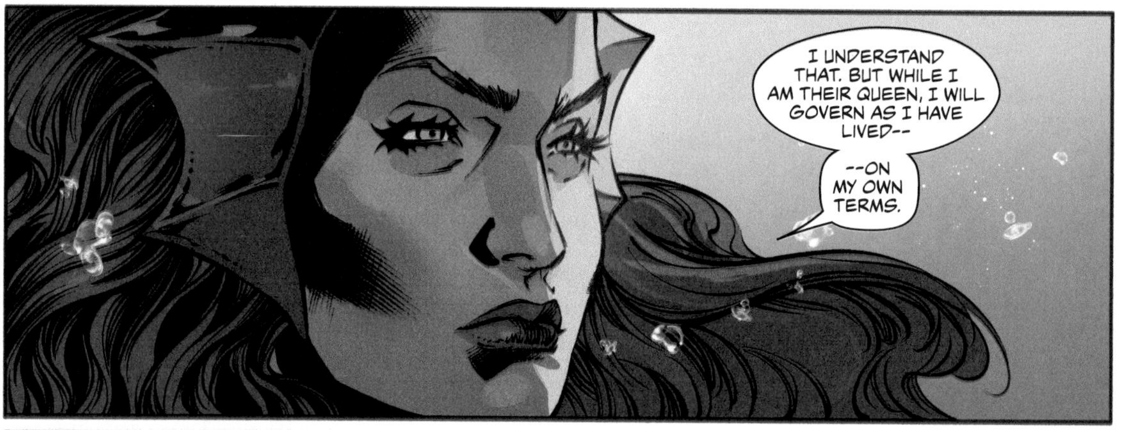
I UNDERSTAND THAT. BUT WHILE I AM THEIR QUEEN, I WILL GOVERN AS I HAVE LIVED--
--ON MY OWN TERMS.

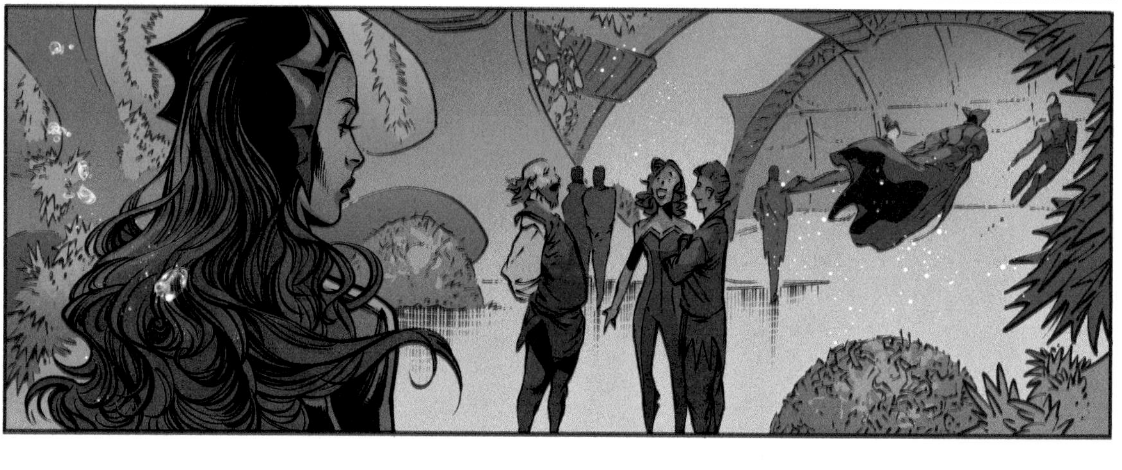

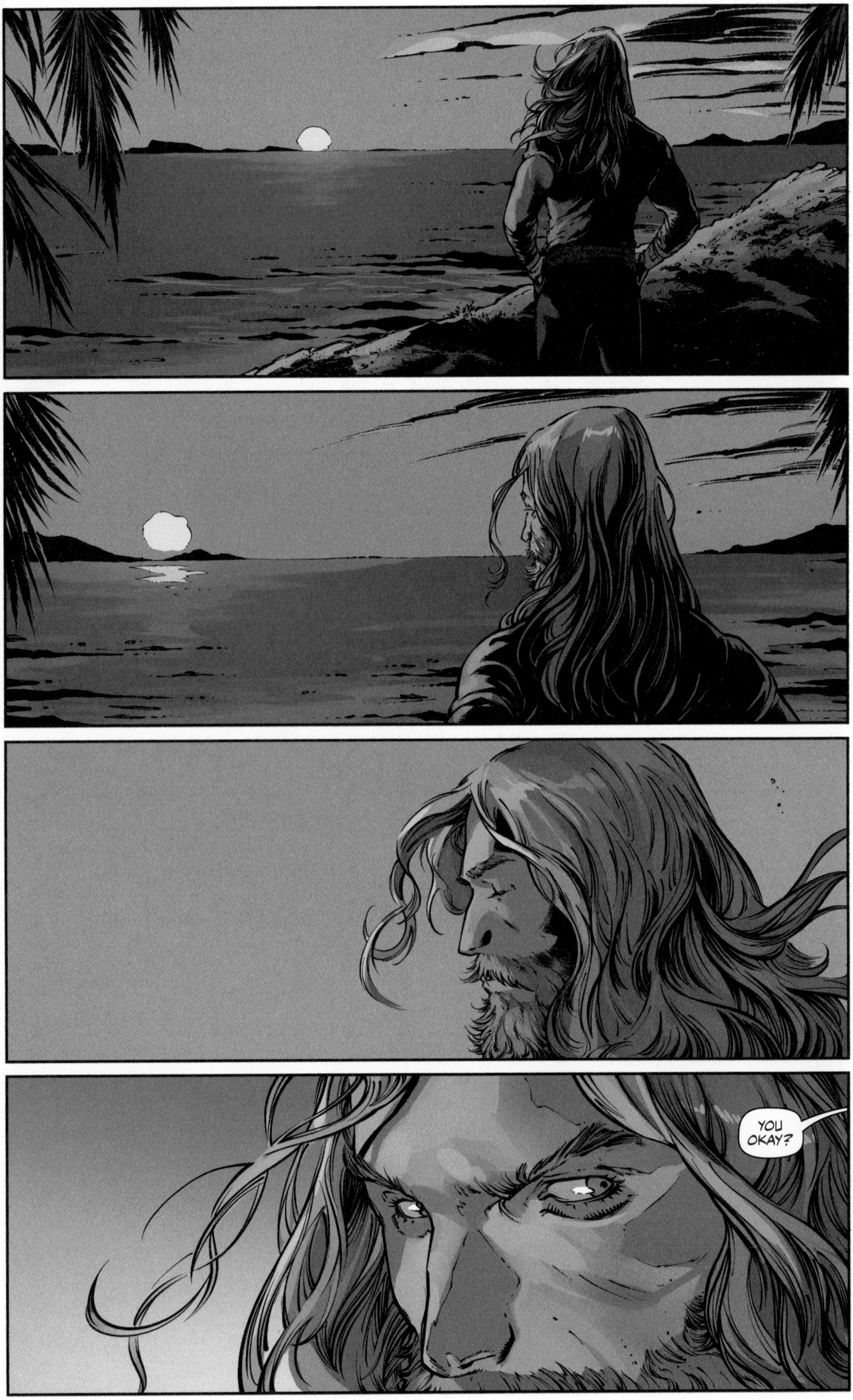
YOU OKAY?

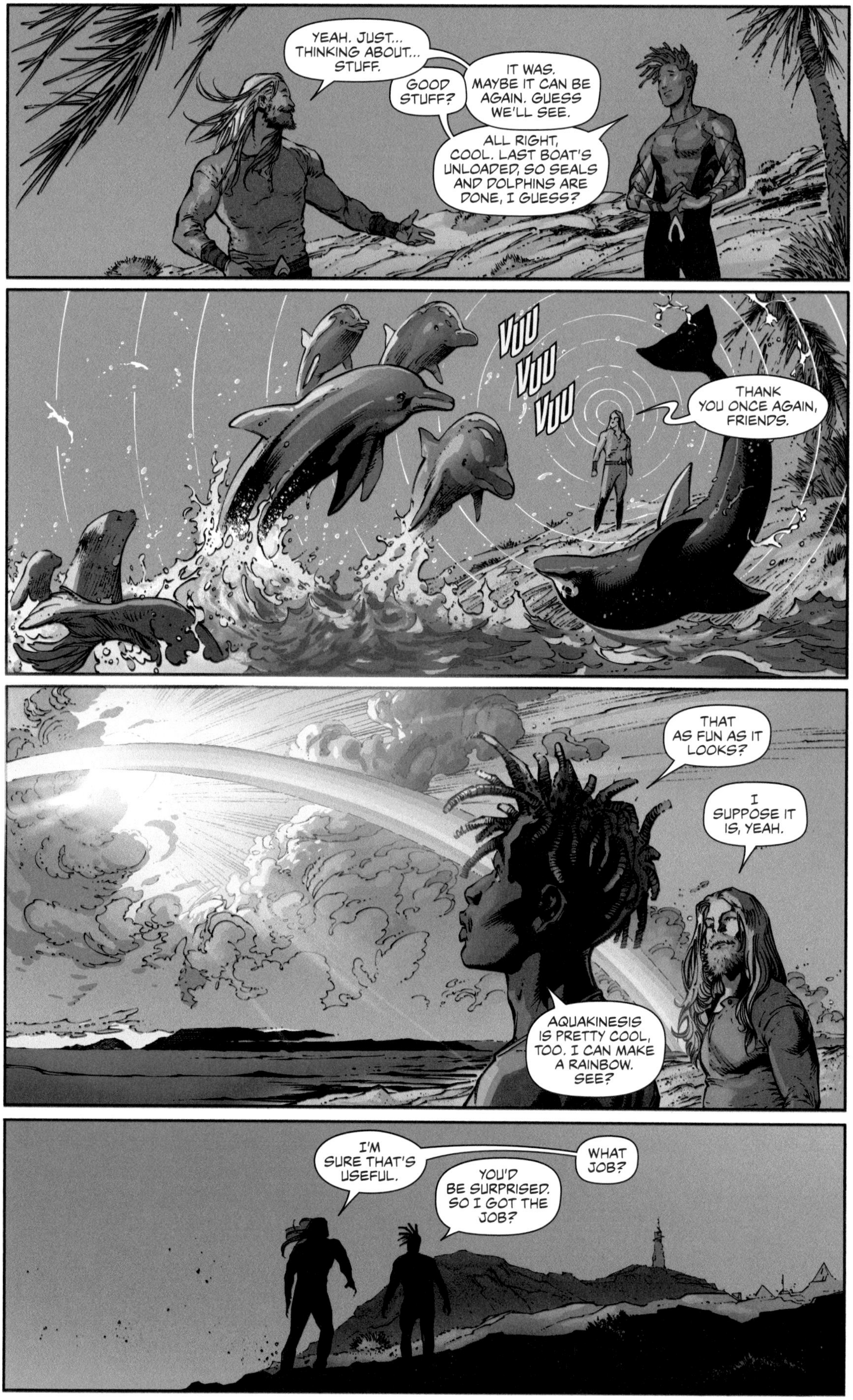
YEAH. JUST... THINKING ABOUT... STUFF.
GOOD STUFF?
IT WAS. MAYBE IT CAN BE AGAIN. GUESS WE'LL SEE.
ALL RIGHT, COOL. LAST BOAT'S UNLOADED, SO SEALS AND DOLPHINS ARE DONE, I GUESS?
VUU VUU VUU
THANK YOU ONCE AGAIN, FRIENDS.
THAT AS FUN AS IT LOOKS?
I SUPPOSE IT IS, YEAH.
AQUAKINESIS IS PRETTY COOL, TOO. I CAN MAKE A RAINBOW. SEE?
I'M SURE THAT'S USEFUL.
YOU'D BE SURPRISED. SO I GOT THE JOB?
WHAT JOB?

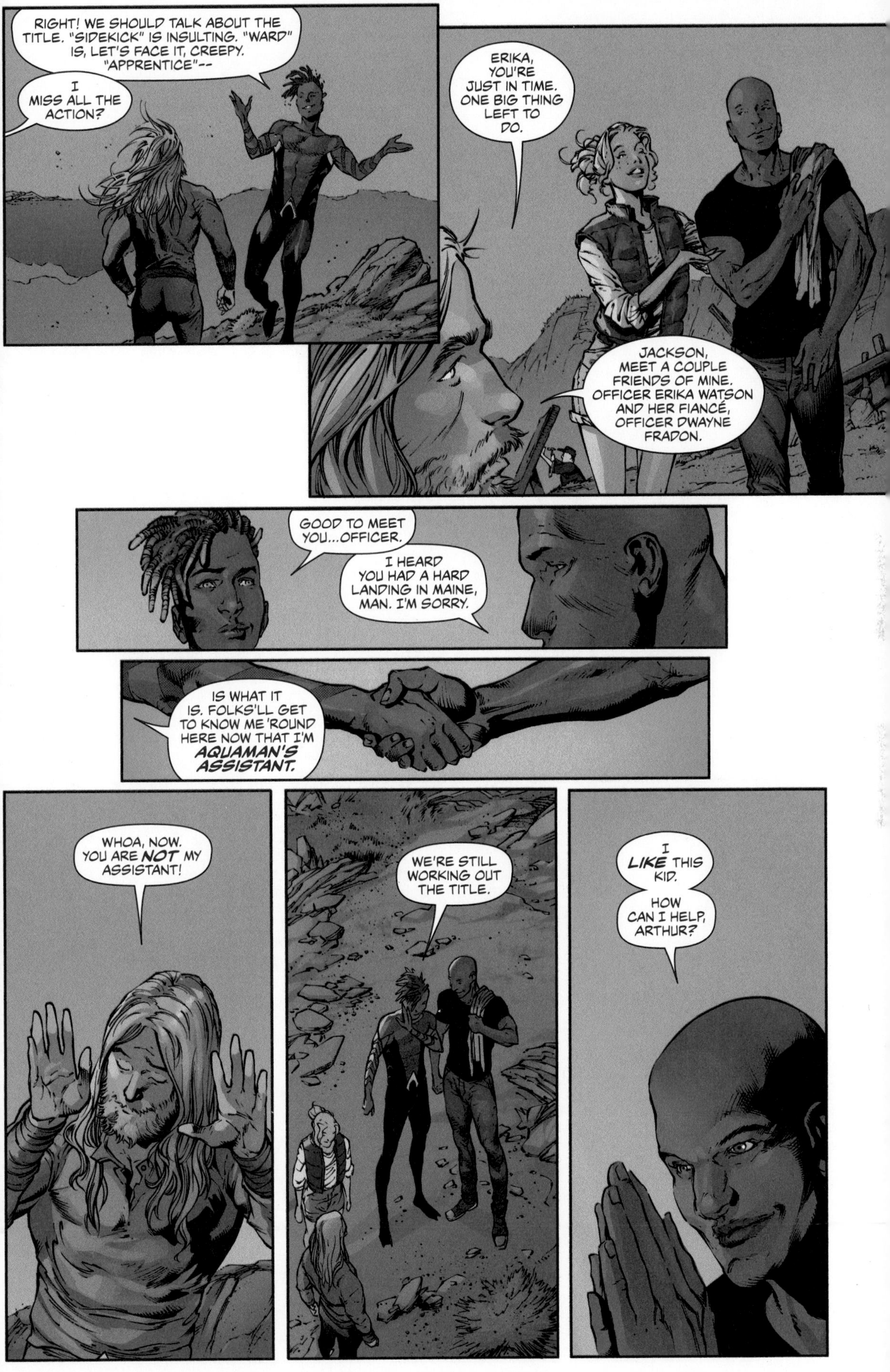
RIGHT! WE SHOULD TALK ABOUT THE TITLE. "SIDEKICK" IS INSULTING. "WARD" IS, LET'S FACE IT, CREEPY. "APPRENTICE"--
I MISS ALL THE ACTION?
ERIKA, YOU'RE JUST IN TIME. ONE BIG THING LEFT TO DO.
JACKSON, MEET A COUPLE FRIENDS OF MINE. OFFICER ERIKA WATSON AND HER FIANCÉ, OFFICER DWAYNE FRADON.
GOOD TO MEET YOU...OFFICER.
I HEARD YOU HAD A HARD LANDING IN MAINE, MAN. I'M SORRY.
IS WHAT IT IS. FOLKS'LL GET TO KNOW ME 'ROUND HERE NOW THAT I'M ***AQUAMAN'S ASSISTANT.***
WHOA, NOW. YOU ARE ***NOT*** MY ASSISTANT!
WE'RE STILL WORKING OUT THE TITLE.
I ***LIKE*** THIS KID.
HOW CAN I HELP, ARTHUR?

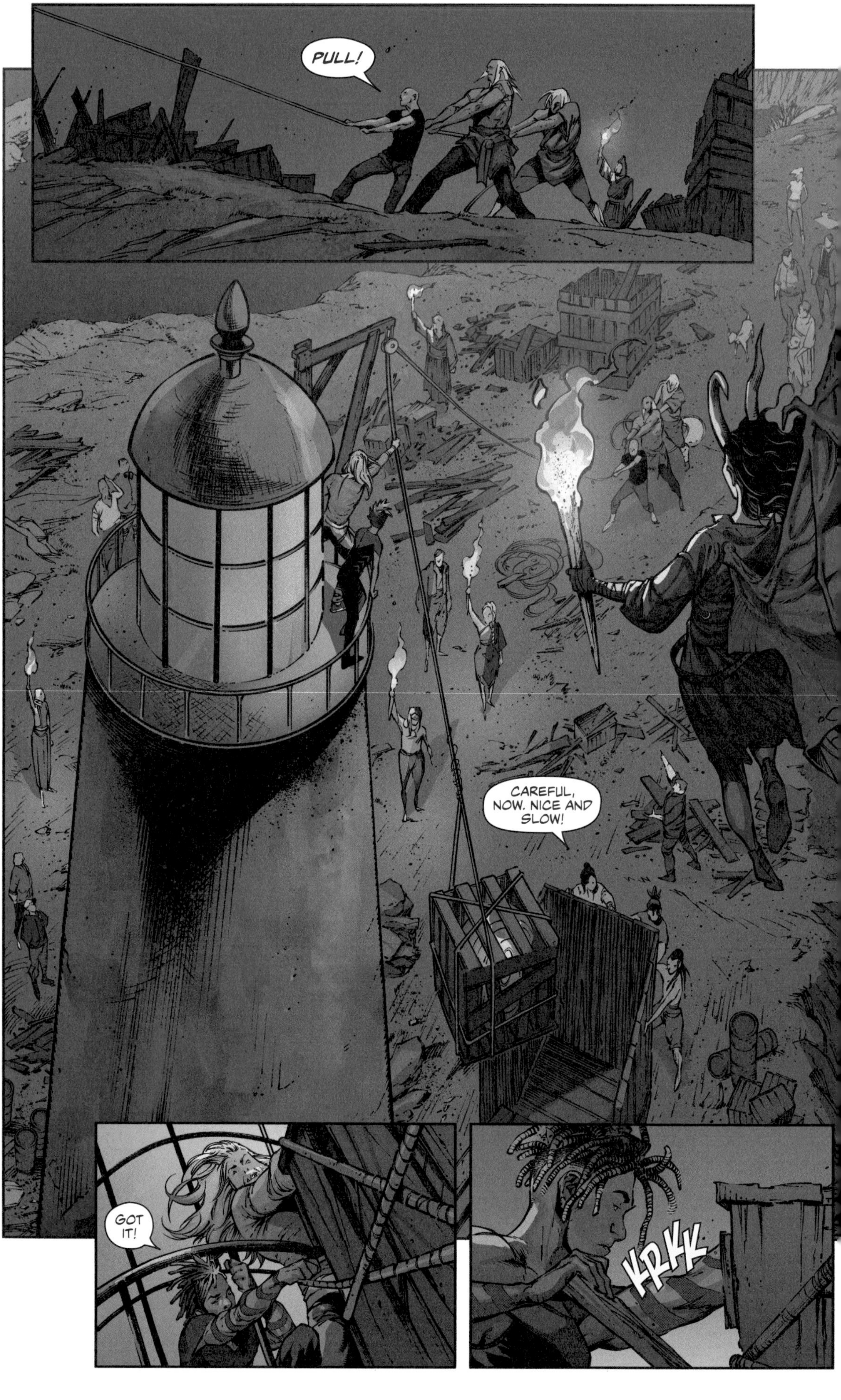
PULL!
CAREFUL, NOW. NICE AND SLOW!
GOT IT!
KRKK

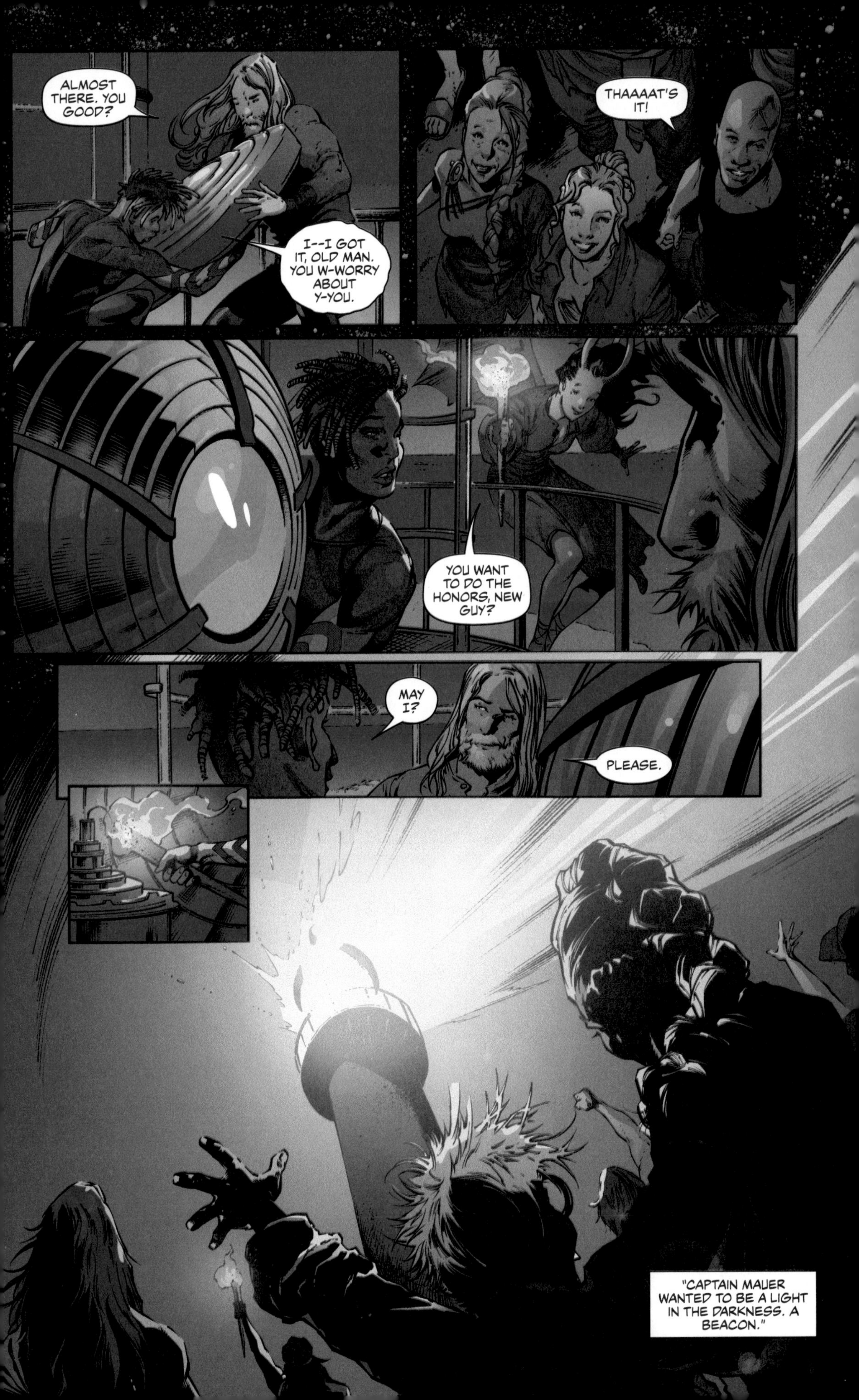
ALMOST THERE. YOU GOOD?
I--I GOT IT, OLD MAN. YOU W-WORRY ABOUT Y-YOU.
THAAAAT'S IT!
YOU WANT TO DO THE HONORS, NEW GUY?
MAY I?
PLEASE.
"CAPTAIN MAUER WANTED TO BE A LIGHT IN THE DARKNESS. A BEACON."

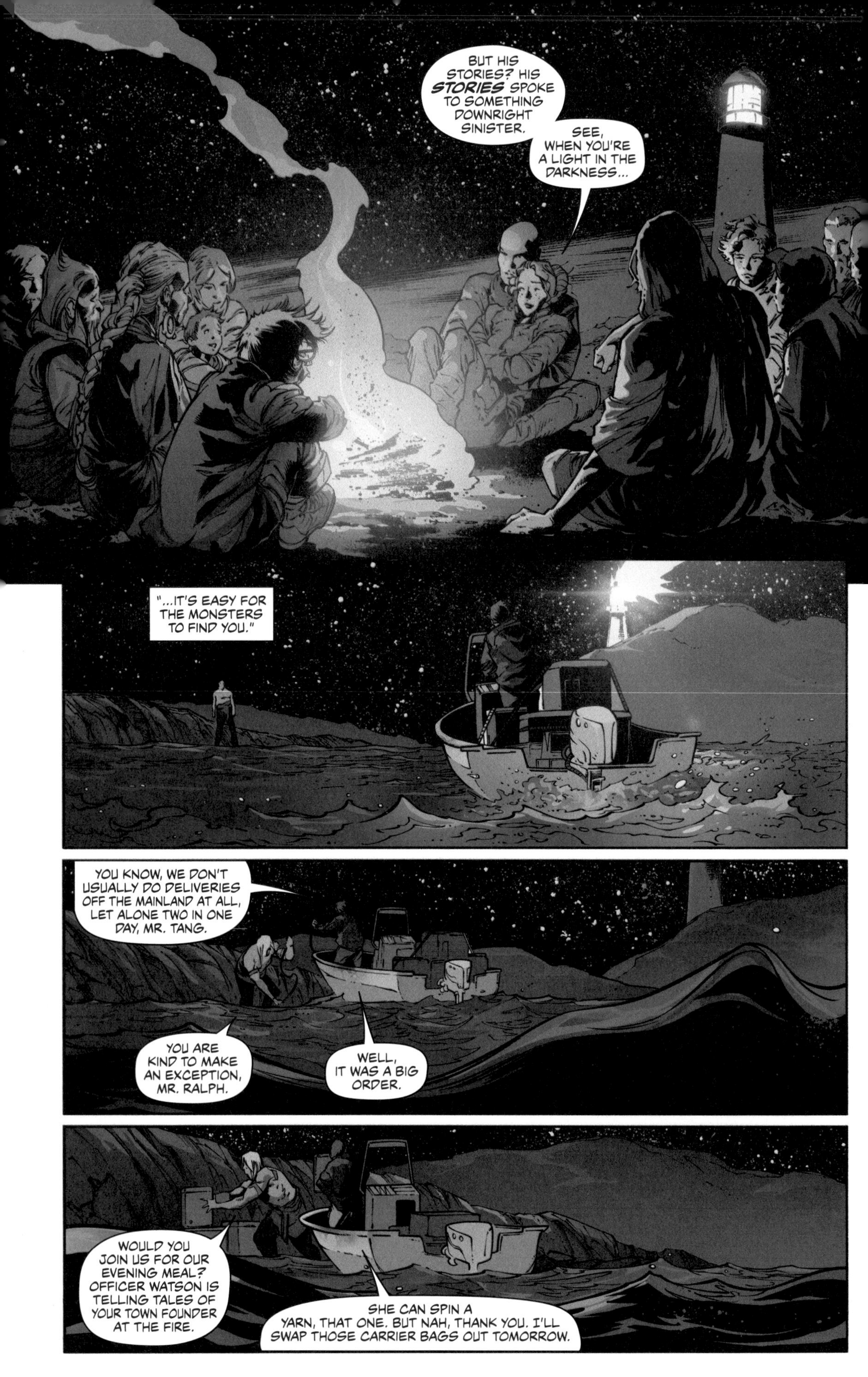
BUT HIS STORIES? HIS STORIES SPOKE TO SOMETHING DOWNRIGHT SINISTER.
SEE, WHEN YOU'RE A LIGHT IN THE DARKNESS...
"...IT'S EASY FOR THE MONSTERS TO FIND YOU."
YOU KNOW, WE DON'T USUALLY DO DELIVERIES OFF THE MAINLAND AT ALL, LET ALONE TWO IN ONE DAY, MR. TANG.
YOU ARE KIND TO MAKE AN EXCEPTION, MR. RALPH.
WELL, IT WAS A BIG ORDER.
WOULD YOU JOIN US FOR OUR EVENING MEAL? OFFICER WATSON IS TELLING TALES OF YOUR TOWN FOUNDER AT THE FIRE.
SHE CAN SPIN A YARN, THAT ONE. BUT NAH, THANK YOU. I'LL SWAP THOSE CARRIER BAGS OUT TOMORROW.

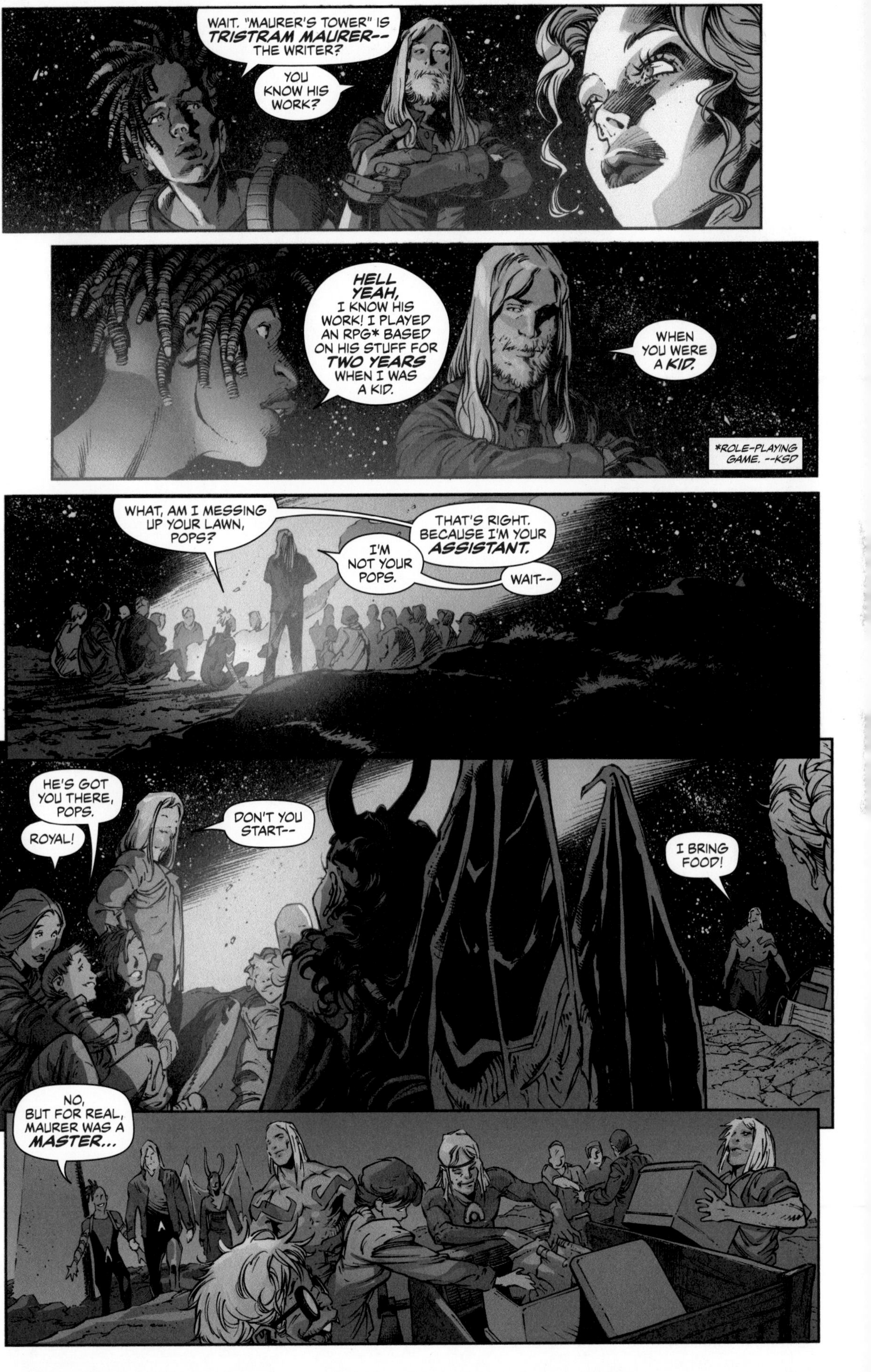

WAIT. "MAURER'S TOWER" IS TRISTRAM MAURER-- THE WRITER?
YOU KNOW HIS WORK?
HELL YEAH, I KNOW HIS WORK! I PLAYED AN RPG* BASED ON HIS STUFF FOR TWO YEARS WHEN I WAS A KID.
WHEN YOU WERE A KID.
*ROLE-PLAYING GAME. --KSD
WHAT, AM I MESSING UP YOUR LAWN, POPS?
I'M NOT YOUR POPS.
THAT'S RIGHT. BECAUSE I'M YOUR ASSISTANT.
WAIT--
HE'S GOT YOU THERE, POPS.
ROYAL!
DON'T YOU START--
I BRING FOOD!
NO, BUT FOR REAL, MAURER WAS A MASTER...

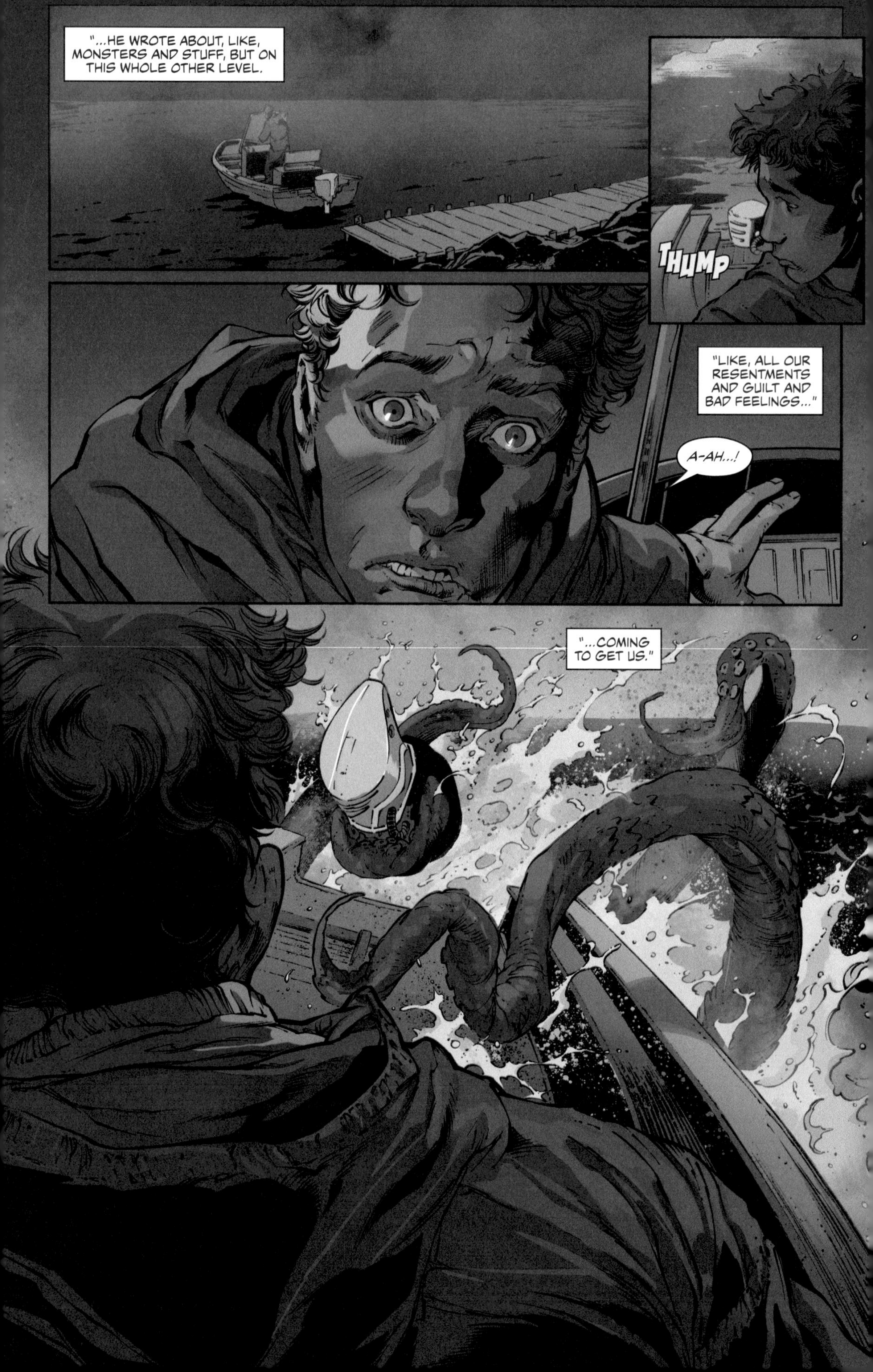
"...HE WROTE ABOUT, LIKE, MONSTERS AND STUFF, BUT ON THIS WHOLE OTHER LEVEL.
THUMP
"LIKE, ALL OUR RESENTMENTS AND GUILT AND BAD FEELINGS..."
A-AH...!
"...COMING TO GET US."

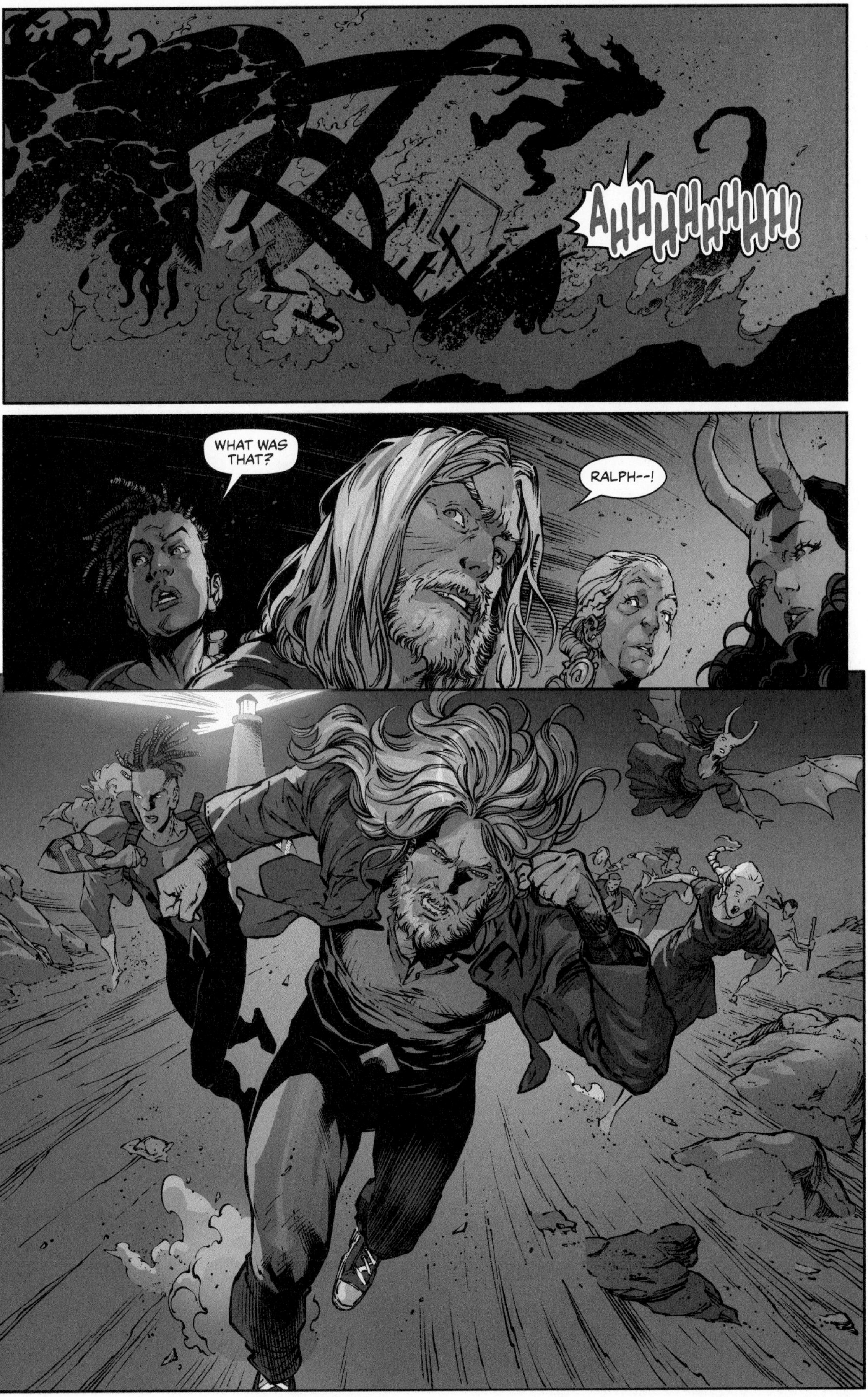
AHHHHHHHHH!
WHAT WAS THAT?
RALPH--!

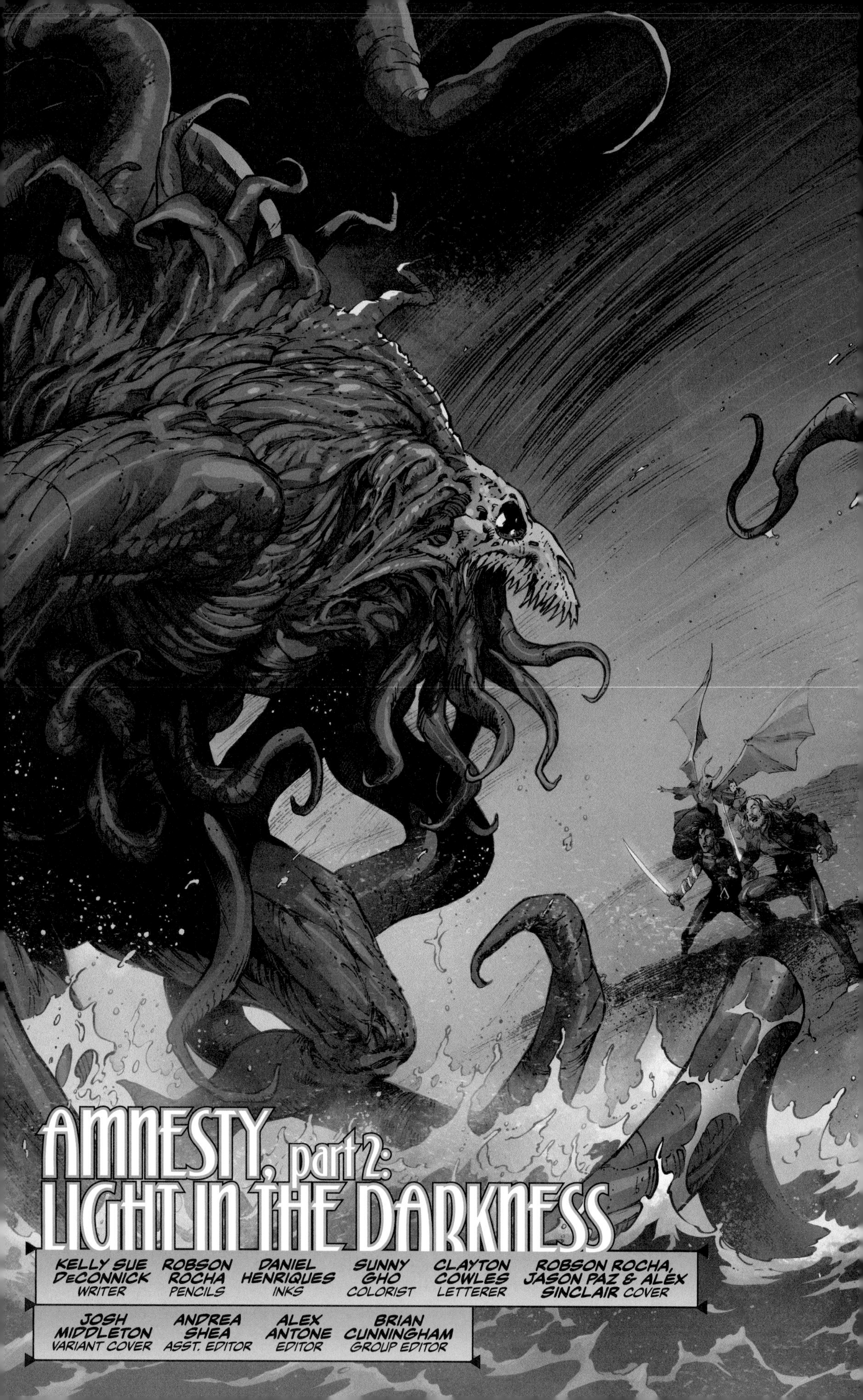
AMNESTY, part 2:
LIGHT IN THE DARKNESS
KELLY SUE DECONNICK WRITER
ROBSON ROCHA PENCILS
DANIEL HENRIQUES INKS
SUNNY GHO COLORIST
CLAYTON COWLES LETTERER
ROBSON ROCHA, JASON PAZ & ALEX SINCLAIR COVER
JOSH MIDDLETON VARIANT COVER
ANDREA SHEA ASST. EDITOR
ALEX ANTONE EDITOR
BRIAN CUNNINGHAM GROUP EDITOR

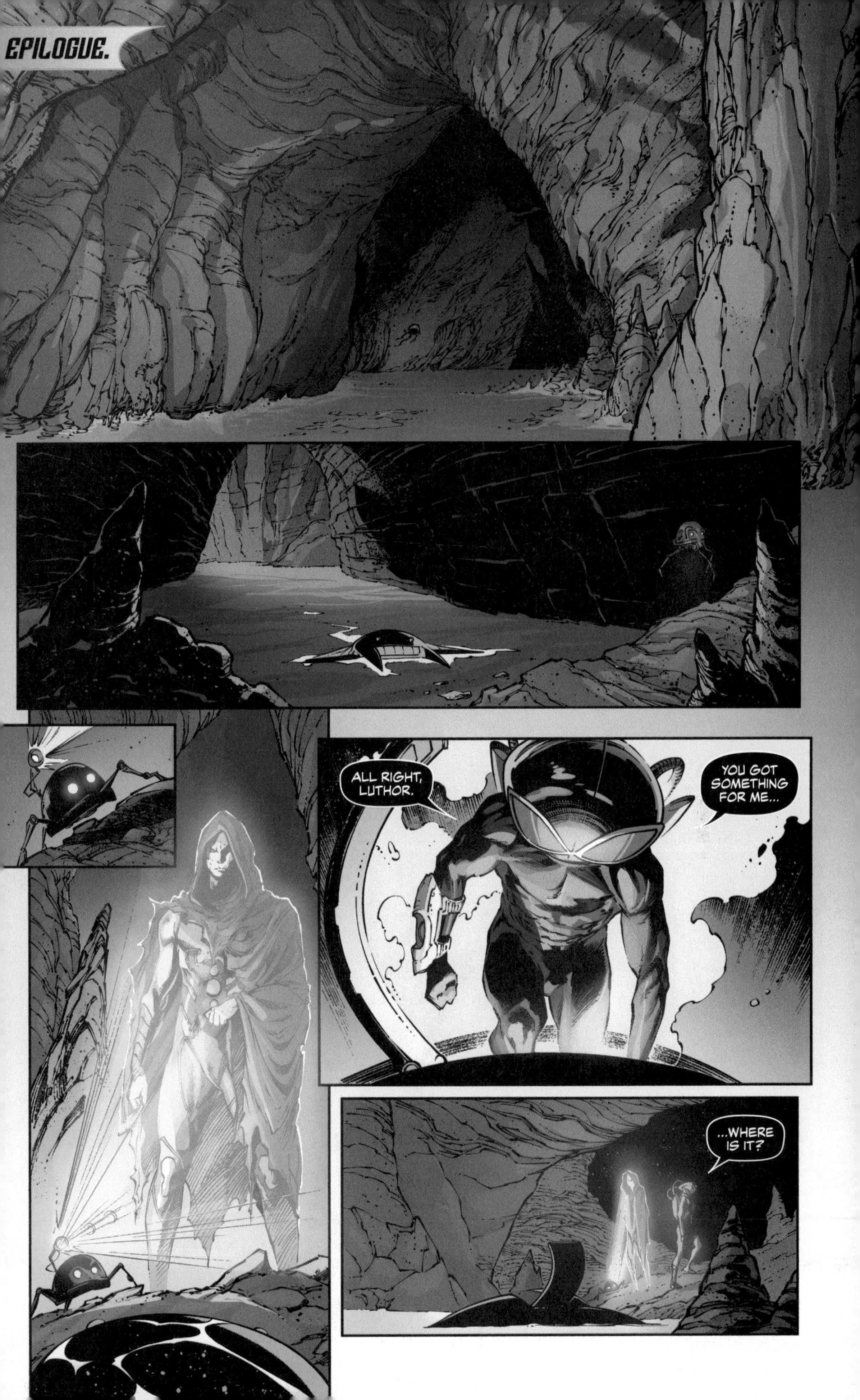
EPILOGUE.
ALL RIGHT, LUTHOR.
YOU GOT SOMETHING FOR ME...
...WHERE IS IT?

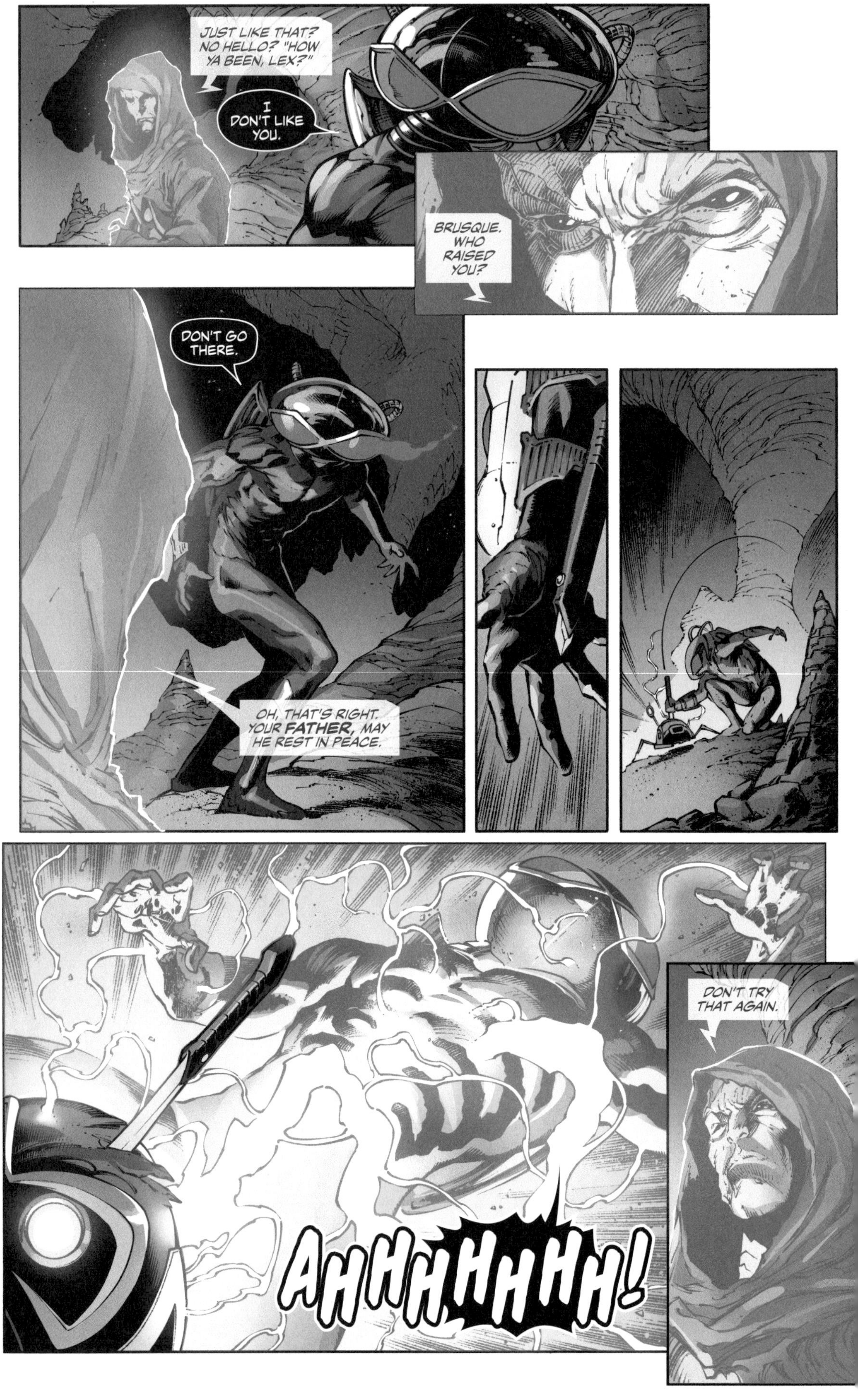
JUST LIKE THAT? NO HELLO? "HOW YA BEEN, LEX?"
I DON'T LIKE YOU.
BRUSQUE. WHO RAISED YOU?
DON'T GO THERE.
OH, THAT'S RIGHT. YOUR FATHER, MAY HE REST IN PEACE.
DON'T TRY THAT AGAIN.
AHHHHHHHH!

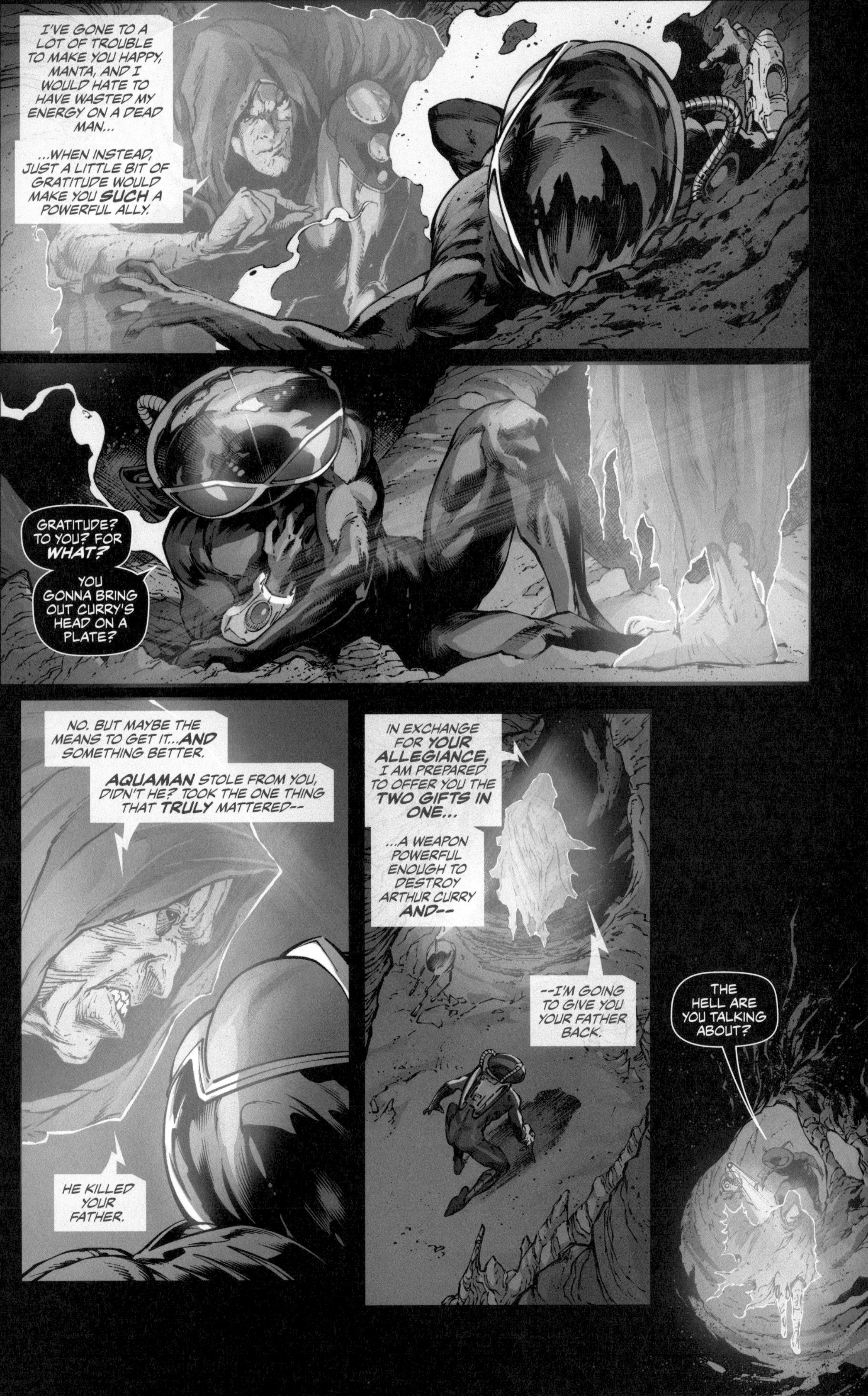

I'VE GONE TO A LOT OF TROUBLE TO MAKE YOU HAPPY, MANTA, AND I WOULD HATE TO HAVE WASTED MY ENERGY ON A DEAD MAN...
...WHEN INSTEAD, JUST A LITTLE BIT OF GRATITUDE WOULD MAKE YOU **SUCH** A POWERFUL ALLY.
GRATITUDE? TO YOU? FOR **WHAT?**
YOU GONNA BRING OUT CURRY'S HEAD ON A PLATE?
NO. BUT MAYBE THE MEANS TO GET IT...**AND** SOMETHING BETTER.
AQUAMAN STOLE FROM YOU, DIDN'T HE? TOOK THE ONE THING THAT **TRULY** MATTERED--
HE KILLED YOUR FATHER.
IN EXCHANGE FOR **YOUR ALLEGIANCE,** I AM PREPARED TO OFFER YOU THE **TWO GIFTS IN ONE...**
...A WEAPON POWERFUL ENOUGH TO DESTROY ARTHUR CURRY **AND--**
--I'M GOING TO GIVE YOU YOUR FATHER BACK.
THE HELL ARE YOU TALKING ABOUT?

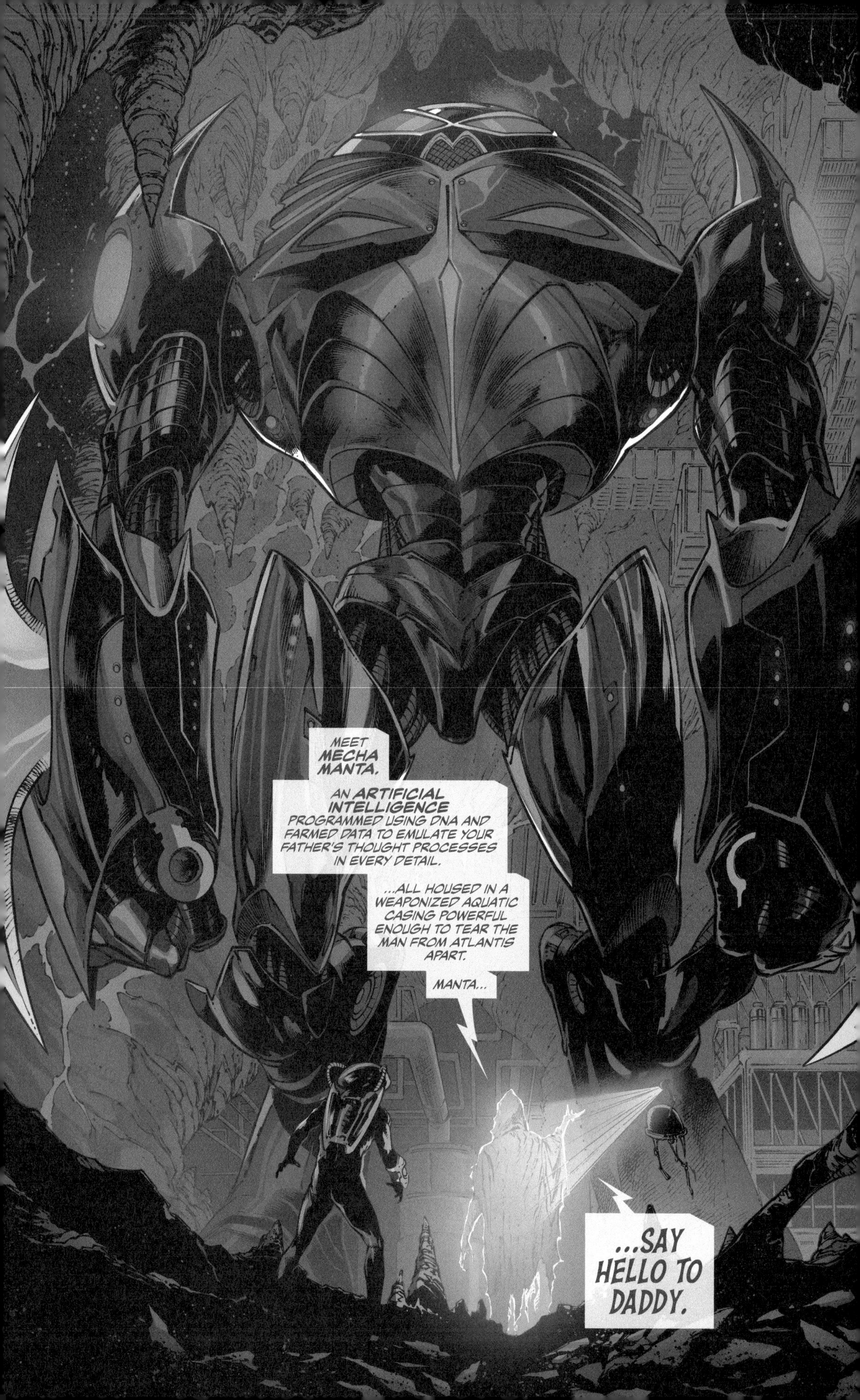
MEET MECHA MANTA,
AN ARTIFICIAL INTELLIGENCE PROGRAMMED USING DNA AND FARMED DATA TO EMULATE YOUR FATHER'S THOUGHT PROCESSES IN EVERY DETAIL.
...ALL HOUSED IN A WEAPONIZED AQUATIC CASING POWERFUL ENOUGH TO TEAR THE MAN FROM ATLANTIS APART.
MANTA...
...SAY HELLO TO DADDY.

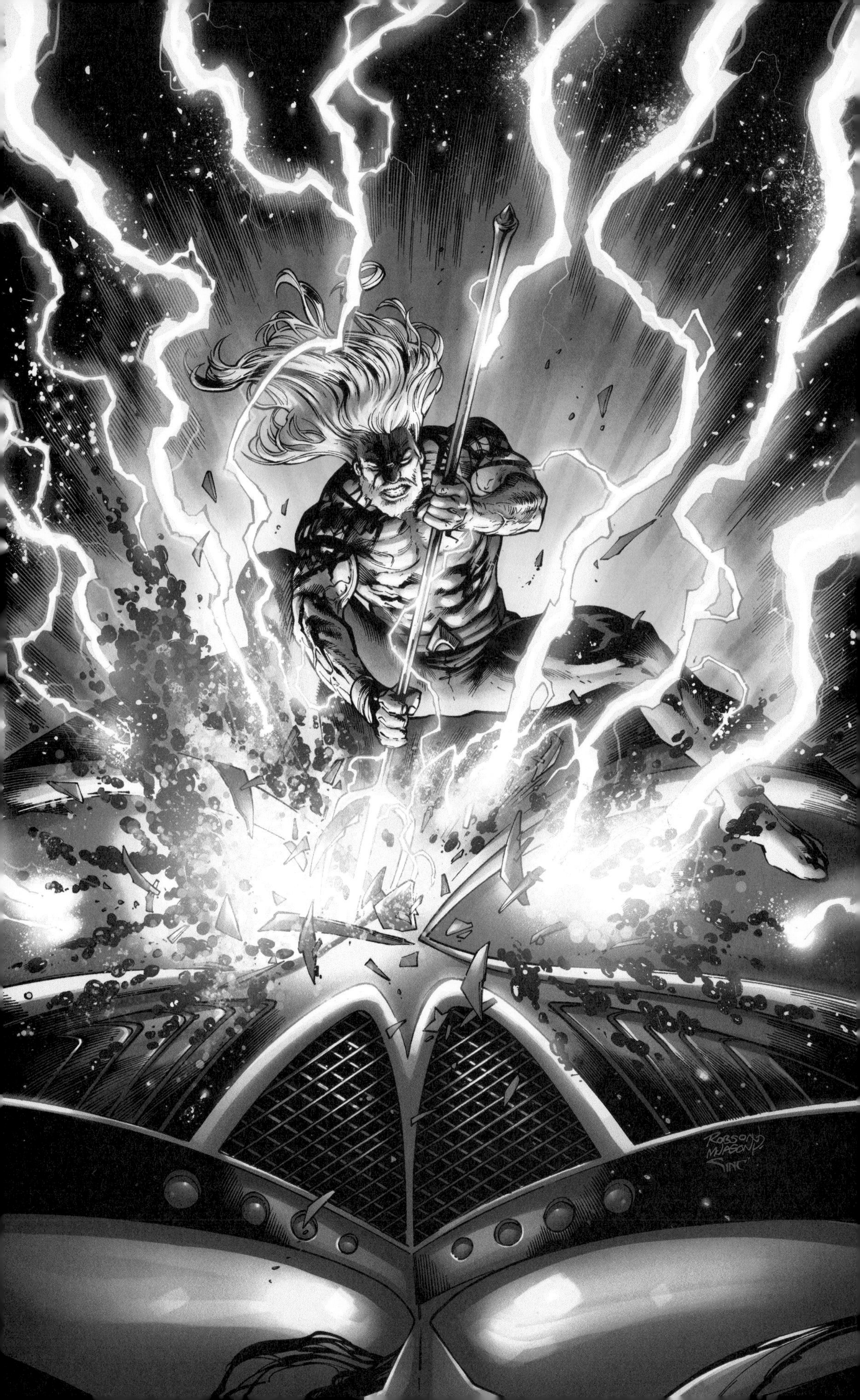

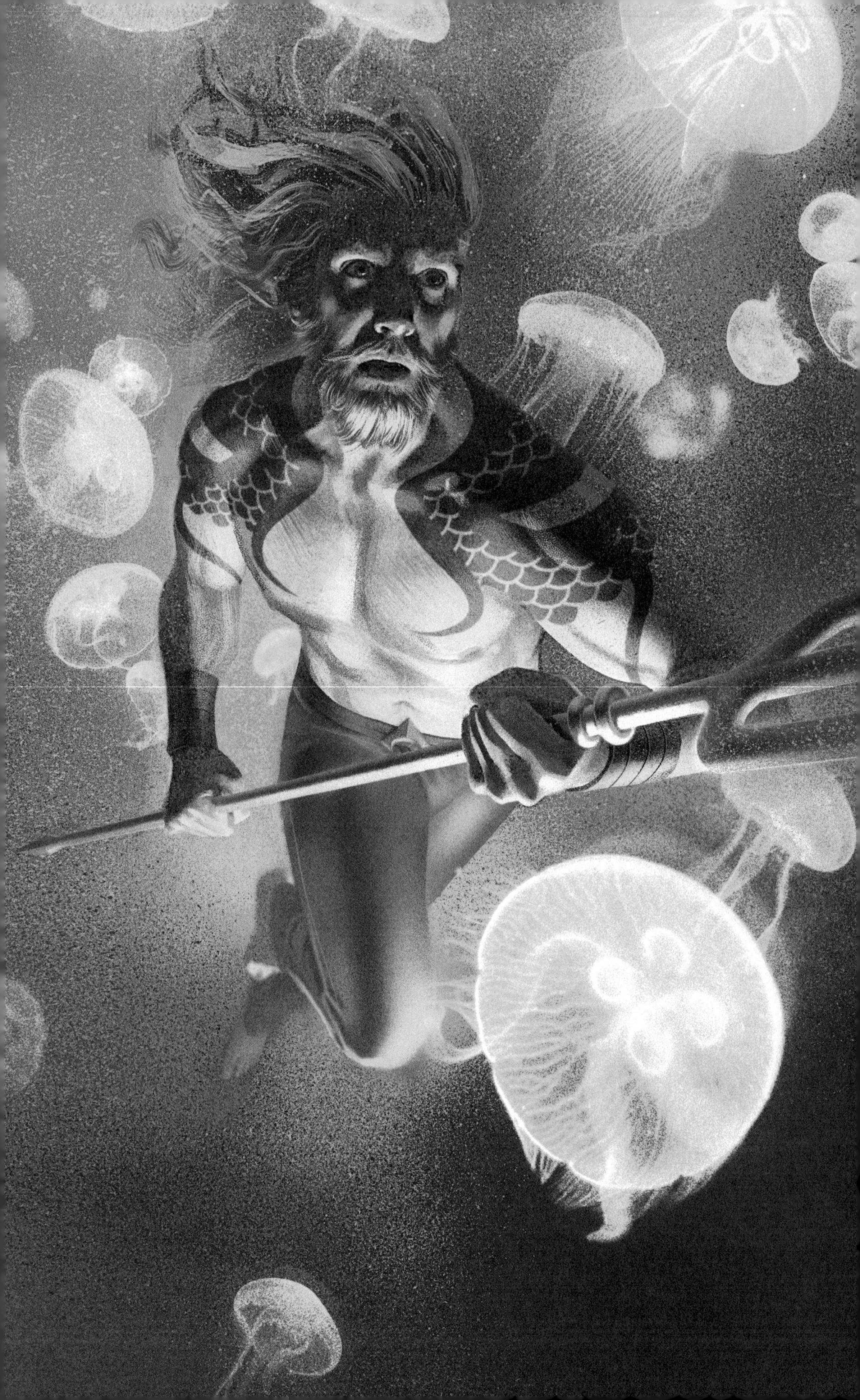

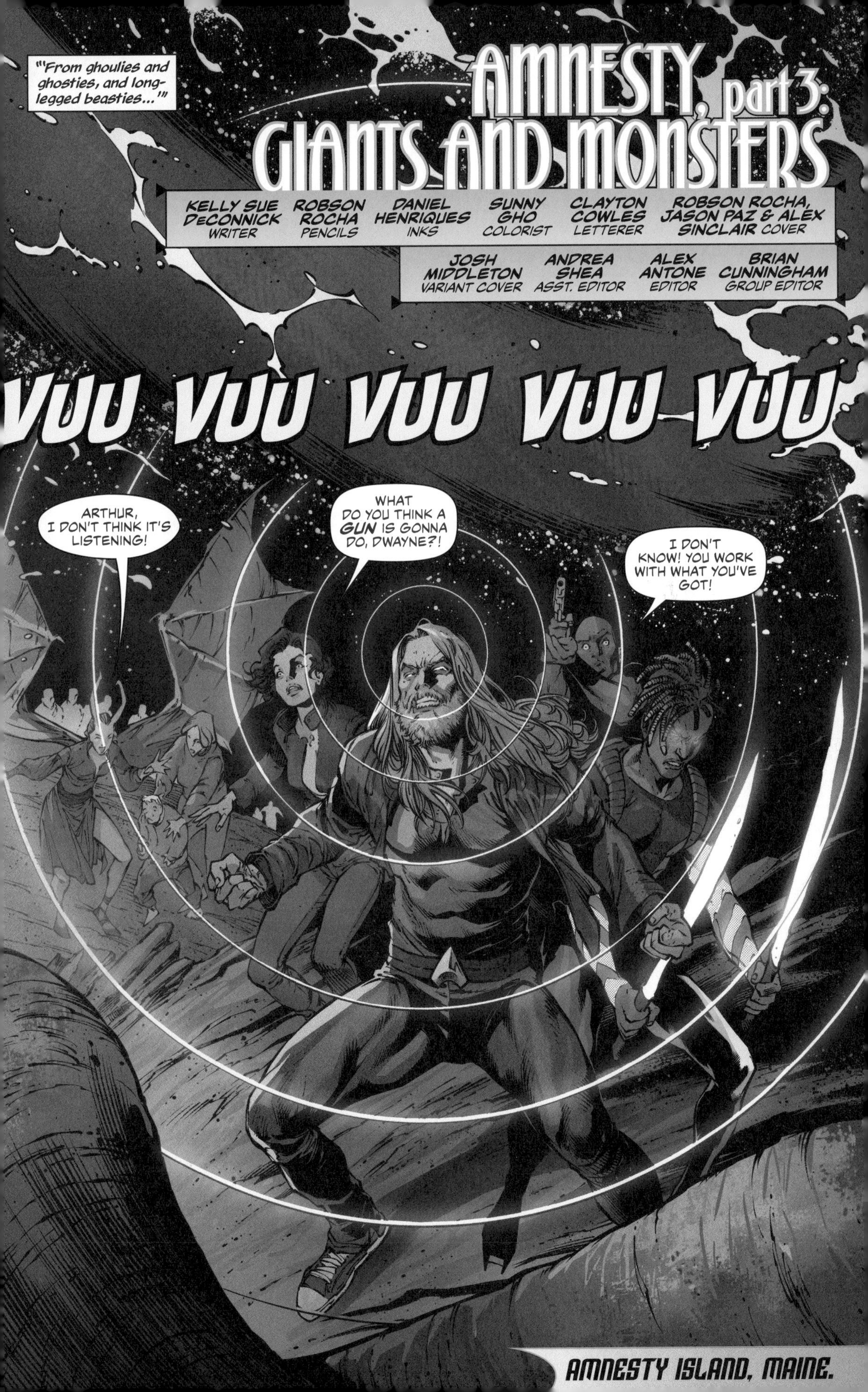
"From ghoulies and ghosties, and long-legged beasties..."
AMNESTY, part 3: GIANTS AND MONSTERS
KELLY SUE DeCONNICK WRITER
ROBSON ROCHA PENCILS
DANIEL HENRIQUES INKS
SUNNY GHO COLORIST
CLAYTON COWLES LETTERER
ROBSON ROCHA, JASON PAZ & ALEX SINCLAIR COVER
JOSH MIDDLETON VARIANT COVER
ANDREA SHEA ASST. EDITOR
ALEX ANTONE EDITOR
BRIAN CUNNINGHAM GROUP EDITOR
VUU VUU VUU VUU VUU
ARTHUR, I DON'T THINK IT'S LISTENING!
WHAT DO YOU THINK A GUN IS GONNA DO, DWAYNE?!
I DON'T KNOW! YOU WORK WITH WHAT YOU'VE GOT!
AMNESTY ISLAND, MAINE.

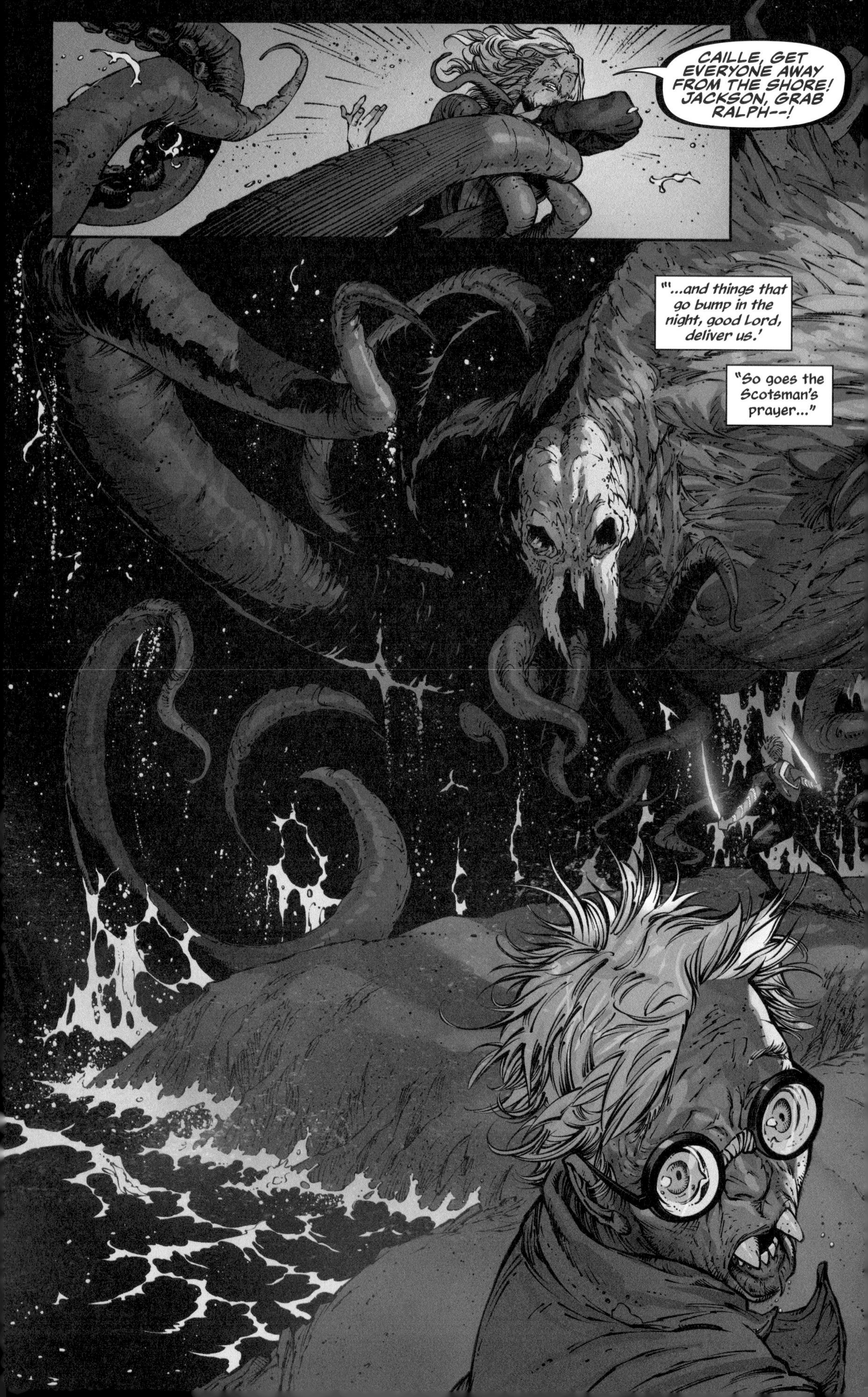
CAILLE, GET EVERYONE AWAY FROM THE SHORE! JACKSON, GRAB RALPH--!
"'...and things that go bump in the night, good Lord, deliver us.'
"So goes the Scotsman's prayer..."

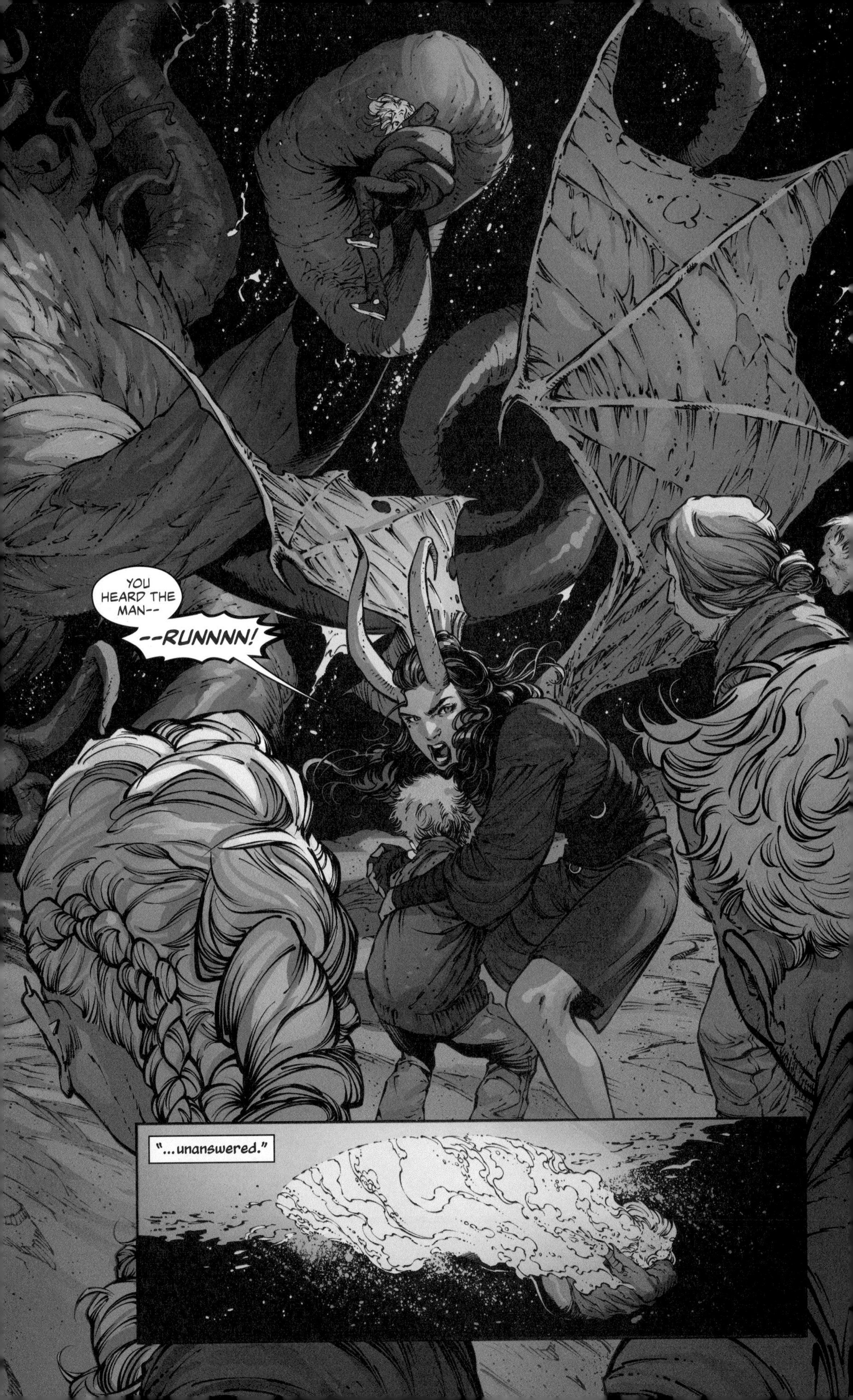
YOU HEARD THE MAN--
--RUNNNN!
"...unanswered."

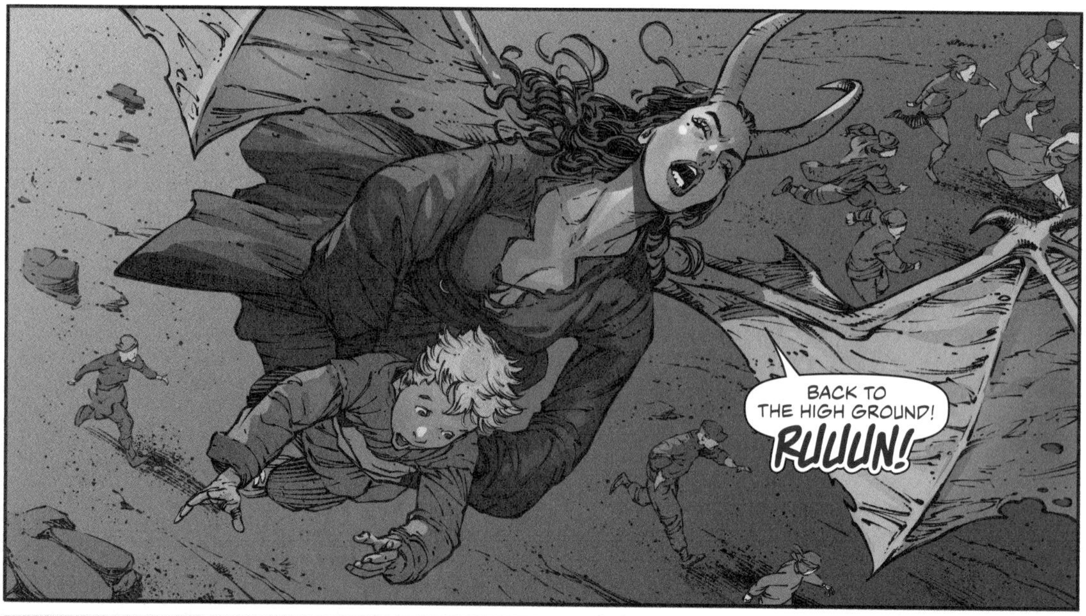
BACK TO THE HIGH GROUND!
RUUUN!

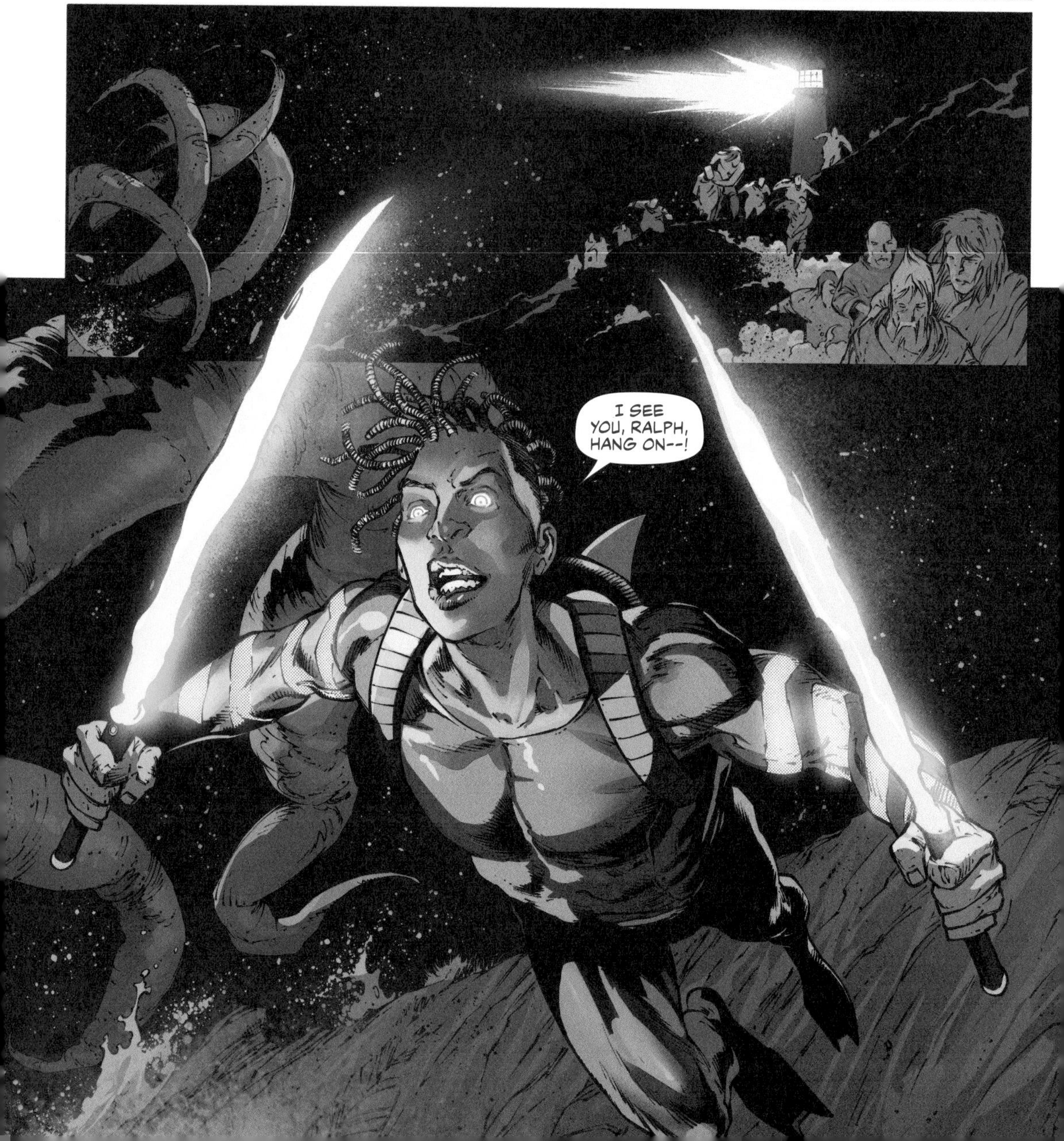
I SEE YOU, RALPH, HANG ON--!

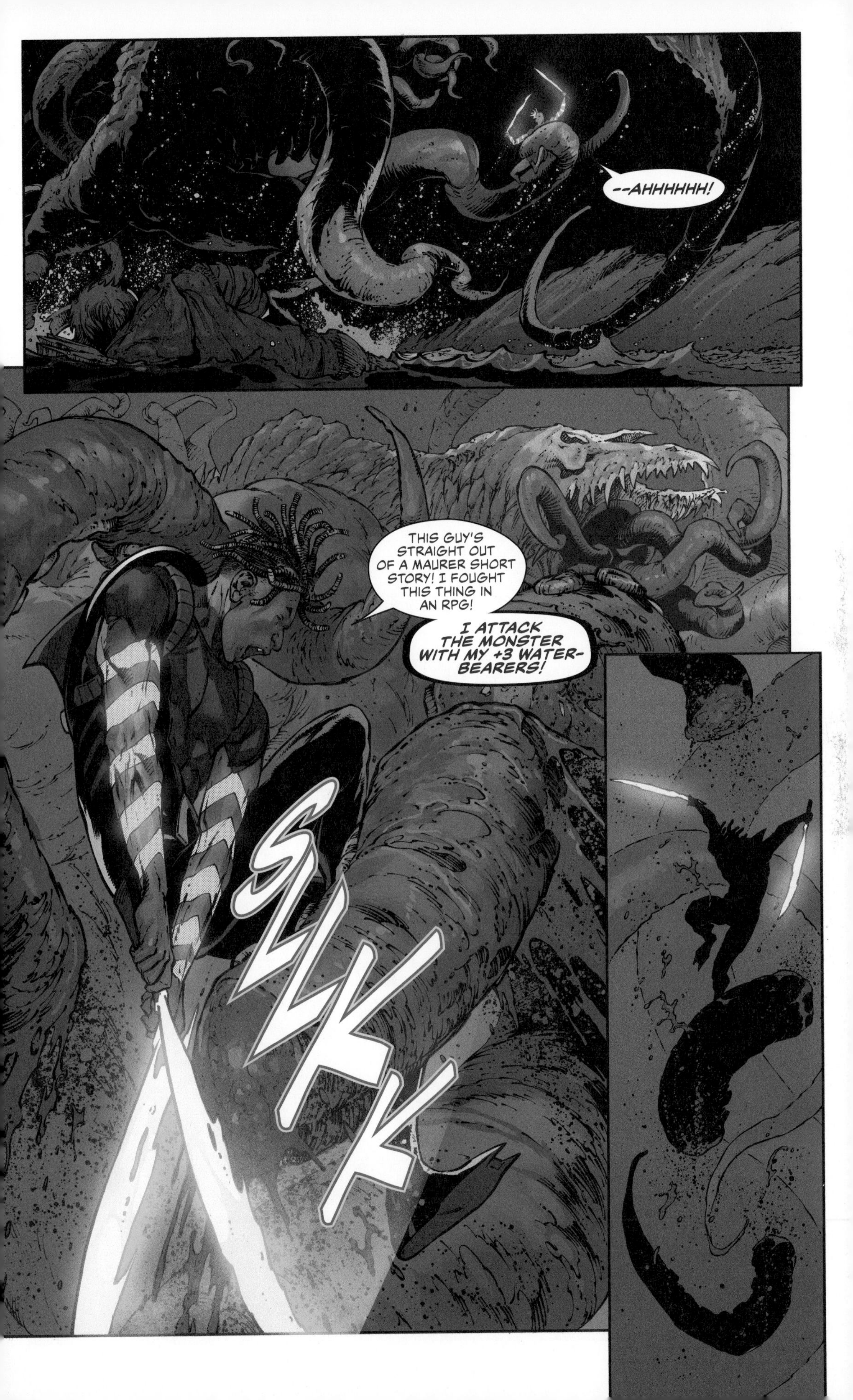
--AHHHHHH!
THIS GUY'S STRAIGHT OUT OF A MAURER SHORT STORY! I FOUGHT THIS THING IN AN RPG!
I ATTACK THE MONSTER WITH MY +3 WATER-BEARERS!
SHUKK

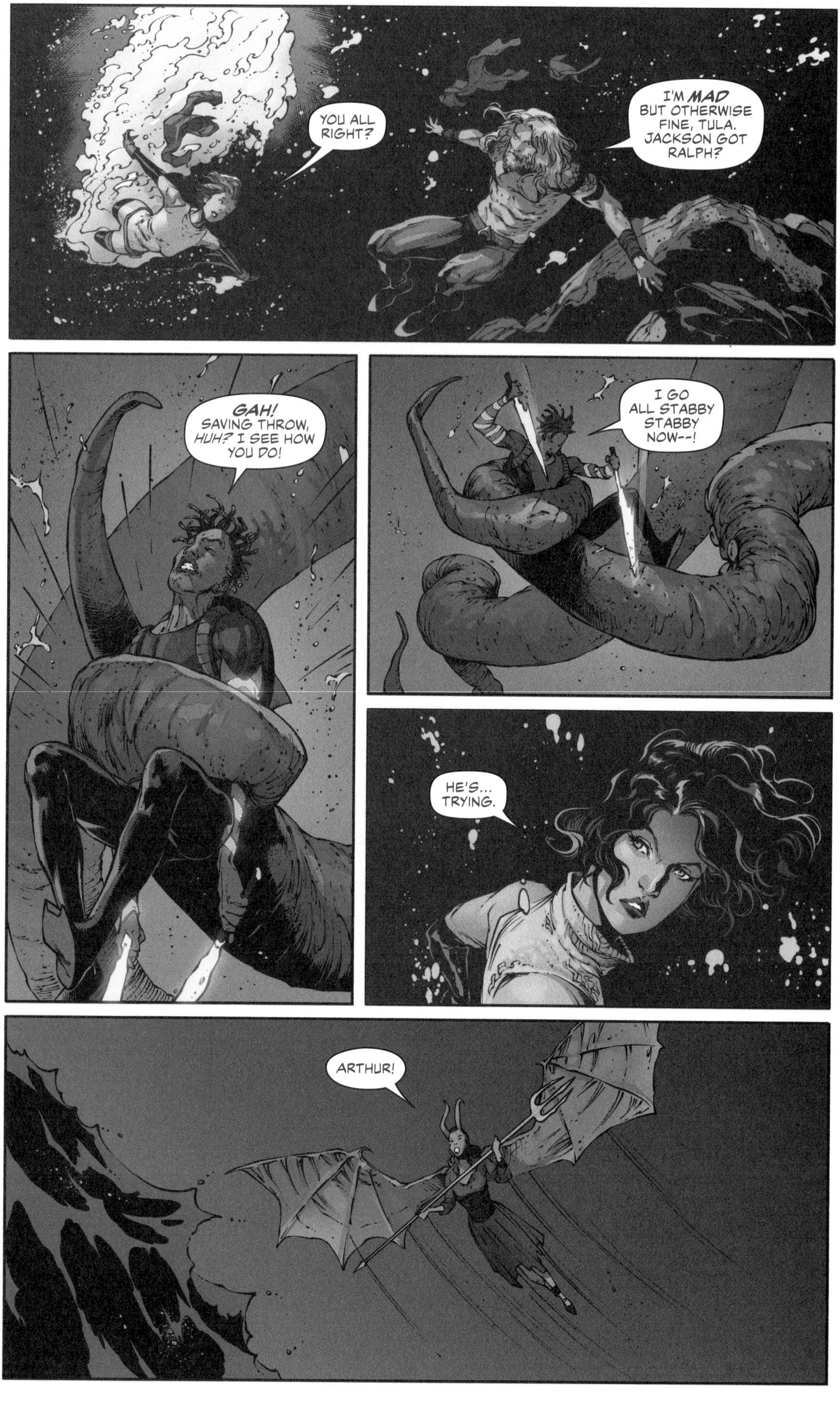
YOU ALL RIGHT?
I'M MAD BUT OTHERWISE FINE, TULA. JACKSON GOT RALPH?
GAH! SAVING THROW, HUH? I SEE HOW YOU DO!
I GO ALL STABBY STABBY NOW--!
HE'S... TRYING.
ARTHUR!

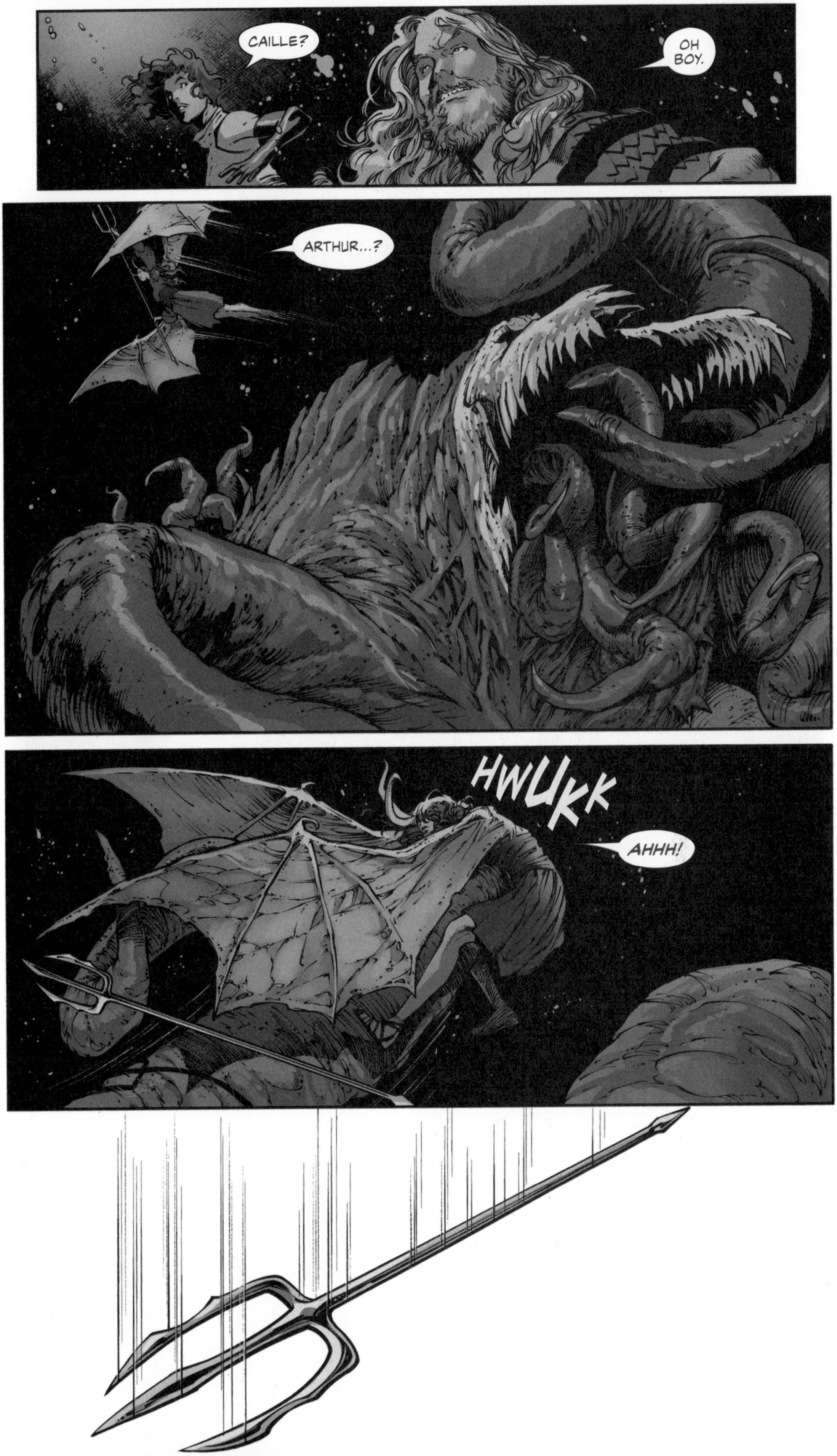
CAILLE?
OH BOY.
ARTHUR...?
HWUKK
AHHH!

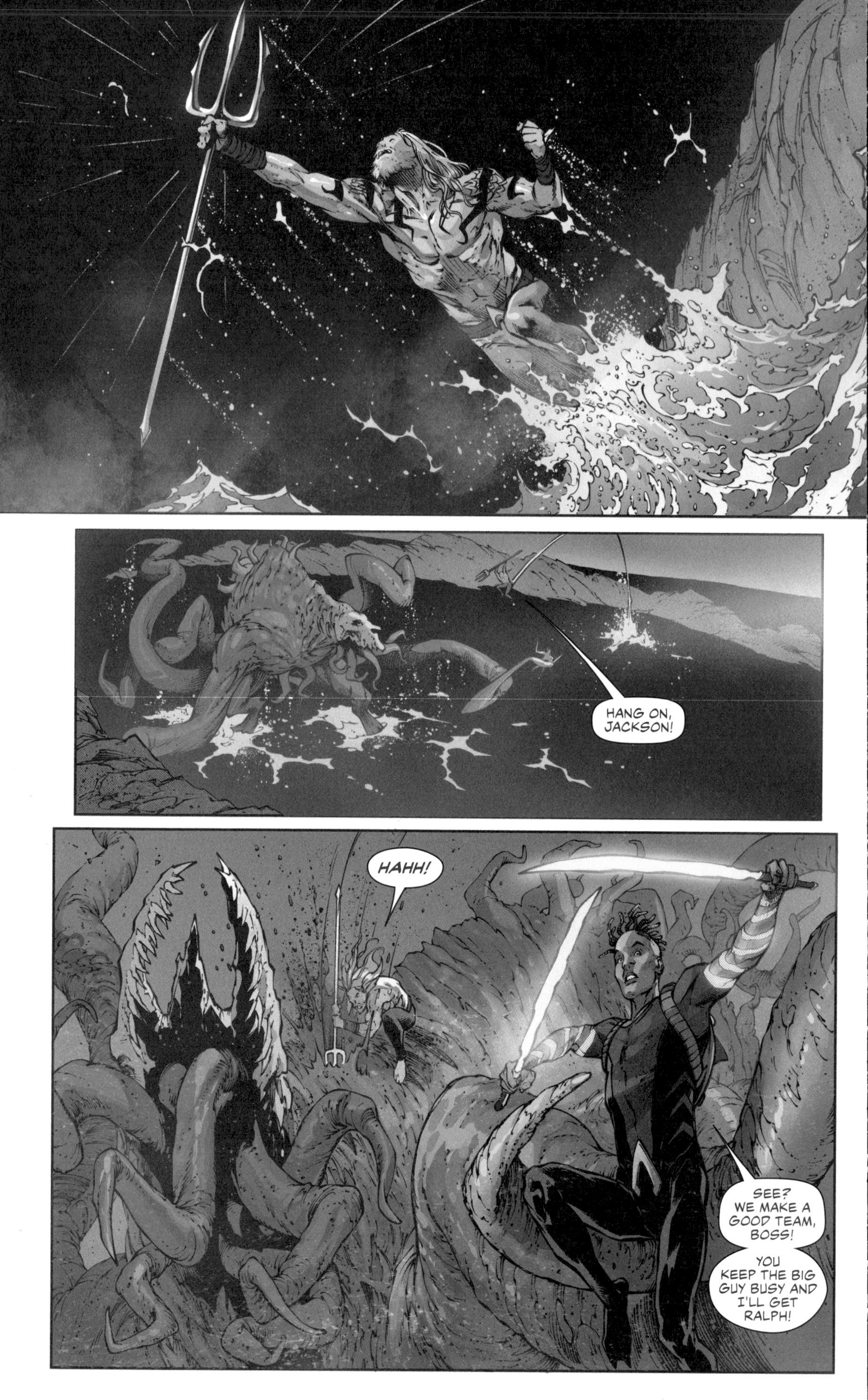
HANG ON, JACKSON!
HAHH!
SEE? WE MAKE A GOOD TEAM, BOSS!
YOU KEEP THE BIG GUY BUSY AND I'LL GET RALPH!

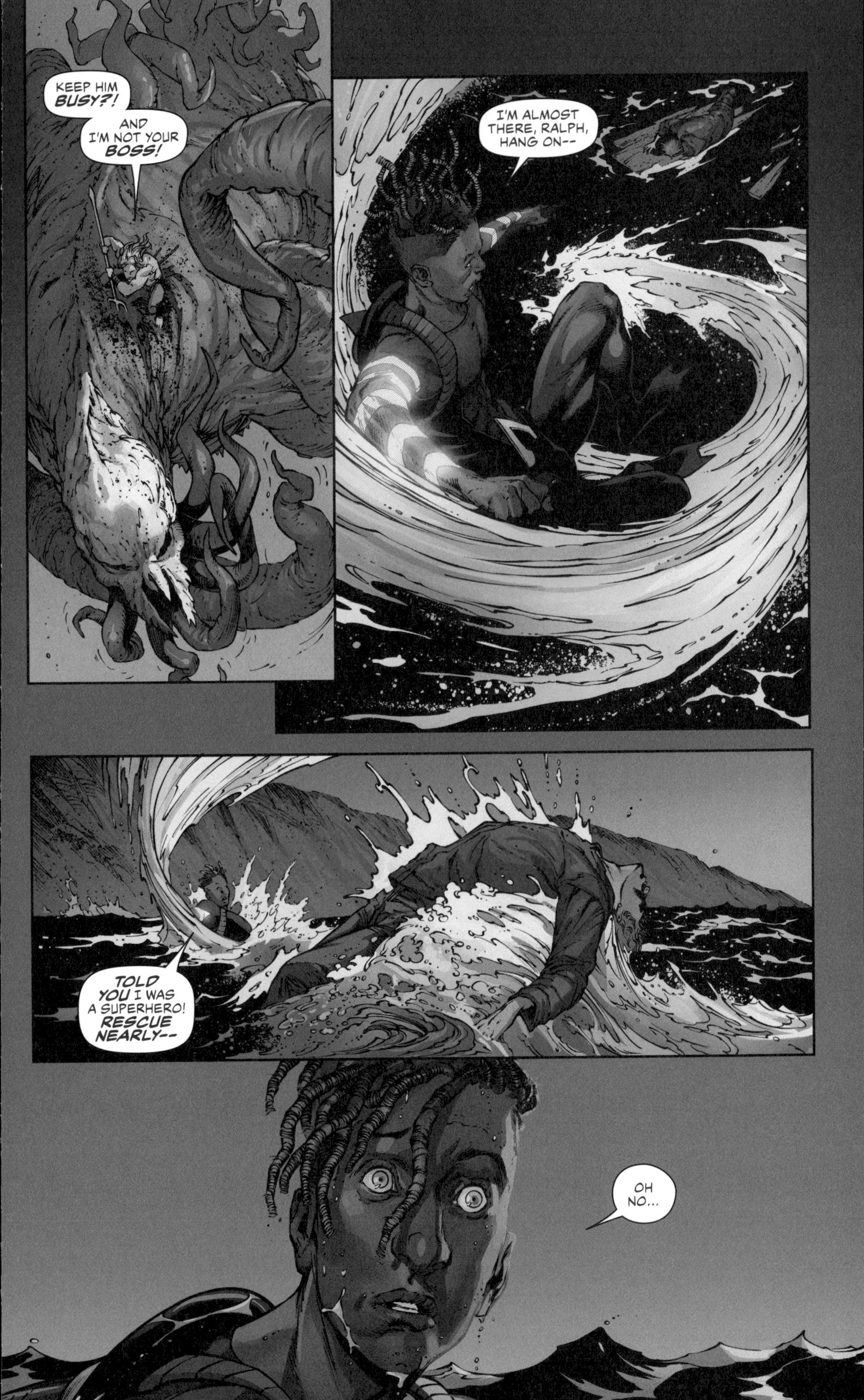
KEEP HIM BUSY?!
AND I'M NOT YOUR BOSS!
I'M ALMOST THERE, RALPH, HANG ON--
TOLD YOU I WAS A SUPERHERO! RESCUE NEARLY--
OH NO...

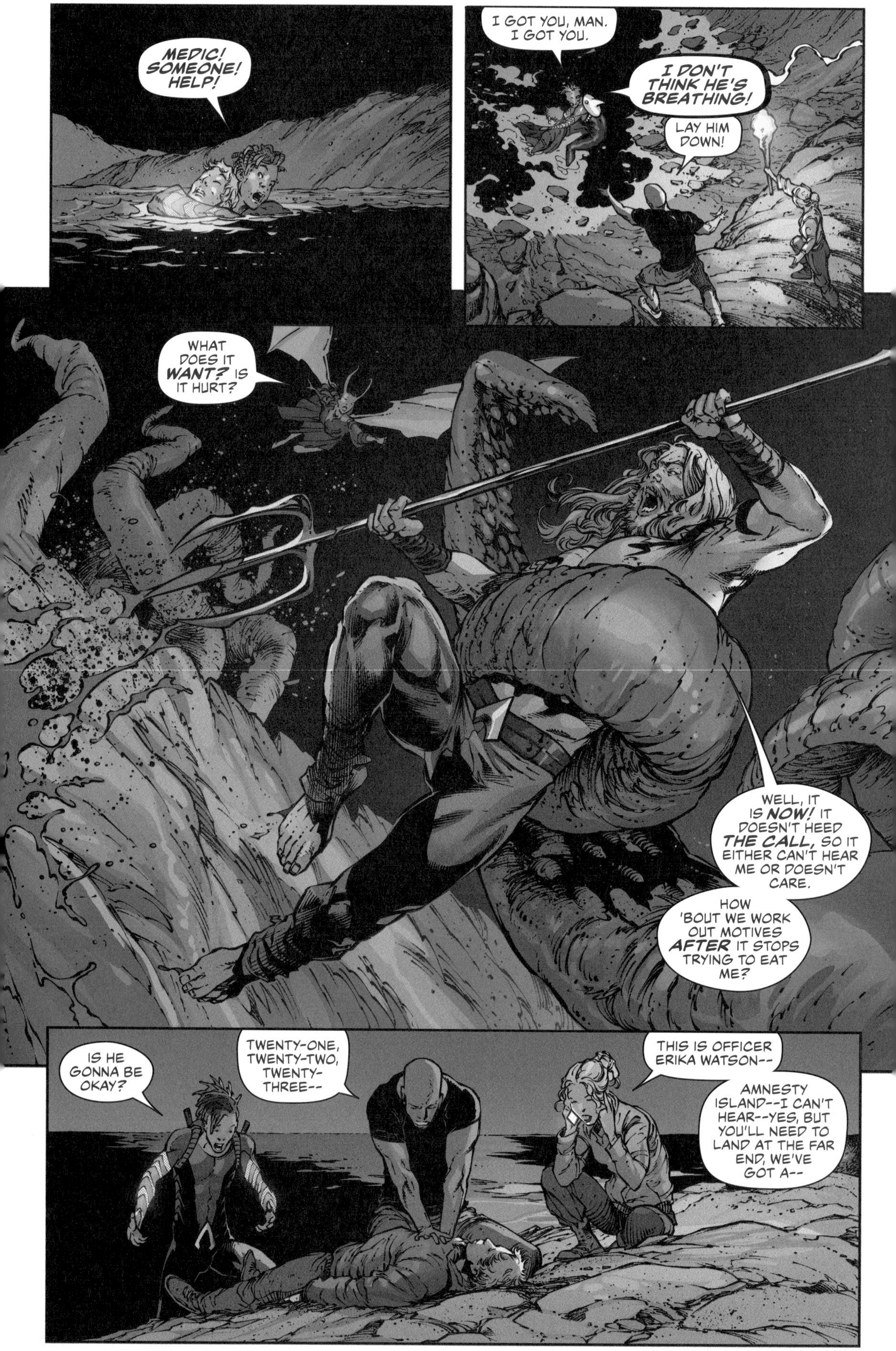
MEDIC! SOMEONE! HELP!
I GOT YOU, MAN. I GOT YOU.
I DON'T THINK HE'S BREATHING!
LAY HIM DOWN!
WHAT DOES IT WANT? IS IT HURT?
WELL, IT IS NOW! IT DOESN'T HEED THE CALL, SO IT EITHER CAN'T HEAR ME OR DOESN'T CARE.
HOW 'BOUT WE WORK OUT MOTIVES AFTER IT STOPS TRYING TO EAT ME?
IS HE GONNA BE OKAY?
TWENTY-ONE, TWENTY-TWO, TWENTY-THREE--
THIS IS OFFICER ERIKA WATSON--
AMNESTY ISLAND--I CAN'T HEAR--YES, BUT YOU'LL NEED TO LAND AT THE FAR END, WE'VE GOT A--

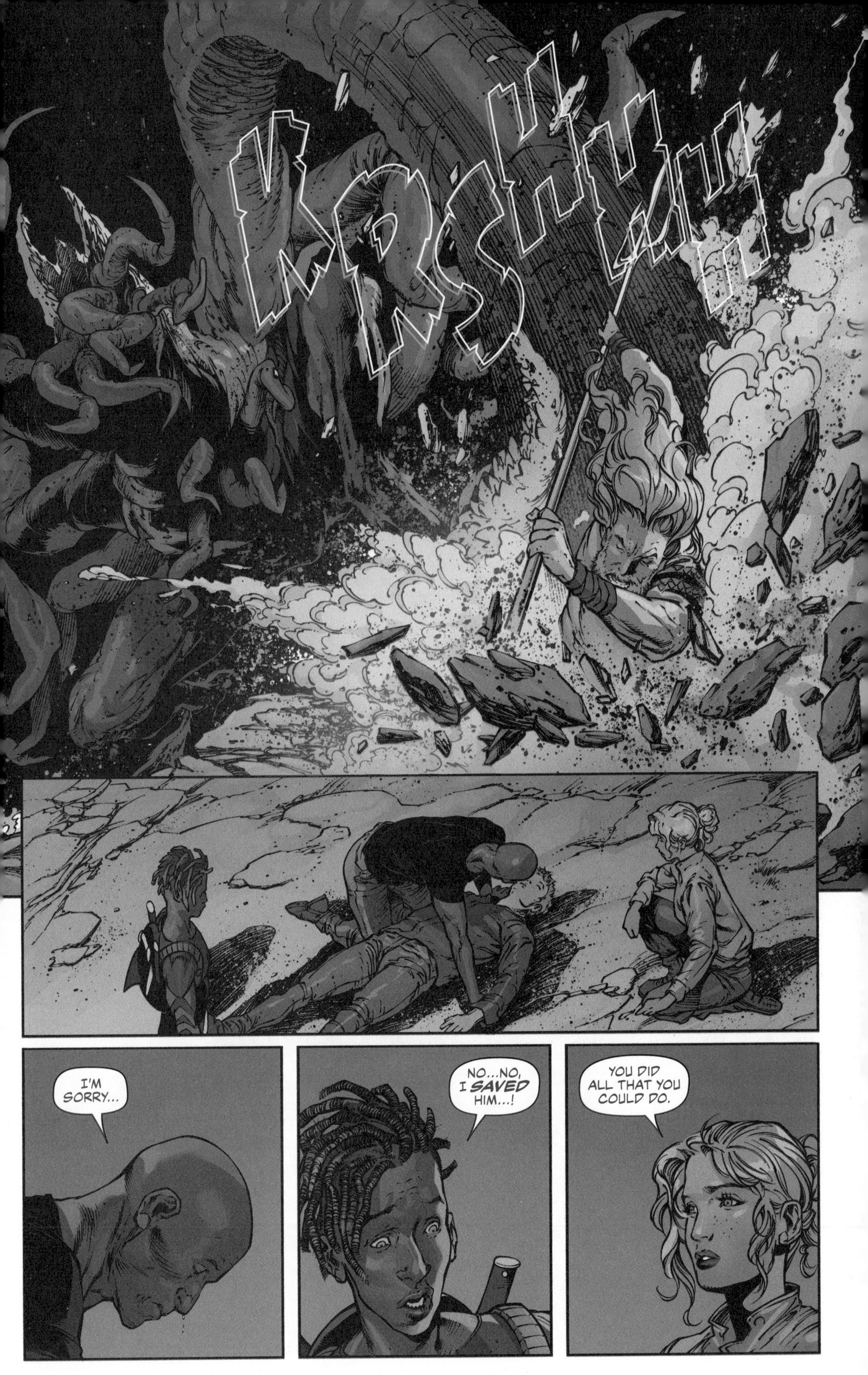
I'M SORRY...
NO...NO, I SAVED HIM...!
YOU DID ALL THAT YOU COULD DO.

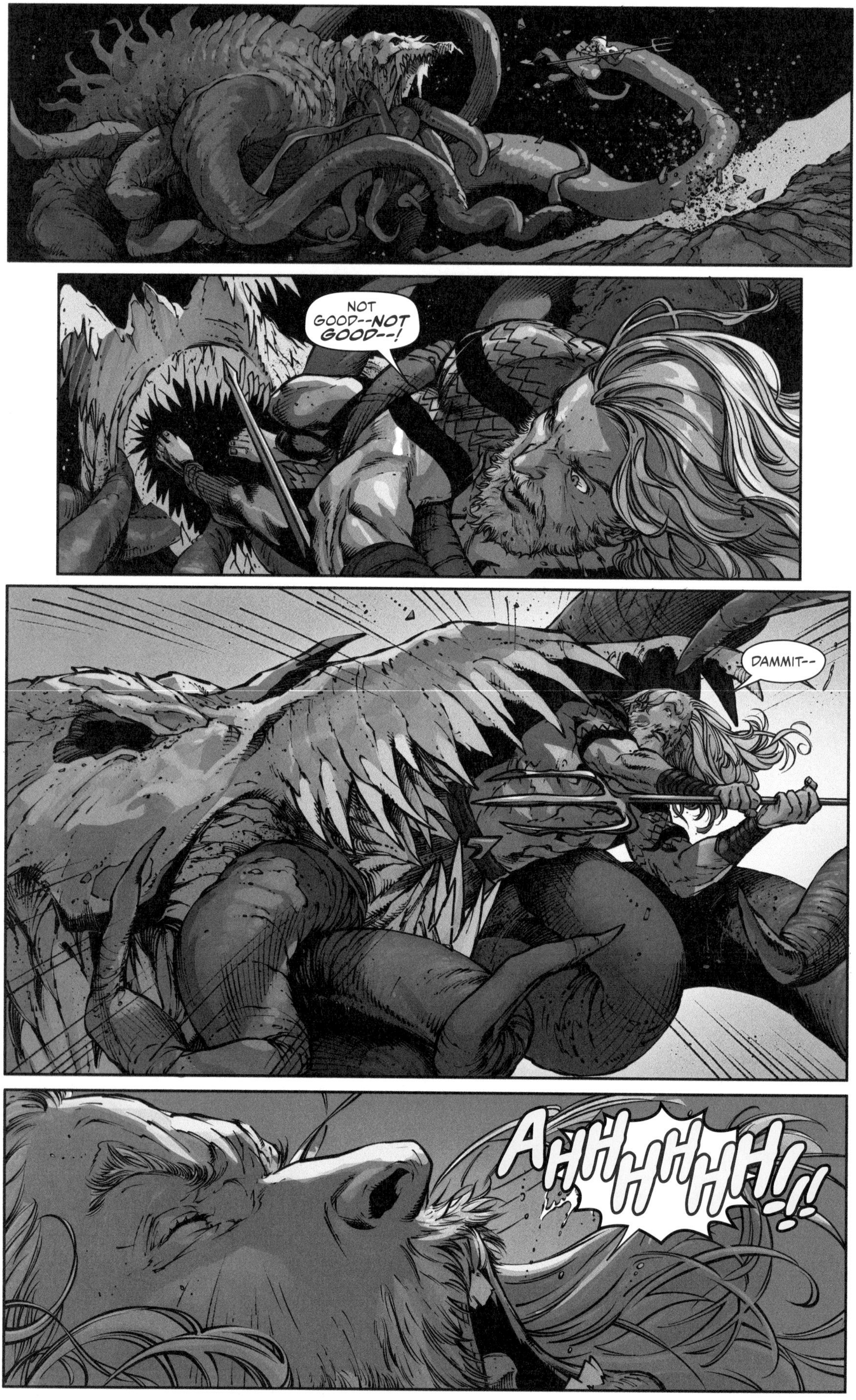
NOT GOOD--NOT GOOD--!
DAMMIT--
AHHHHHHH!!!

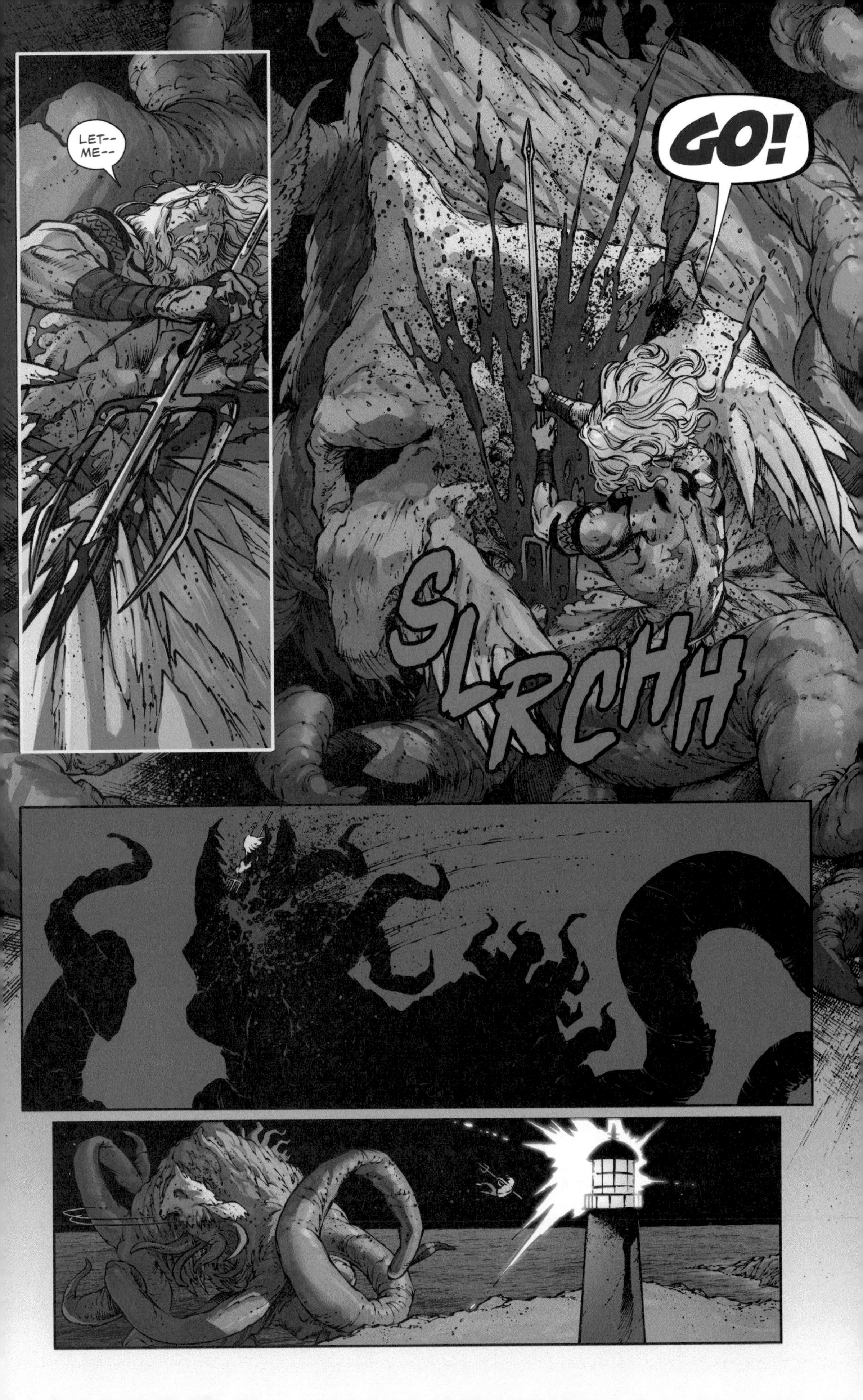

LET--
ME--
GO!
SLRCHH

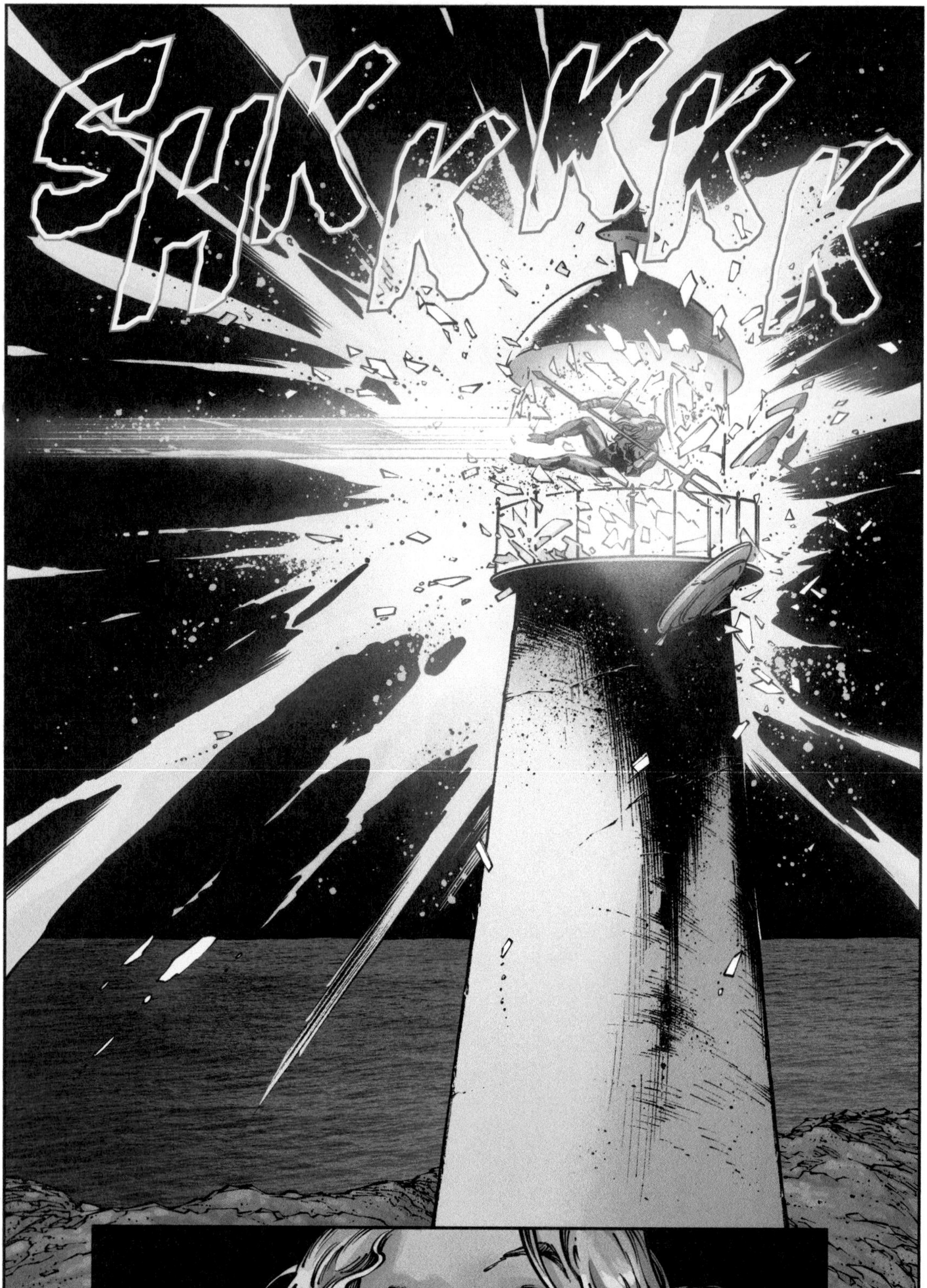
SHKKKKK
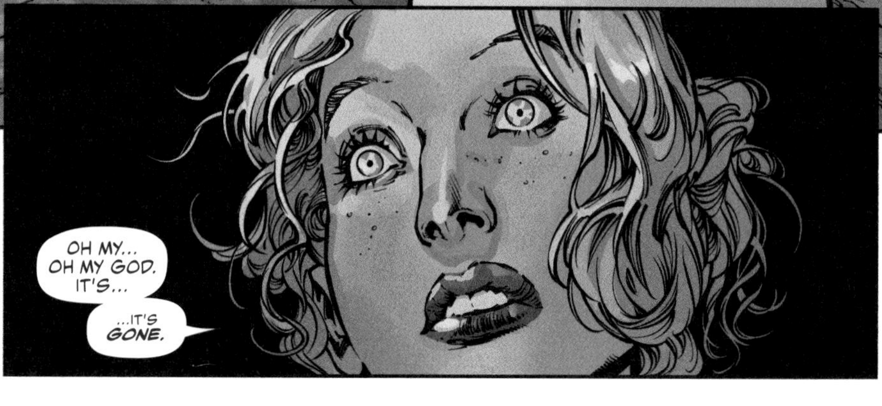
OH MY... OH MY GOD. IT'S...
...IT'S GONE.

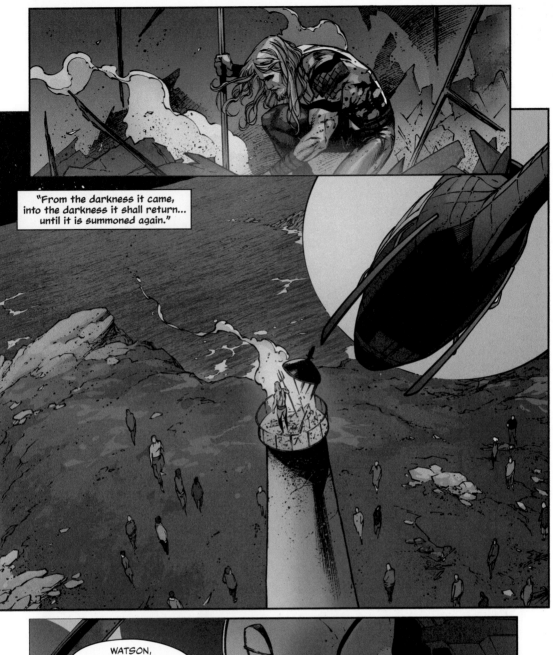

"From the darkness it came, into the darkness it shall return... until it is summoned again."

WATSON, WE'RE NOT SEEING THE HAZARD. ASSUMING THE SITUATION IS REMEDIED?

COPY?

...THE MONSTER, IT'S JUST... GONE.

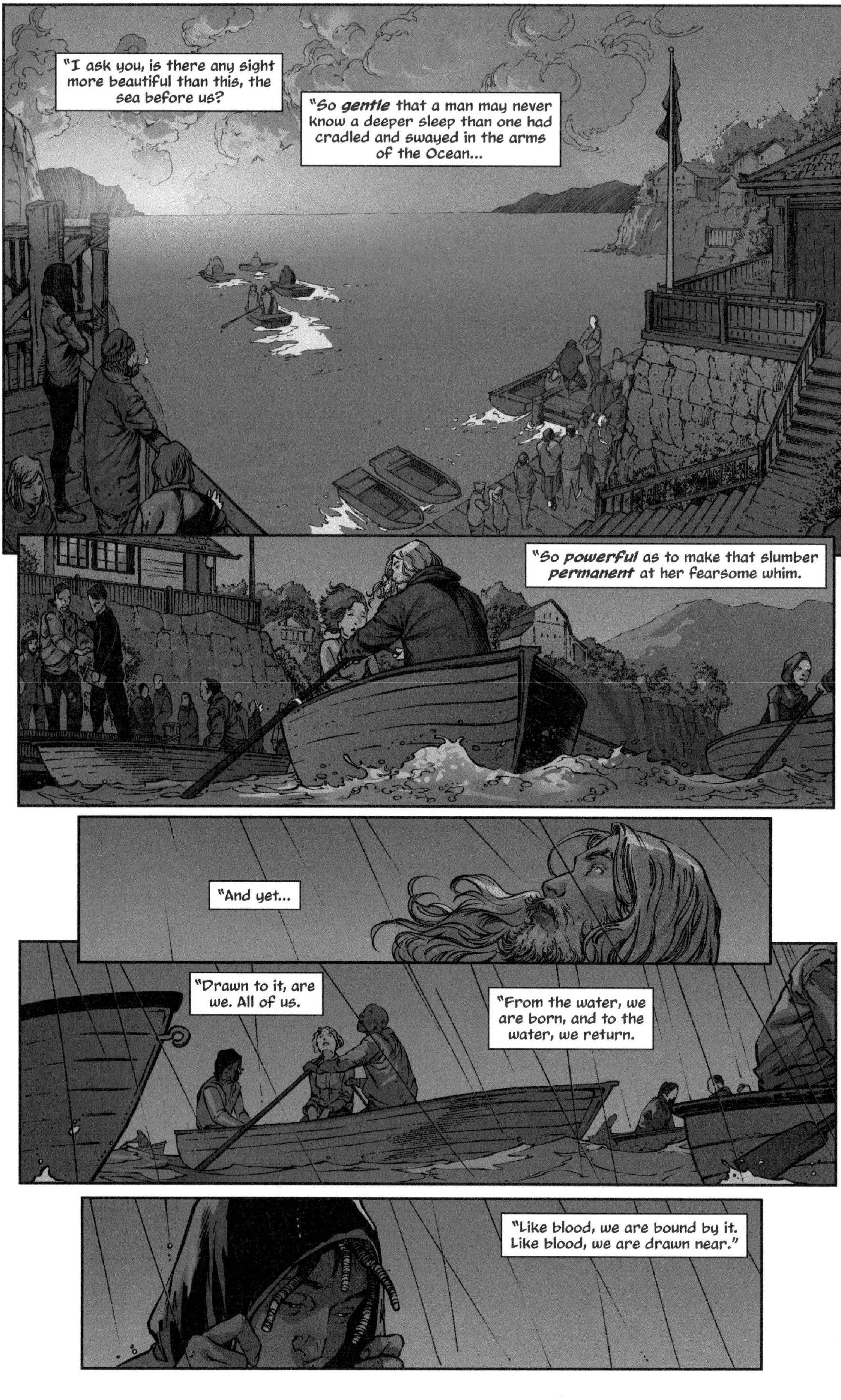
"I ask you, is there any sight more beautiful than this, the sea before us?
"So *gentle* that a man may never know a deeper sleep than one had cradled and swayed in the arms of the Ocean...
"So *powerful* as to make that slumber *permanent* at her fearsome whim.
"And yet...
"Drawn to it, are we. All of us.
"From the water, we are born, and to the water, we return.
"Like blood, we are bound by it. Like blood, we are drawn near."

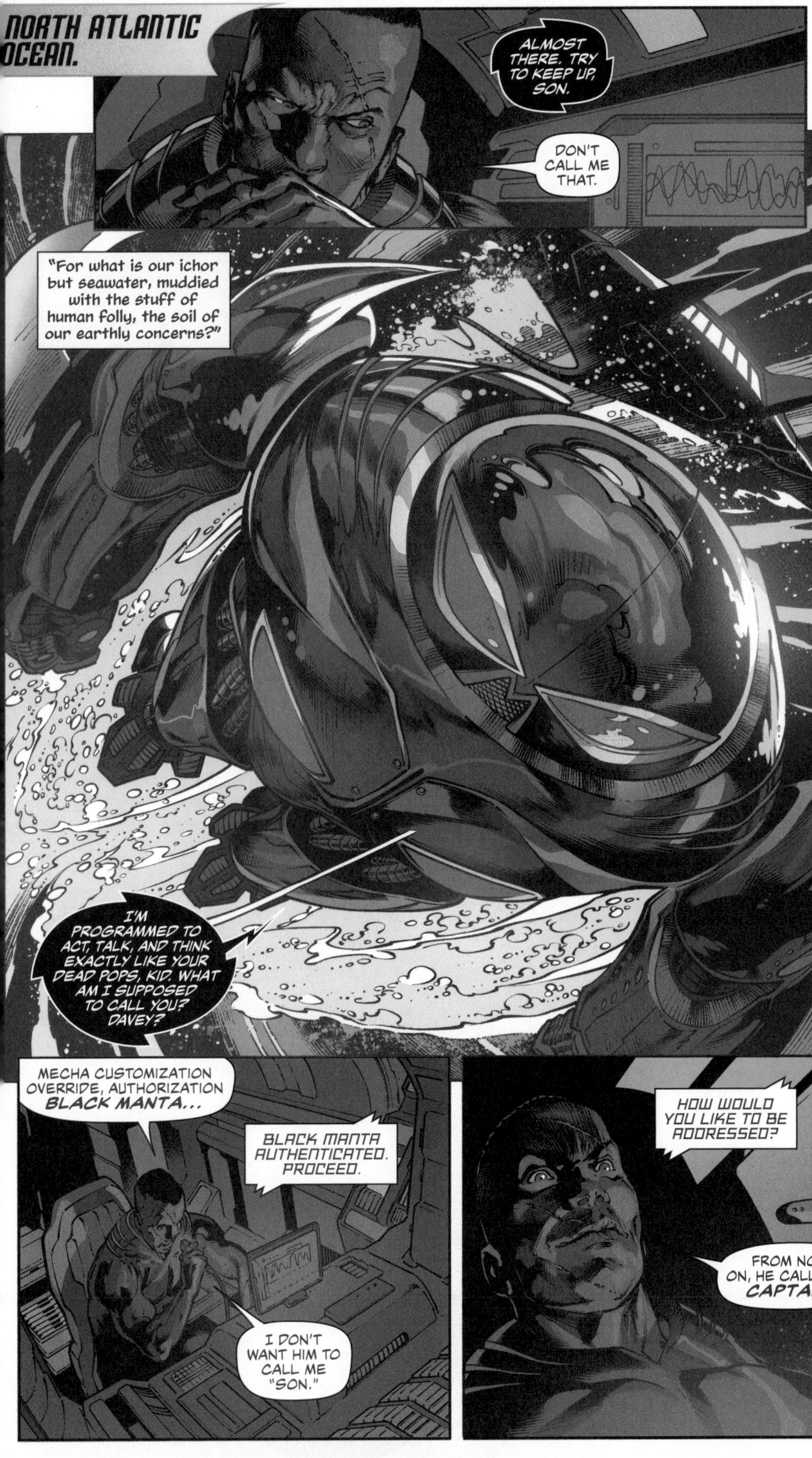
NORTH ATLANTIC OCEAN.
ALMOST THERE. TRY TO KEEP UP, SON.
DON'T CALL ME THAT.
"For what is our ichor but seawater, muddied with the stuff of human folly, the soil of our earthly concerns?"
I'M PROGRAMMED TO ACT, TALK, AND THINK EXACTLY LIKE YOUR DEAD POPS, KID. WHAT AM I SUPPOSED TO CALL YOU? DAVEY?
MECHA CUSTOMIZATION OVERRIDE, AUTHORIZATION BLACK MANTA...
BLACK MANTA AUTHENTICATED. PROCEED.
I DON'T WANT HIM TO CALL ME "SON."
HOW WOULD YOU LIKE TO BE ADDRESSED?
FROM NOW ON, HE CALLS ME CAPTAIN.

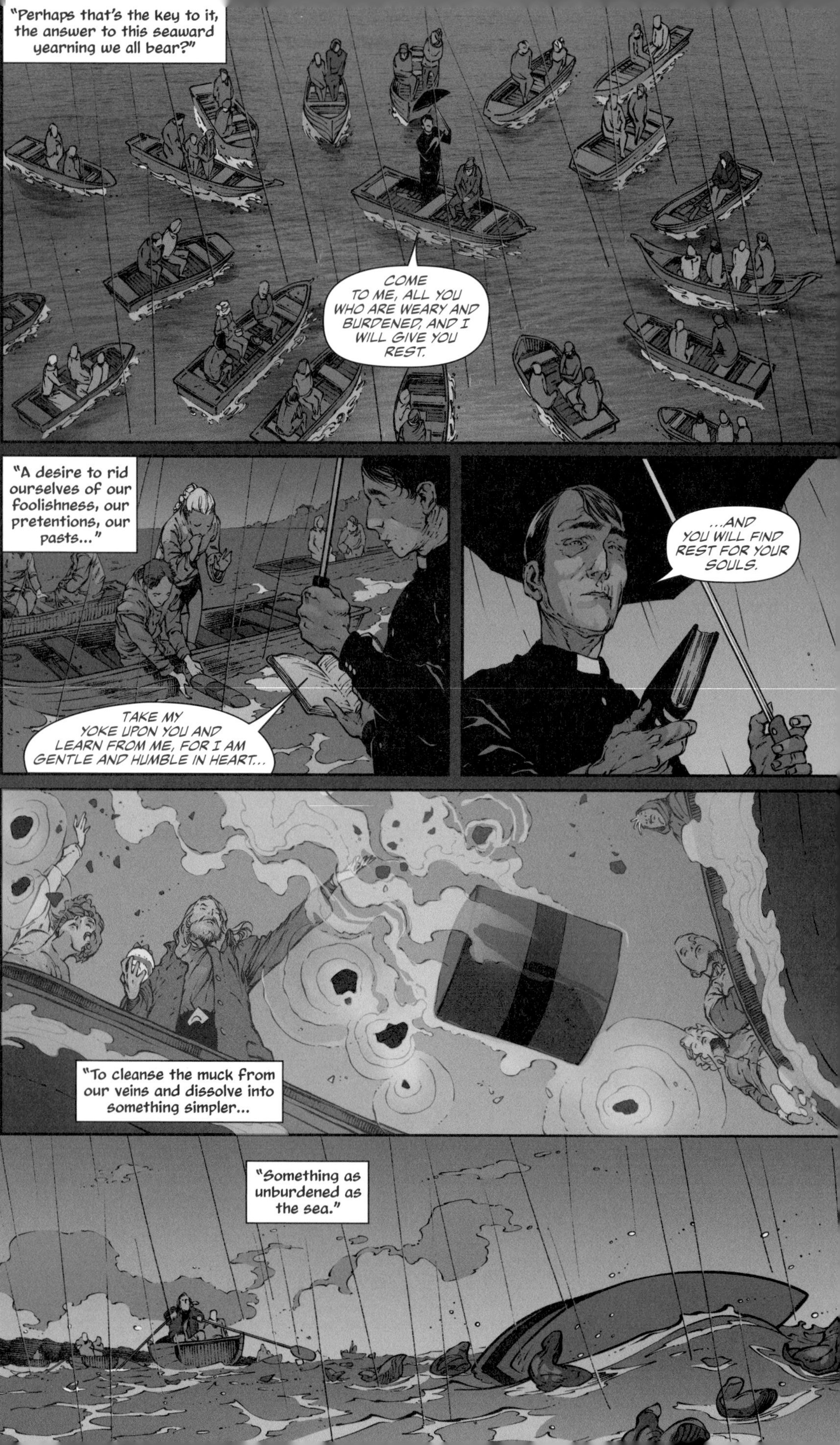
"Perhaps that's the key to it, the answer to this seaward yearning we all bear?"
COME TO ME, ALL YOU WHO ARE WEARY AND BURDENED, AND I WILL GIVE YOU REST.
"A desire to rid ourselves of our foolishness, our pretentions, our pasts..."
TAKE MY YOKE UPON YOU AND LEARN FROM ME, FOR I AM GENTLE AND HUMBLE IN HEART...
...AND YOU WILL FIND REST FOR YOUR SOULS.
"To cleanse the muck from our veins and dissolve into something simpler...
"Something as unburdened as the sea."

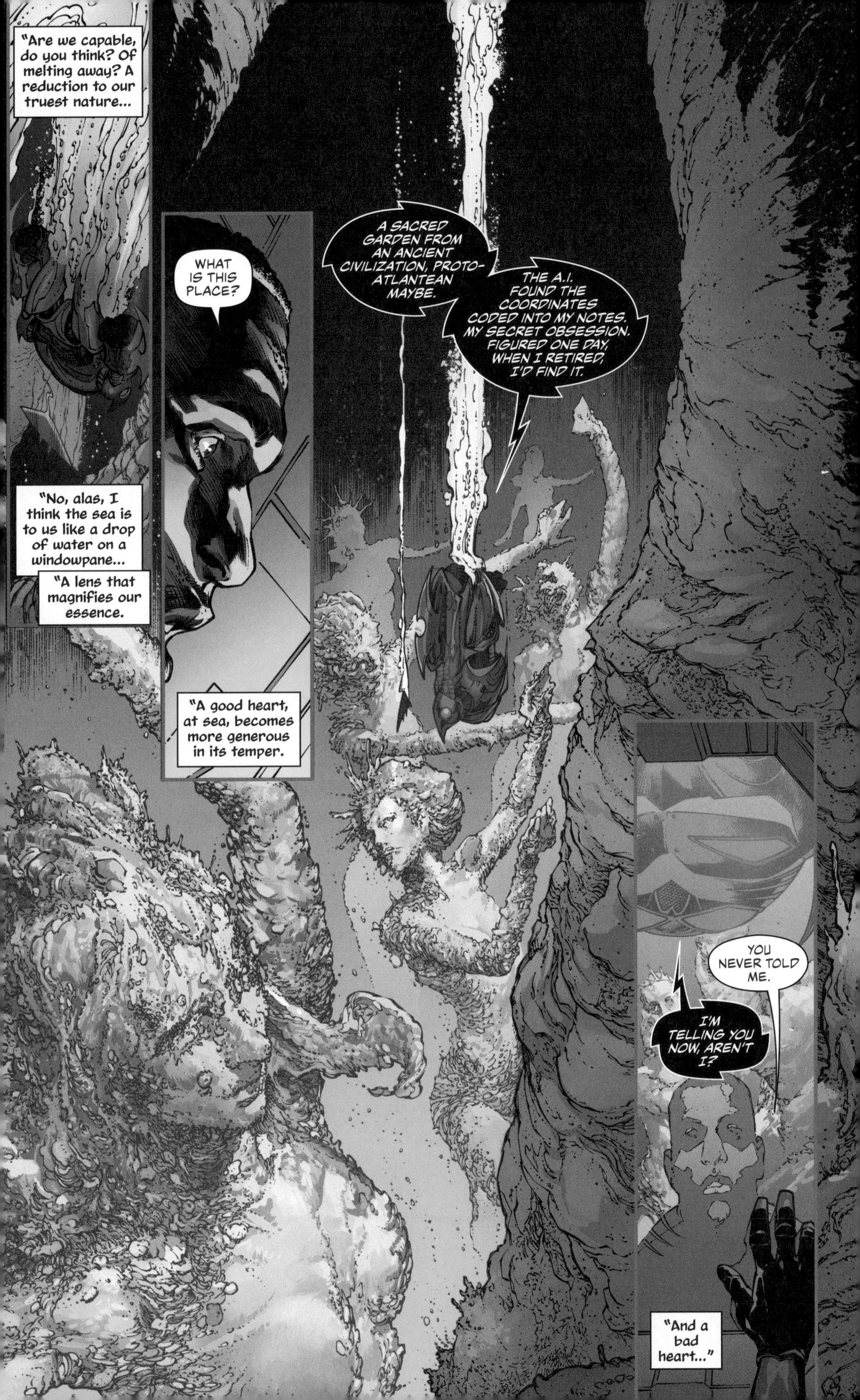
"Are we capable, do you think? Of melting away? A reduction to our truest nature...
WHAT IS THIS PLACE?
A SACRED GARDEN FROM AN ANCIENT CIVILIZATION, PROTO-ATLANTEAN MAYBE.
THE A.I. FOUND THE COORDINATES CODED INTO MY NOTES. MY SECRET OBSESSION. FIGURED ONE DAY, WHEN I RETIRED, I'D FIND IT.
"No, alas, I think the sea is to us like a drop of water on a windowpane...
"A lens that magnifies our essence.
"A good heart, at sea, becomes more generous in its temper.
YOU NEVER TOLD ME.
I'M TELLING YOU NOW, AREN'T I?
"And a bad heart..."

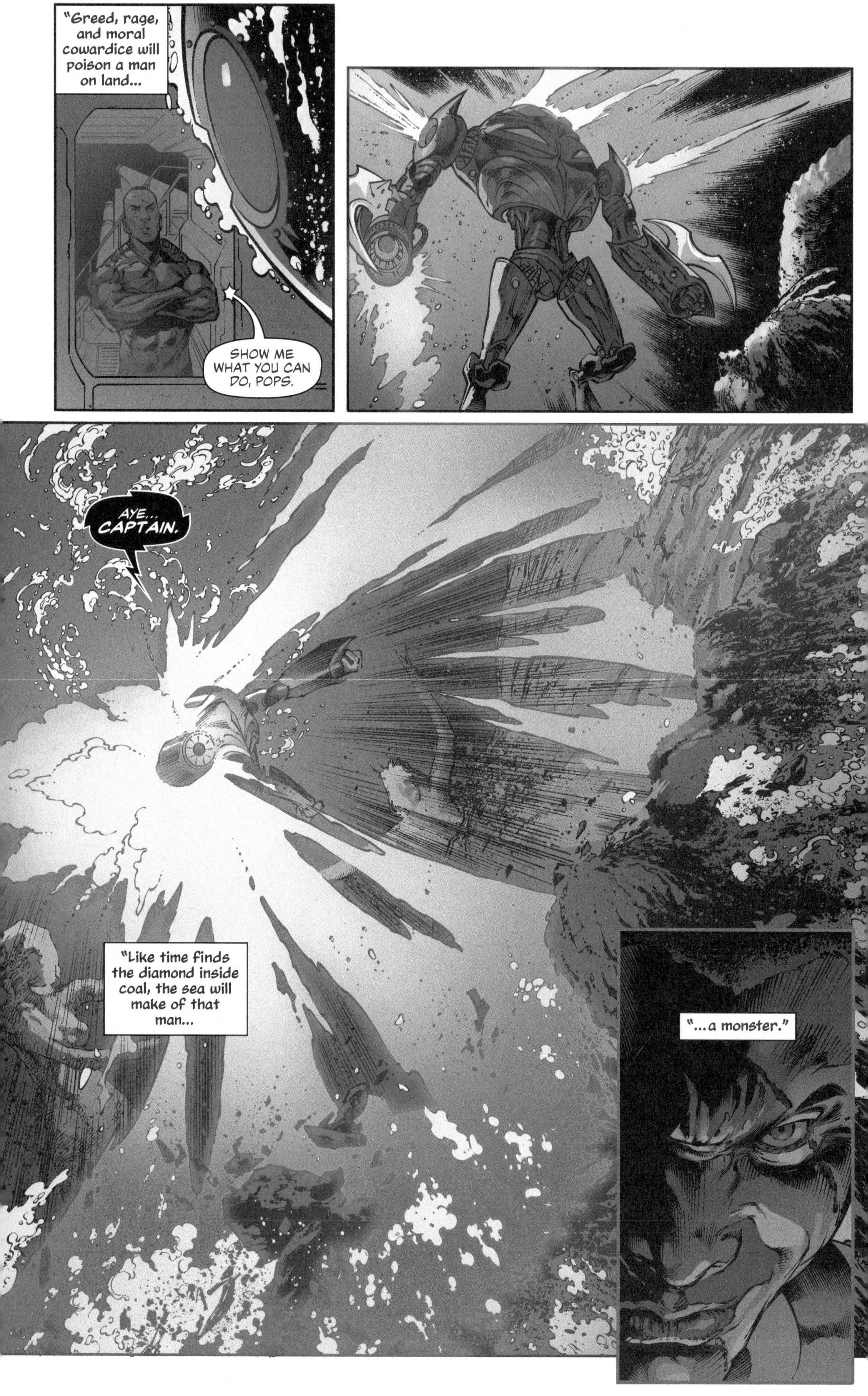
"Greed, rage, and moral cowardice will poison a man on land...
SHOW ME WHAT YOU CAN DO, POPS.
AYE... CAPTAIN.
"Like time finds the diamond inside coal, the sea will make of that man...
"...a monster."

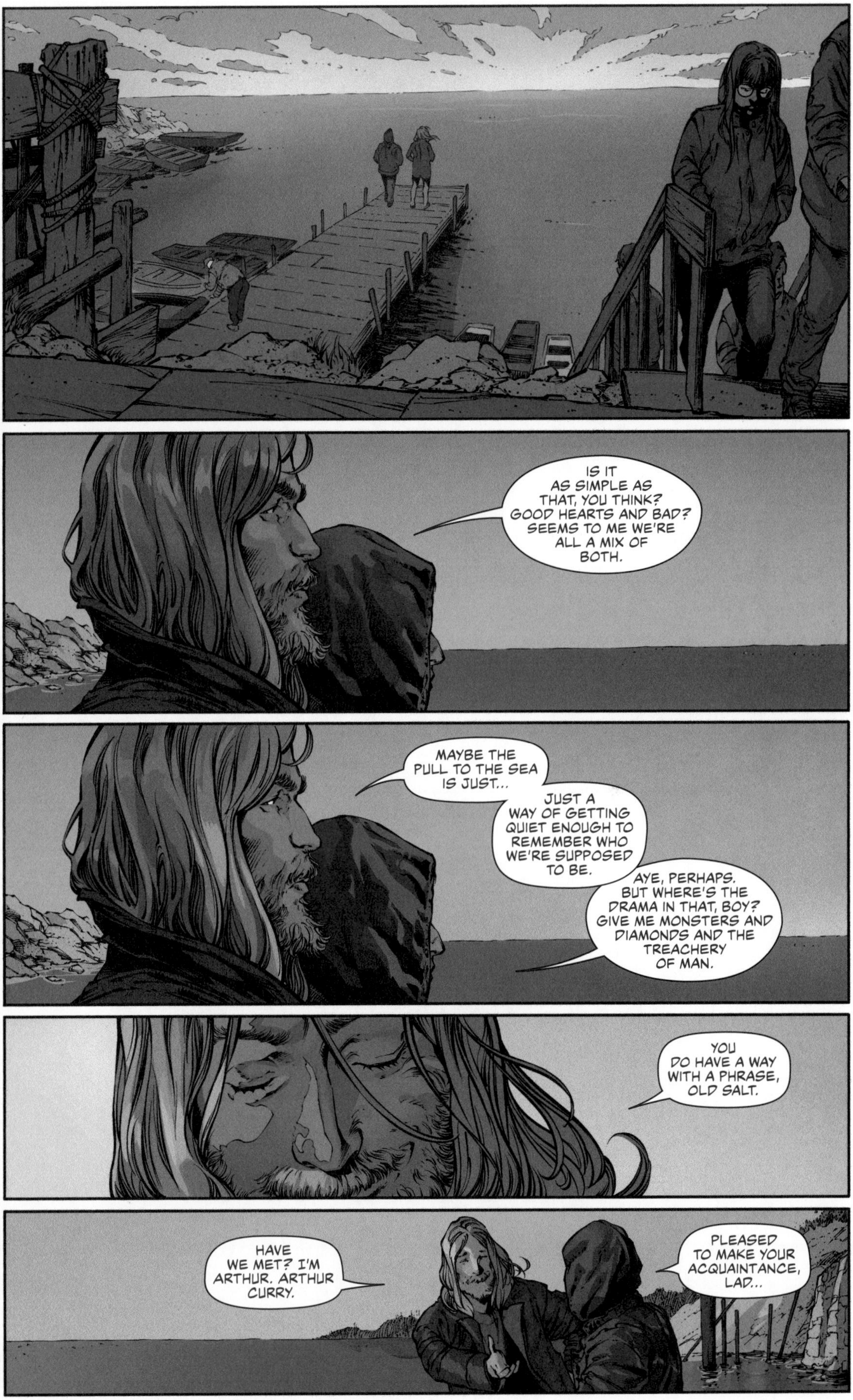
IS IT AS SIMPLE AS THAT, YOU THINK? GOOD HEARTS AND BAD? SEEMS TO ME WE'RE ALL A MIX OF BOTH.
MAYBE THE PULL TO THE SEA IS JUST...
JUST A WAY OF GETTING QUIET ENOUGH TO REMEMBER WHO WE'RE SUPPOSED TO BE.
AYE, PERHAPS. BUT WHERE'S THE DRAMA IN THAT, BOY? GIVE ME MONSTERS AND DIAMONDS AND THE TREACHERY OF MAN.
YOU DO HAVE A WAY WITH A PHRASE, OLD SALT.
HAVE WE MET? I'M ARTHUR. ARTHUR CURRY.
PLEASED TO MAKE YOUR ACQUAINTANCE, LAD...

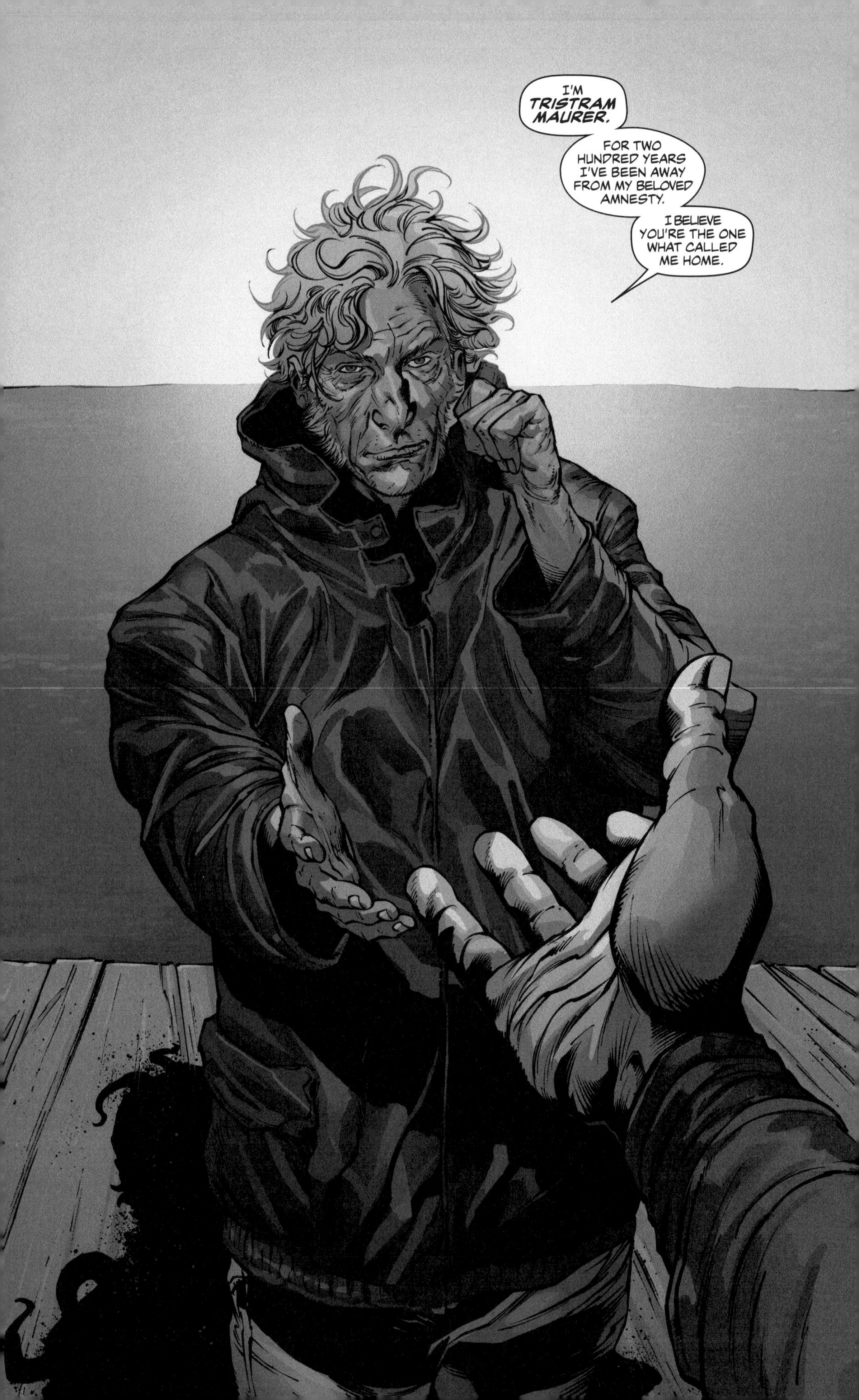
I'M TRISTRAM MAURER.
FOR TWO HUNDRED YEARS I'VE BEEN AWAY FROM MY BELOVED AMNESTY.
I BELIEVE YOU'RE THE ONE WHAT CALLED ME HOME.

SKETCHBOOK BY VIKTOR BOGDANOVIC

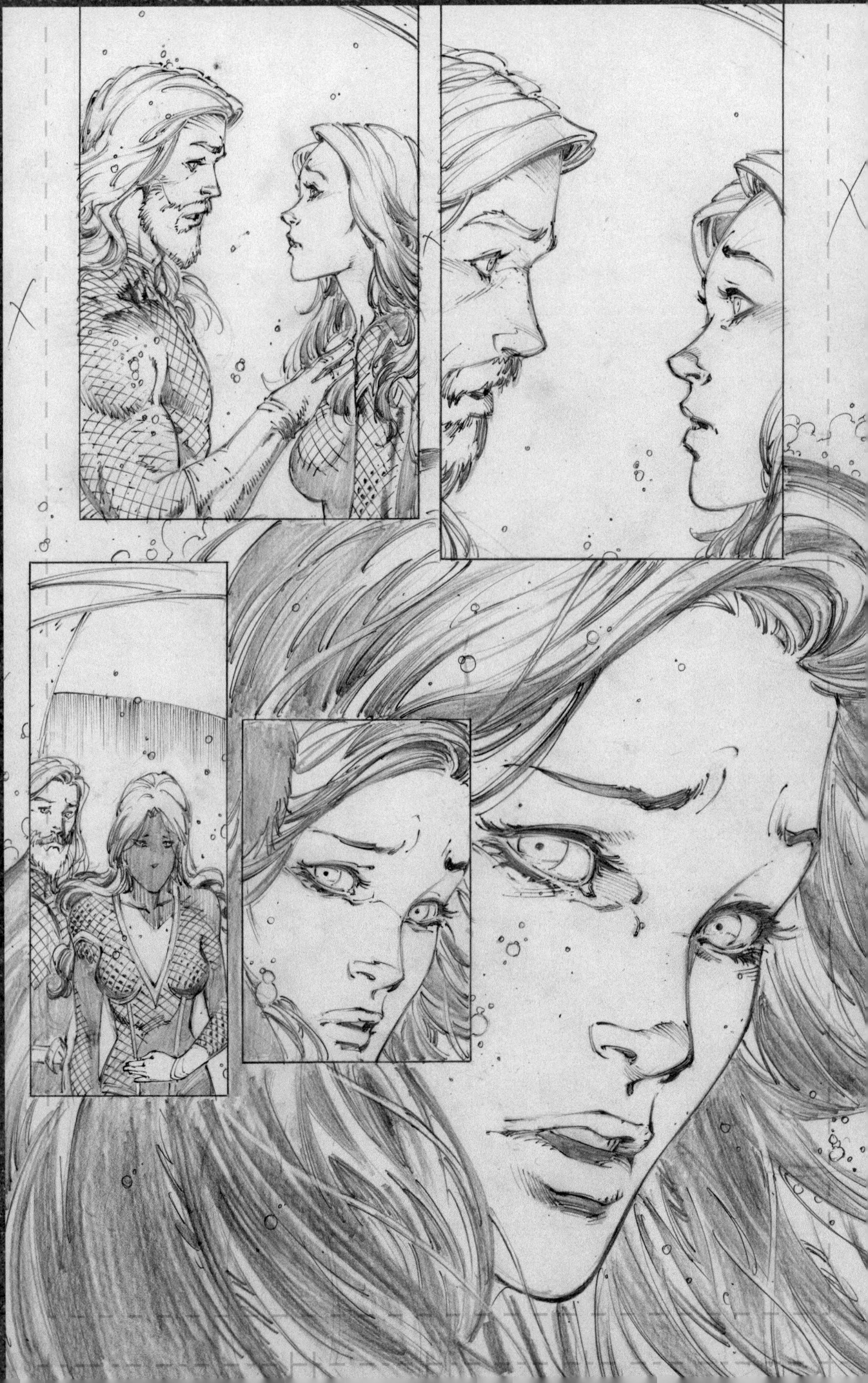

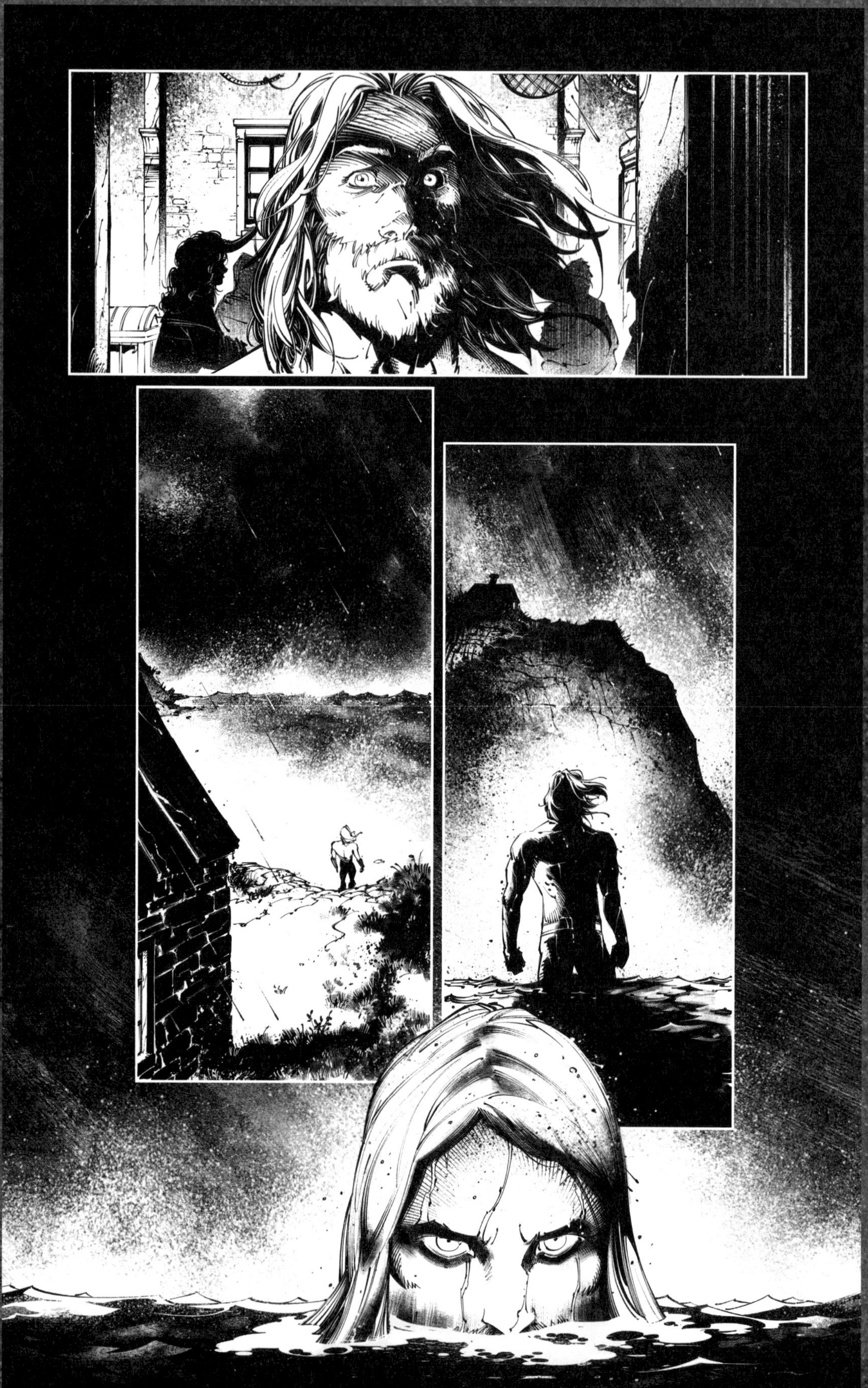

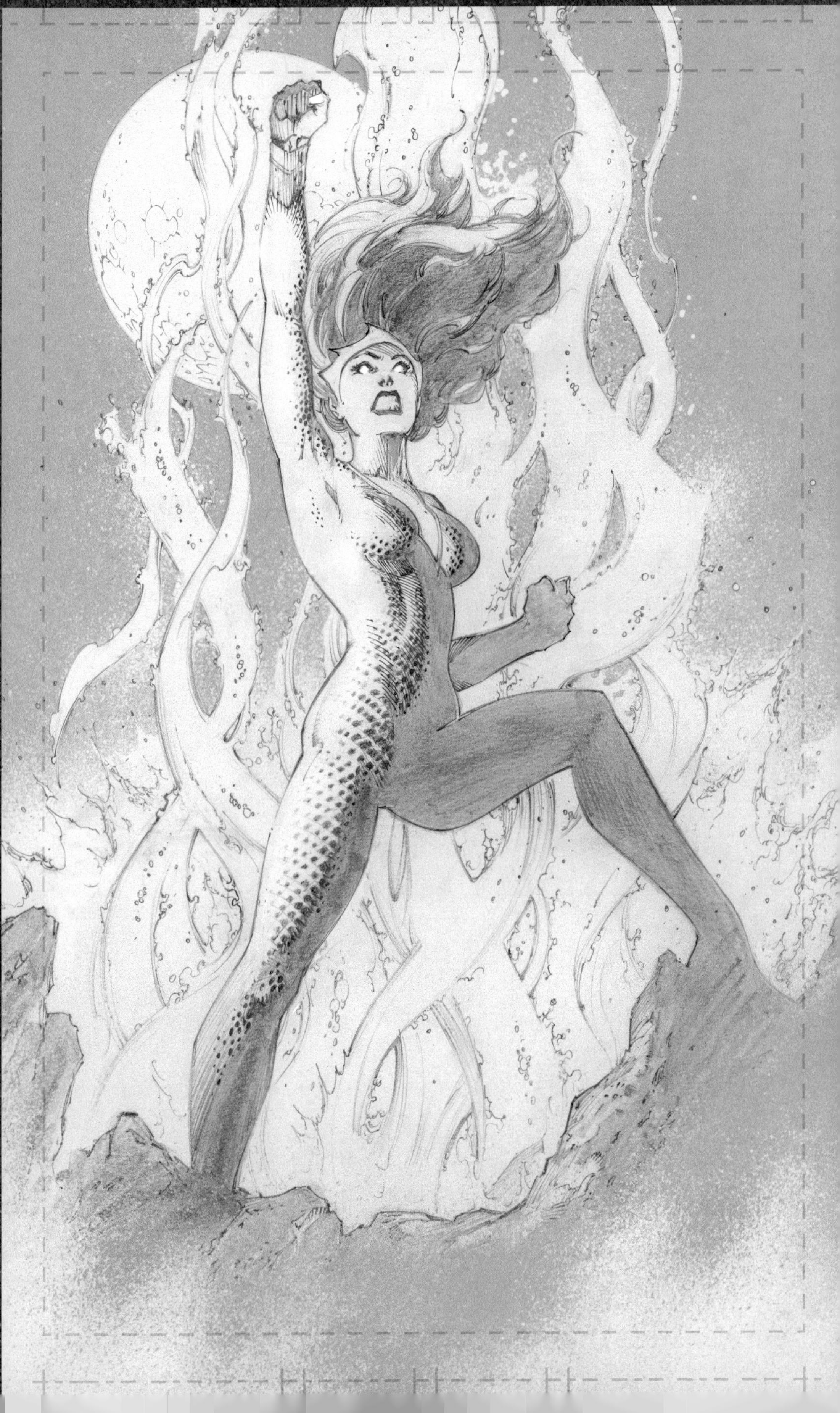

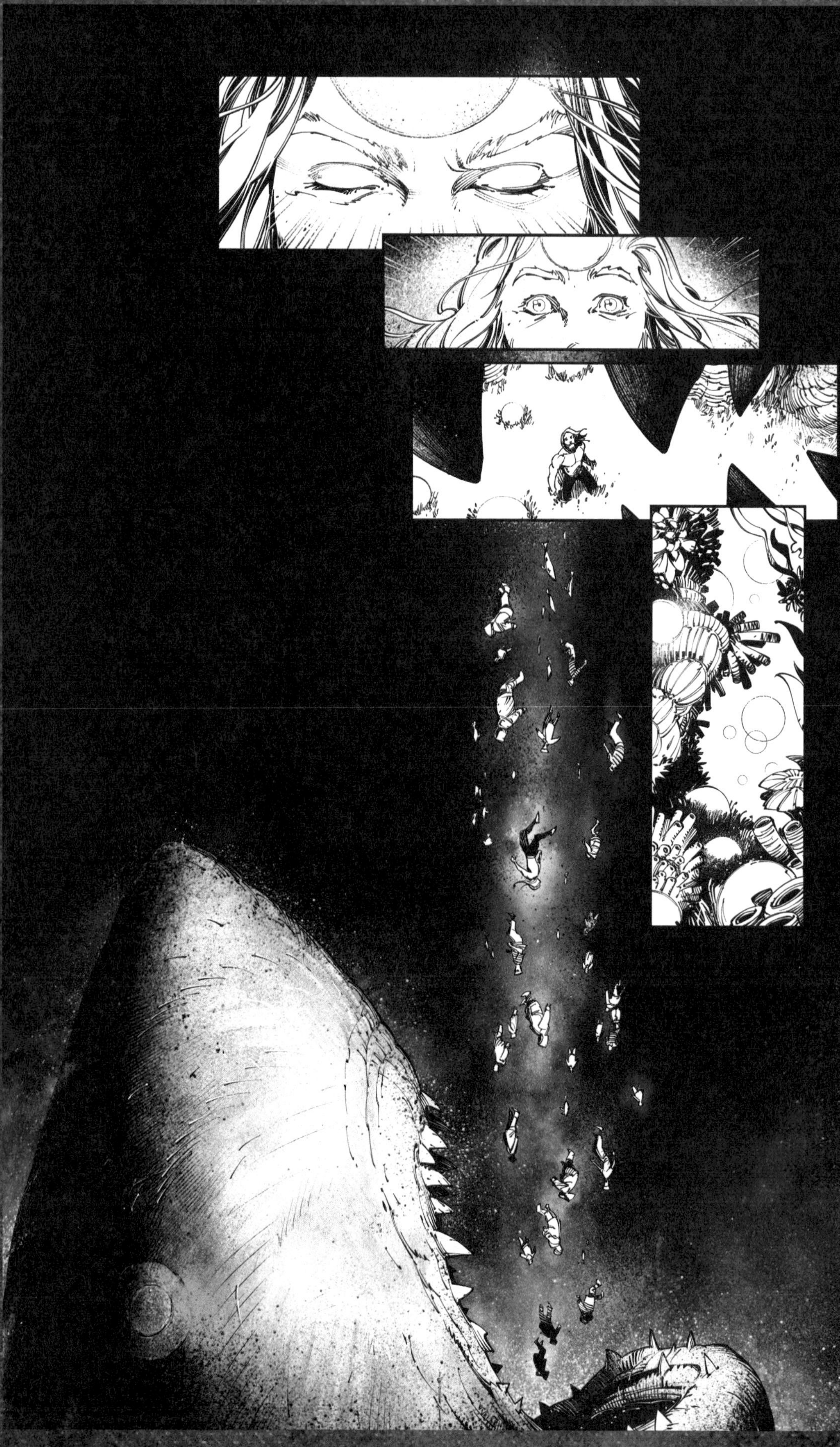